BORROWED PLUMES

All rights reserved. No part of this publication may be reproduced, stored in a retrieval system or transmitted, in any form or by any means, electronic, mechanical, photo-copying, recording or otherwise, without the prior permission of the publisher.

© 1994 Peter Farrer.   **ISBN** 0 9512385 2 3
Published by Karn Publications Garston,
63 Salisbury Road, Garston, Liverpool L19 0PH.

Phototypeset and printed in Great Britain by Wilton Printing Company,
239B Preston Road, Wembley, Middlesex HA9 8PE.

BORROWED PLUMES

**LETTERS FROM EDWARDIAN NEWSPAPERS
ON MALE CROSS DRESSING
Edited by PETER FARRER**

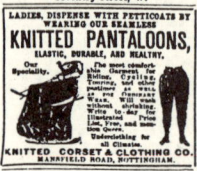

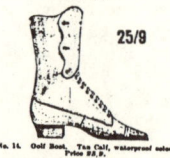

1. Advertisements. *The Queen*, 17th November 1900.

ACKNOWLEDGEMENTS

Some of the letters from *Modern Society* and *Photo Bits* were printed in issues 50 and 52 (1990) of *The Glad Rag*, the journal of the Transvestite/Transsexual Support Group (UK), a registered charity.

I wish to thank Anthea Jarvis, Keeper of The Gallery of English Costume, Platt Hall, Manchester, and also former Keepers, for help with research into *The Queen* newspaper; Jacqueline Bailey, formerly Librarian of the Art and Design Library of Liverpool Polytechnic (now Liverpool John Moores University), for permission to consult, and help with, The Liddell Hart Collection; and Janet Kent for finding the illustration of the riding habit.

I should also like to thank the Librarians and staff of the Arts, Language and Literature Department of Birmingham Central Library (*The Queen*), The Bodleian Library, The British Library, The Newspaper Library, Colindale, The Liverpool City Libraries and The Liverpool University Library.

Finally, may I thank Chris Wilson for indispensable help with production, and my wife, Anne Brogden, for her continuing support and for finding the illustrations.

2. Parisian Afternoon Dress. *The Ladies' Field*, 2nd March 1901, p.477.

CONTENTS

ACKNOWLEDGEMENTS 5

I – INTRODUCTION 11

II – THE QUEEN, THE LADY'S NEWSPAPER

INTRODUCTION 17

DRESS AND THE TOILETTE 33
Answers to Correspondents by Ardern Holt

III – THE DAILY MIRROR 47

IV – MODERN SOCIETY

INTRODUCTION 49

THE CORRESPONDENCE 57

V – PHOTO BITS

INTRODUCTION 83

THE CORRESPONDENCE 95

LIST OF ILLUSTRATIONS

COLOUR AND PHOTOGRAPHIC PLATES

Facing Page 32   i.   Ardern Holt in the Court gown she wore when she was presented by her mother as a debutante of 17. *The Queen*, 3rd February 1926.
© Manchester City Art Galleries.

Facing Page 33   ii.   Toilettes de Casino pour Villes d'eaux. *The Queen*, 3rd April 1909.
© Manchester City Art Galleries.

Facing Page 48   iii.   Toilettes de Casino pour Villes d'eaux. *The Queen*, 3rd April 1909.
© Manchester City Art Galleries.

Facing Page 49   iv.   Ardern Holt at the last Court of 1924. *The Queen*, 3rd February 1926.
© Manchester City Art Galleries.

Facing Page 80   v.   Fancy Dress Suggestions for Christmas Parties. *The Queen*, 19th November 1910.

Facing Page 81   vi.   W.A. Bolton as Georgiana Tidman in *Dandy Dick* by Sir Arthur Pinero, Easter 1903. *Courtesy of A.D.C. Theatre Executive Committee, Cambridge.*

Facing Page 96   vii.   G.E. Hubbard as Ida Pinkerton in *Pinkerton's Peerage* by Sir Anthony Hope Hawkins, June 1905. *Courtesy of A.D.C. Theatre Executive Committee, Cambridge.*

Facing Page 97   viii.   M.E. Hawtrey as Belinda Trehearne, G.F. Kidd as Belvawney and Justin Brooke as Minnie Symperson in *Engaged* by W.S. Gilbert, Easter 1907. *Courtesy of A.D.C. Theatre Executive Committee, Cambridge.*

ILLUSTRATIONS IN THE TEXT

Page

1. Advertisements. *The Queen*, 17th November 1900. 4
2. Parisian Afternoon Dress. *The Ladies' Field*, 2nd March 1901. 6
3. Visiting Gowns. *The Woman at Home*, April 1903. 10
4. Newest Shapes in Unmade Sequin Robes. 14
   Catalogue Summer 1904, D.H. Evans & Co. Ltd.

ILLUSTRATIONS IN THE TEXT (contd.)

		Page
5.	The Correct Form Corsets. *Catalogue Summer 1904*, D.H. Evans & Co. Ltd.	20
6.	Costumes for Girls. *Catalogue Summer 1904*, D.H. Evans & Co. Ltd.	24
7.	The Apron Riding Skirt. *The Ladies' Tailor*, September 1906.	32
8.	Stockings. *Catalogue Summer 1904*, D.H. Evans & Co. Ltd.	38
9.	Bridesmaids and Attendants. *The Designer*, June 1902.	45
10.	Exquisite French Lingerie. *Catalogue Autumn & Winter 1904*, Wooland Brothers.	46
11.	The Latest Corset and Skirt from Paris. *Lady's Pictorial*, 1st April 1905	52
12.	Bathing Outfit. *Every Woman's Encyclopædia*, Vol. VIII (1912).	56
13.	Fashions for Cowes Week. *The Lady's Realm*, May 1906.	62
14.	Ladies' Costumes. *Catalogue Spring and Summer 1906*, Pryce Jones, Ltd.	68
15.	Corsets. *Catalogue Spring and Summer 1906*, Pryce Jones, Ltd.	74
16.	Frocks for Girls. *Femina*, 15th October 1906.	79
17.	Hats and Parasols. *Every Woman's Encyclopædia*, Vol. VIII (1912).	81
18.	Tennis Frocks. *The Girl's Own Paper*, 31st August 1907.	82
19.	A New Garden Party Frock. *The Woman At Home*, May 1908.	88
20.	A Dinner Gown. *The Woman At Home*, June 1908.	94
21.	Charming Skirts. *Catalogue Autumn 1908*, Oxendales, Manchester.	102
22.	High-Class Underskirts. *Catalogue Autumn 1908*, Oxendales, Manchester.	108
23.	Semi-Tailored Dresses. *The Girl's Own Paper*, October 1908.	112
24.	Embroidered Silk and Jet Stoles. *Catalogue Summer 1909*, Dickens & Jones.	116
25.	Two Late Summer Costumes. *The Lady's Realm*, September 1910.	122
26.	Fashionable Underskirts. *Catalogue*, c. 1910, William Whiteley Ltd.	126
27.	Elegant Tailor Costume. *The Lady's Realm*, July 1912.	134
28.	Child's Summer Frock. *Every Woman's Encyclopædia*, Vol. VIII (1912).	140
29.	French Day-Wear. *Le Miroir Des Modes*, August 1910.	144

3. Visiting Gowns. *The Woman at Home*, April 1903, p.89.

I

INTRODUCTION

In my conclusion to *Men in Petticoats*, I promised a further collection of letters about cross-dressing. This is a continuation of that book, taking the collection up to 1912. I have called the newspapers Edwardian because in each of the newspapers concerned the series of letters started and reached its climax within the Edwardian period. In the case of *Modern Society* and *Photo Bits*, the relevant letters come to an end only a year or two into the next reign. In his book *Fashion and Fetishism* (Totowa, New Jersey: Rowman and Littlefield, 1982, p. 233), David Kunzle wrote, "I have been unable to bridge the gap in fetishist correspondence between 1900 and 1909." This book partly bridges that gap. In each chapter or section devoted to the letters from a particular newspaper there is an introduction giving a brief history of the paper so far as it is known or relevant, and a summary of the letters and subject matter covered. Here I will make some general comments about the contents of the collection and the papers included.

Of the newspapers included in *Men In Petticoats*, *Society* ceased publication in 1900. While *The Family Doctor* continued until 1918, I have not found any similar correspondence after 1895. I have, however, come across two letters which I had previously overlooked, which I am taking the opportunity to reproduce now. They are useful additions to the group of letters already taken from that newspaper, revealing innocent male enjoyment in dressing up for theatricals or sensual pleasure.

TIGHT LACING 5th January 1889

Your fair correspondent, "Sweet Seventeen," seems to doubt that men ever really wear corsets. Permit me to set her mind at rest upon this point, as I myself am an enthusiastic votary of the corset, though not an excessively tight lacer–21inches for a height of 5ft. 7ins. I am a pupil in a civil engineer's office here, and twenty years of age. it may be vain, and it may be effeminate, but I mean to stick to it in spite of the "warning voice," and if England ever is in danger I dare say I shall do my duty, as I am a member of a corps of rifle volunteers.

I am now studying a girl's part in a piece we are going to do at a large house where I am invited this Christmas (my people are abroad), and find a good deal of fun in rehearsing my lines in costume at home every evening, and I can assure you there are many worse looking young ladies than yours truly,
Hull, Dec. 18, 1888. W.R.

HIGH HEELS AND TIGHT LACING 17th September 1892

I was very pleased to see in one of your late issues, one of those charming letters from "Science and Art" concerning "High Heels and Tight Lacing," giving a description of the deliciously stilted heels worn by the Maltese ladies.

I may state that I have worn both high-heeled boots and corsets for some years, though, on account of my height, I have rarely ventured to appear out of doors with heels over 2¾ in. high. In the house, however, I have often donned complete feminine attire, preferring it in every way to the baggy habiliments I am constrained by the foolish custom of my sex to wear.

As regards boots for indoor wear, I have high lacing boots of glove kid, with small

11

pointed patent-leather toes and narrow French heels, from 4 to 5in. high, and I must say that the sensation caused by the wearing of these is infinitely delightful. Respecting corsets, I have not as yet tried lacing as tightly as some of your correspondents; but when ordering my new corsets, I intend the waist measurement not to exceed 20in.–my present stays, which are loose for me, being 24in. in the waist. I do not consider the latter to be large, seeing that my height, without heels, is 5ft. 10in.

At the risk of being thought vain, I may say that my features, being of a decidedly feminine cast, and my figure slender and well-proportioned, I have always, when clad in female attire, called forth the admiration of my acquaintances; and I quite agree with them in saying that it is a thousand pities that I was not born a girl, as then I would have been able to have indulged in the delightful practice of wearing high heels and tight corsets to the fullest extent. If you would do me the favour of inserting these few lines in your valuable paper, you would oblige, yours very truly,
Edinburgh   MARIANUS

The first newspaper to be represented in this new collection is *The Queen, The Lady's Newspaper*, founded in 1861. If there had been sufficient space in *Men in Petticoats* two or three articles of the 1860's would have found a place in that. What I now include is a selection of replies to readers on questions on dress and fashion by Ardern Holt from 1901 to 1910, with a stray one from 1913.

That I am able to include *The Queen* at all is the result of following up a reference which I have known about for over forty years, but have not had the time or the energy to pursue before. On 26 July 1941 *London Life* printed a letter from their regular correspondent, "Ino," which included this statement:

> In *The Queen* of about thirty years ago, there is a long article upon "Pages for Weddings," and the writer suggests the 1855 boy's costume, when velvet and silk frocks and the most elaborate and conspicuous frilled white knickers were the rage for all small boys.

This sounds clear and specific, but "about 30 years" before July 1941 could mean two or three years on either side of 1911 and the perusal of thousands of pages, the paper normally being bound in four volumes a year. I also had grave doubts about the reliability of "Ino's" memory. I decided, however, that there was no point in quoting this paragraph without trying to find the article mentioned. At least I could say that I hadn't found it. Well, I didn't find that particular article in the form described, but I found much more that I didn't expect which made the search well worth while.

On 18 November 1911, Ardern Holt did in fact give a correspondent some advice on pages' costume, but she recommended the costume of the pages of honour at the coronation of George IV (CXXX, 920). Each week there were articles on "Fashionable Marriages" and pages were included in the elegant engravings of the participants. While some of them wore knee-length white satin tunics, there were none in Victorian boys' frocks. The nearest thing I could find to the supposed quotation was in an article on "Children's Fancy Dress" by Mrs. Jack May on 19 November 1910:

> Our artist has accorded an equal amount of consideration to boys, and offers in the case of the tiny of from four to five years a picture of the orthodox everyday get-up of a little boy about 1823. It will be quickly surmised how this is effected either in white or brown holland stitched with fine black silk braid. The style is unmistakable; it is absolutely typical of that phase of history, and would by no means ill become a child of fair, attractive countenance, the shady hat and hoop enhancing the general summery suggestion.

As can be seen from the illustration which I reproduce there are no frilled drawers and the date is 1823 not 1855. Perhaps "Ino" has confused the two items and thought she remembered a page in a boy's frock, and of a later period. As I had expected, however, there was no long article on "Pages for Weddings." On the other hand some of Ardern Holt's correspondents seemed to be asking curious and intriguing questions. I therefore continued my examination of *the Queen* back into earlier years. In due course I came across this question in the issue for 13 June 1908 (CXXIII, 1012): "How long should boys be dressed in Corsets and Petticoats?" Holt replied that this would be unusual after the age of three or at most four, and very unusual for a boy of seven, apparently the age of the boy concerned. She added: "Possibly in South Africa it would not be so remarkable," with the implication that the boy was going to live there.

This question and answer reminded me of another letter from "Ino" in *London Life*. On 2 August 1941 she had quoted from memory "some details from the correspondence column of a ladies' magazine published about thirty-five years ago." The alleged advice was to the effect that there would be no harm in a boy of *eleven* (my emphasis) wearing white frilled petticoats, etc. under his kilt "in a remote Continental country." Again "Ino's" memory is defective in important respects. The date is about right, but the country has been changed and the age of the boy much increased. I believe that in both these examples "Ino" is basing her remarks on articles in *The Queen*, but in her mind she has exaggerated the original in the direction she desires, namely an older boy being dressed in a girlish manner. Her pseudonym, "Ino," was the name of the wife of Athamas, King of Orchomenus, who was entrusted with rearing Dionysus as a girl to save him from the wrath of Hera, Dionysus being the son of Zeus by Semele.

Going further back I found sufficient replies by Ardern Holt from the years 1902 to 1910 to make a complete chapter, the first being remarkable advice to a "mere man" on "the Complete Outfit for Riding," namely a safety habit for riding side-saddle (4 January 1902, CXI, 25). After that there were questions about stays for boys and men, the correct underwear for boys in kilts, whether dressing boys as girls had a beneficial effect and costumes for amateur theatricals. My last reply of hers trespasses into 1913. Ardern Holt ceased to edit The Answers to Correspondents column early in 1914.

Although "Ino's" quotations were wrong, they contained important clues to the actual contents of *The Queen's* question and answer columns. It means that the newspaper I present first in this collection and gets pride of place is the eminently respectable *The Queen, The Lady's Newspaper*. It shows that the readers of that paper were no less interested in tight-lacing, corsets for men and girls' clothes for boys than the readers of *Modern Society* and *Photo Bits*. There is also the advantage that the views and opinions of the readers of *The Queen* come to us via the editorship of Ardern Holt, a well known writer on costume and fashion. She provides confirmation that even the most extraordinary letters have indeed been received in the post as enquiries directed to her. We also hear her contemporary opinion of those letters and if she disapproved of her correspondents' views, she told them so in no uncertain terms.

In my introduction to the selection from *The Queen* I have given a fairly extensive history of that paper as well as a review of the career of Ardern Holt herself. This is needed because apart from the historical notes in the centenary issue of 3 August 1961 there is no official history of *The Queen* as there is of *The Field* and what information various writers have given about the early years of the paper is mostly wrong.

The next paper to figure in this collection is *The Daily Mirror*, which was founded in 1903. In 1906 it printed a few letters on tight-lacing, some of which mention men in stays and female attire. These form a separate chapter.

Up to 1900 *Modern Society* provided much material for *Men in Petticoats* and *In Female Disguise*. As in the case of *The Family Doctor* there are more letters which could have been included in the former. I begin this selection with four letters from the years 1898 and 1899 about boys wearing stays. Letters about corsets for both sexes, high heels and earrings continued to appear from time to time throughout the period 1901 to 1908. In the years 1907 to 1909 there are a few on stays for boys, and my extracts recommence. From 13 November 1909 to 8 January 1910 inclusive *Modern Society* ran a correspondence page headed "Slaves of the Stay-Lace," certainly one of the most concentrated batches ever of letters on this subject.

D. H. EVANS & COMPANY, LTD.,   OXFORD STREET, LONDON, W.

LACE DEPARTMENT.

NEWEST SHAPES IN UNMADE SEQUIN ROBES.

When ordering please quote No. 245 FB.
UNMADE SEQUIN ROBE.
With Bodice and Sleeves in all Black. Price **21/-**
Black and Steel or White and Silver.
Price **24/6**

When ordering please quote No. 246 FB.
NEW MAURESQUE LACE ROBE.
Unmade, in Cream or Ecru with Bodice and Sleeves. Price **42/-**

73

4. Newest Shapes in Unmade Sequin Robes.

Catalogue Summer 1904,
D.H. Evans & Co. Ltd., p.73

Some were concerned with the figure training of boys. This was followed by a number of letters about effeminate men, that is to say, men who enjoyed wearing women's clothes. "Jupon" on 19 February 1910 was the first man to confess this personally in the columns of *Modern Society*. Another special feature of this paper in the years 1910 and 1911 was the column, "Frills and Furbelows," signed by "Suzanne." From 20 November 1909 she invited readers to send in enquiries and like Ardern Holt she found herself having to answer questions about corsets for men and kilts and petticoats for boys. She was less hostile to the combination of petticoat and kilt for boys than Ardern Holt and some of her replies are rather like those attributed to *The Queen* by "Ino," but I do not think that "Ino" had ever seen *Modern Society*. It would have interested her and she would have remembered at least something about it and mentioned it in *London Life*.

It is interesting that other papers in 1908 gave space to the corset and tight-lacing. *The Daily Chronicle* printed correspondence on this subject from 25 to 31 August 1908 and I believe there is more to find in that newspaper. Perhaps the most striking and influential treatment was, as David Kunzle has pointed out (*op. cit.* p. 233), the publication by *The Tatler* of a photograph of the actress Polaire on 30 December 1908 (p. 357), under the heading, "The Smallest Waist in the World." Two more photographs of women with small waists were printed on 13 January and 17 February 1909.

These photographs and their captions undoubtedly encouraged the pin-up magazine *Photo Bits* to go in for pictures of tight-lacing and correspondence about it. Their first article on this theme was on 29 May 1909, entitled "Who Has the Smallest Waist in the World?" and they also printed a photograph of Polaire. It took a few weeks for their programme to get under way, but for about two-and-a half years from the autumn of 1909 to March 1912, *Photo Bits* was a unique vehicle for the pictorial and written exposition of female impersonation, corporal punishment and every kind of what has been called fetishism. The leaders in this enterprise were the editor, G. Gascoine; an American writer of fiction, Derk Fortescue; and two columnists who expatiated on the fetish of the week, first, "The Amorist," and when he died, another American who called himself "Cosmopolite." Both stories and articles were illustrated by appropriate drawings and photographs. "Cosmopolite" had studied Krafft-Ebing, but he never conveyed any sense that there was anything morally or medically wrong with "kinks," and "fetishes." They were there to be enjoyed. This is a very modern attitude. Magnus Hirschfeld's *Die Transvestiten* was published in 1910. In his investigations of "The Effeminate in Man," "Cosmopolite" was the first writer in English to discuss these matters, anticipating Havelock Ellis's volume on "Eonism" first published in 1928 by several years. After the death of Fortescue reported on 16 March 1912, this style of presentation collapsed and, soon after, Gascoine and "Cosmopolite" left the paper.

I am sure that other newspapers published material on tight-lacing before the First World War, and I have read that possible candidates for research are *The Daily Telegraph* and *The Morning Post*. A "comic" paper, in the classification of the time, which certainly did, was *New Photo Fun*, which had started life as *Photo Fun* on 16 June 1906, changing its name on 2 October 1909. It began a correspondence on corporal punishment on 12 November 1910, and extended its scope to "petticoat punishment" on 25 November 1911. This paper continued to thrive in this way under a succession of different names right through the war until 1920, finishing as *Bits of Fun*. I hope to bring out a collection of those letters in due course.

A more serious journal which published letters about boys in petticoats, in the sense of skirts, at this time was *Notes and Queries*. On 23 July 1910 the writer and genealogist, G.H. White, contributed a letter about the custom in some parts of Ireland of quite large boys continuing to wear petticoats. He cited an article in *Harpers Magazine* for May about boys on the Aran Islands wearing long petticoats until the age of ten or eleven, and another in *The Hospital* of 1905 mentioning boys of twelve and fourteen in petticoats in Connemara, where the mothers claimed it was done to protect them from the fairies. White mentioned similar practices in India and in the Far East and wondered whether there was any trace of this superstition in other parts of the U.K.. D.K.T. replied to this on 13 August 1910:

> Sixty years ago, when I was a child at Brighton, my elder brothers wore petticoats, as I did myself until we were seven or eight years old, at which age we were "breeched." I have still in my possession a silhouette of us as we appeared in those days (taken on the old Chain Pier); and other boys were attired in a similar manner. I remember one of our playmates in Sussex Square being kept in petticoats by his mamma until he was twelve years old, which caused him much chaff from boys and girls of his own age.
>
> I dare say some of your readers can corroborate my statement as to boys being dressed similarly to girls at that period. I never heard that it had anything to do with the fairies, but "knickerbockers" were then unknown in England.

White made this comment on D.K.T.'s letter: "Apparently there is no clear trace of the superstition in England. Probably D.K.T.'s Brighton playmate, who was kept in petticoats until the age of twelve, owed this experience to some other cause. I have been told of a much more recent case in the same town, in which two brothers were dressed as girls until the ages of ten and eight respectively, but the reason alleged was simply the mother's disappointment at not having girls."

As in the case of *Men in Petticoats*, I shall normally include only letters which give examples of men wearing complete female dress. Thus I shall omit letters describing men wearing corsets, high heeled shoes or earrings and no other items of feminine apparel. On the other hand I shall now include examples of female clothes being used as some form of punishment for the male sex. The first printed evidence of this having happened that I have been able to discover is to be found in the Supplement to *The Englishwoman's Domestic Magazine* of April 1870. This was in a letter signed by "Etonensis." The incident related probably took place in the second quarter of the nineteenth century. There is further reference to it in *Town Talk* in the eighties, and in *Society* in the nineties. Contributors to *The Family Doctor* from 1885 to 1895 favoured what they called "corset discipline," which involved subjecting boys to tight stays. I hope to reprint these letters in a future collection. Ardern Holt knew about the correspondence in *The Family Doctor* as she gave the dates of it to one enquirer. She did not of course agree with tight stays for boys and told a correspondent that it was absurd on 1 May 1909.

In *Modern Society* "Tamed" (22 July 1899) was a victim of corset discipline, and several examples were reported in 1910, "A.I." claiming on 1 January that the brother of a friend of hers was at the age of thirteen dressed as a girl by his nurse for any exhibition of boyish spirits. Even now this practice has never been examined or described by a historian of costume or childhood. Yet in *Photo Bits* it was fully explored and discussed by "Cosmopolite" in a series of articles in 1910 and 1911 with the titles, "The Cultivation of the Cub" and "The Cub and the Kilt." "Cosmopolite" is the only writer who has ever done this. With the encouragement of the paper readers contributed details of their own experiences.

The period covered by these letters 1901 to 1912 falls within "La Belle Epoque," but important changes in fashion had begun by 1908. This is not the place to describe those changes but we have selected illustrations from a variety of contemporary sources to show different aspects of fashion over the years. The actual events described in some of the letters obviously fell in the nineteenth century, but these are the sort of pictures of women's clothes that the correspondents would have been seeing at the time of writing. Poiret's designs with a vertical silhouette, high waist, and narrow skirts came out in 1908. He did not, as he claimed, abolish the corset, but he did help to alter the shape of it. He freed the bust, but tied the legs. It is a curious fact that just when fashion had taken a decisive turn away from the wasp waist, there was a sudden flurry of interest in the practice of tight-lacing. This was evident at all levels, just as much in *The Queen* as in *Photo Bits*.

II

THE QUEEN, THE LADY'S NEWSPAPER

INTRODUCTION

The Queen, "an illustrated journal and review," as it was described in the title plate, in which Windsor Castle formed the background, was founded by Samuel Beeton (1831-1877) on 7 September 1861 as a weekly paper for women at the price of sixpence. According to a notice printed in the bottom right-hand corner of the last page, the imprint, the paper was printed by Charles Wyman, of Cox and Wyman and "published by Samuel Orchart Beeton, at the office of "THE QUEEN," No. 248, Strand, in the Parish of St. Clement Danes, in the County of Middlesex." This was the address of Beeton's publishing business and the home of *The Englishwoman's Domestic Magazine*, started by Beeton in May 1852. There is no information in the pages of *The Queen* about the editor nor do any names appear under the articles. According, however, to J.W.Robertson-Scott (*The Story of the Pall Mall Gazette*, O.U.P., 1950, p.118), the first editor was Frederick Greenwood (1830-1909), a friend of Beeton's, who later became sub-editor of *The Cornhill Magazine*, and founded *The Pall Mall Gazette* on 7 February 1865. No doubt the section, "Novelties in Needlework," incorporated in a four page "Work-Table Supplement" from 9 November 1861, was the responsibility of Isabella Beeton, but this did not appear every week.

The Beetons did not, however, persevere: the paper was sold within a year. Perhaps it had become too much of a burden on top of their other publications. Curiously enough, none of the biographers of the Beetons, Nancy Spain (*Mrs. Beeton and her Husband*, Collins, 1948 and *The Beeton Story*, Ward, Lock & Co., 1956), H. Montgomery Hyde (*Mr. and Mrs. Beeton*, Harrap, 1951) and Sarah Freeman (*Isabella and Sam*, Victor Gollancz, 1977), correctly report this change in the ownership and running of the paper. Hyde places the change after Isabella Beeton's death on 6 February 1865, her fourth child having died on 29 January 1865 (p.13); Spain does not mention it at all; while Freeman puts it in July 1863 (p.184).

The essential key to what happened is the change of imprint. On 12 April 1862 the imprint reads: "London: Printed and Published by JOHN CROCKFORD, at 346, Strand, W.C., in the Parish of St. Mary-le-Strand, Middlesex." When we turn to the front page, we find that the engraving incorporating the title at the top is exactly the same in every detail as in previous issues, except that the number 346 has replaced 248 in the address. *The Queen* had moved a few blocks to the west, to the offices of *The Field* in fact, because Beeton had sold the paper to Edwin William Cox (later Serjeant-at-Law), proprietor of *The Field* and *The Law Times*. Cox, a distinguished barrister and writer on legal matters, was born in Taunton in 1809, founded *The Law Times* on 8 April 1843 and acquired *The Field* with effect from 25 November 1854. John Crockford, also of Taunton, and the founder, in 1858, of the famous *Clerical Directory*, which was known as *Crockford's Clerical Directory* from 1860, was entrusted with the business side of Cox's newspaper interests. The offices of these papers changed quite frequently and *The Field* of 23 October 1858 printed the following announcement: "Mr. Crockford announces that the businesses of THE FIELD, THE CRITIC, THE LAW TIMES, THE CLERICAL JOURNAL and other publications will move to 346, Strand and 19, Wellington-street, North" (XII, 323). From 12 April 1862 Crockford was printer and publisher of both *The Field* and *The Queen* and probably of Cox's other papers as well.

This information comes partly from examining the newspapers themselves and partly from the centenary history of *The Field* by R.N. Rose (*The Field 1853-1953*, Michael Joseph, 1953), and it is important that Beeton's sale of *The Queen* in 1862 should be more widely known and accepted. It means that the correspondence in *The Queen* on tight-lacing from 1862 to 1864 and on corporal punishment from December 1865 to February 1866 was not only not inspired or encouraged by Beeton, it actually preceded Beeton's extended correspondence column in *The Englishwoman's Domestic Magazine*, which did not begin until January 1867. It therefore looks as if the earlier correspondence in *The Queen* was one of the factors which influenced Beeton in allowing correspondence on these subjects to develop in *The Englishwoman's Domestic Magazine* from 1867 onwards. It is also amusing to reflect that the name which can legitimately be associated with the first set of letters, on the female figure and stays, is not that of the supposedly raffish Beeton, but that of the eminently respectable chronicler of Victorian ecclesiastical personnel.

The change of ownership produced an immediate and drastic change in the character of the paper. Beeton's *Queen* had its merits. There were splendid engravings of fashionable occasions, public events and disasters, rather in the manner of *The Illustrated London News* or *The Graphic*. There were also humorous illustrations, explained in a whimsical commentary, in the manner of *Punch*, such as "Marriage in the East and Marriage in the West," a skit on the different styles of weddings in the East and West Ends of London (2 Nov. 1861, pp.161-162). On 5 April 1862, in both *The Queen* and *The Field* there was an elaborate announcement, a column long, setting out the changes that were to take place in the former. Of Beeton's biographers, only Hyde shows awareness of this announcement, but he did not appreciate that a change of ownership was taking place at the same time. Freeman ignores both the announcement and the change of imprint, with the result that her whole chapter on *The Queen*, (xvi), is flawed and requires revision, particularly pages 184 and 185. All the developments mentioned by her came into effect after the sale to Cox. In view of the complete change in the paper after 5 April 1962, negotiations for its sale and preparations for the new format must have been going on for some weeks beforehand. The last couple of pages on "Needlework" appeared on 22 March 1862 (II, 56-7) and the last full "Work-Table Supplement" on 8 March 1862 (II, 17-20).

As it happened, "The Work-Table Supplement" was the only section of the paper to be retained by the new management (except the chess problem which only lasted until 7 June 1862 (II, 265). The whole of the rest of the paper was entirely different. There were no more engravings of public affairs, only a few small portraits, only a few more humorous sketches. The illustrations were confined to objects connected with needlework, house and garden, objects of art and natural history and advertisements for corsets and carriages. What happened was that the paper was redesigned specifically as a woman's paper, which it had not been up till then. This was explained in the announcement:

> In the following expanded plan for the contents of "THE QUEEN," it will be seen that the Conductors have determined to make it as complete a Lady's Journal as is possible. It will be unrivalled as a record of that which is fashionable, elegant, and ornamental—useful as a Guide and Companion in the Domestic Household and Circle, and as a Collection of Information and Facts.
>
> The price of "THE QUEEN" will remain at 6d. weekly, as heretofore.
>
> "THE QUEEN" will be EDITED by a LADY.

(*The Queen*, II, 82)

At the same time, not surprisingly, the paper was remodelled on the lines of *The Field*. There were four aspects to this. As announced on 5 April 1862, the paper was divided, like *The Field*, into Departments, departments, of course, appropriate to a woman's paper. I list those of 12 April 1862: Notes on Dress, Court News, Household Economy and Domestic Science, Society, Rural Economy, Natural History, The Ladies' Library, Law and Justice, Church News, Births, Marriages and Deaths, and Miscellaneous. To this were added: Lyra Domestica (verses by lady writers), Pastimes (most important this), Fine Arts, Music and the Drama and others, while some of the headings of 12 April fell out of use.

Secondly, and something which is most important for my present purposes, readers were encouraged to write in to the editor. This was a definite invitation to readers in the original announcement formulated in three different ways:

> SOCIETY.—Under this heading will be given letters from Lady Subscribers on Domestic and Social Questions, and Letters containing such hints for "THE QUEEN," and its readers as cannot be classified under any of its various departments.
> ....
> NOTES AND QUERIES, and ANSWERS TO NOTES AND QUERIES, will be inserted under each department of the paper, thus opening to readers a medium of intercommunication and information on each and every of the subjects treated of in "THE QUEEN."
> ....
> TO CONCLUDE: Lady Readers are invited to communicate freely to the Editress their suggestions, hints, experiences, and observations. All will have a fair hearing in the columns of "THE QUEEN." (II, 82)

The announcement of 5 April was reproduced in the issues of 12 April (p.96) and 19 April (p.121) with minor alterations: for example the paper "is" edited by a Lady. Also a new column of readers' letters under the significant heading of "CONFIDENCES" is announced on 19 April in the following terms:

> Our invitation of last week has met with a heartier response than we had ventured to anticipate. We have, therefore, added "Confidences" as a department to THE QUEEN, and now print some of the letters which the week has produced from among our subscribers. (See page 127). Other communications, obviously intended as hoaxes (but of a very bungling kind), have been consigned to the waste-paper basket. The purpose of this department is to afford to the ladies of the kingdom an opportunity of speaking out upon some of the semi-social, semi-domestic questions, which so nearly affect their interests, but which hitherto have lain utterly neglected and un-agitated. . . . (II, 121)

It is interesting to have a paper at this early date reporting the receipt of bogus letters from the public. We are given a glimpse of the editorial process at work. The reader may think that some of the letters in the present collection are also hoaxes, though perhaps of a less bungling kind.

The third aspect of *The Field* which affected *The Queen* was the identity of the staff employed. The announcement of 5 April simply stated "new Contributors have therefore been retained." In fact, some of these already wrote for *The Field* and were brought in to contribute articles for the sister paper. Frank Buckland, surgeon and naturalist (1826-1880) and W.B. Tegetmeier (1816-1912) contributed articles on natural history, Francis Francis (1822-1886) on angling. A reader, "Free-lance," writing to *The Field* on 31 May 1862 welcomed this. He was gratified to find " 'Firefly,' Mr. Buckland, Mr. Francis, Mr. Grantley Berkeley and others also contribute to *The Queen*." (p.495). There were, of course, other contributors, and the fourth similarity to *The Field* was that their articles were usually signed, even if only with initials or a *nom de plume*.

Notable for their amusing contributions on various matters concerning the dress, habits and lives of women were Anson Hartley Turnour, a woman possibly related to Francis Francis, his married sister perhaps (his mother's maiden name was Hartley and the name "Anson" may be a tribute to the family's naval forbears: R.N. Rose, *op. cit.* p.66); "Peregrine," who admitted in a letter of 6 September 1862 (III, 14) that his name was Gage Earle Freeman and wrote "Letters" to "Cousin Kate;" J.J.B., presumably John James Britton, who published a couple of novels, and contributed articles under the heading "The Girls," usually citing the views of an imaginary old bachelor, "Mr. Surly Hardbake;" and R.B., joining on 24 January

1863 and writing on many subjects, sometimes invoking the activities of a typical Englishwoman he names "Anglicana," as in "Anglicana at the Derby" on 23 May 1863 (IV, 236). I have not able to discover his identity.

To reflect and emphasise the reorientation of the paper, it was now subtitled "The Lady's Weekly Journal," so that the words "The Queen; The Lady's Weekly Journal" appear at the top of each page. On 14 June 1862 the words "The Lady's Journal and Review" were incorporated into the title engraving in place of "An Illustrated Journal and Review." Thus only the three words on the left-hand scroll were changed.

Although in their publicity, the proprietors, or "the Conductors," as they called themselves, of *The Queen* laid great stress on the fact that the new *Queen* was to be edited by a Lady, they never told the reader who she was. A tantalising glimpse of her is perhaps provided by a series of five articles which ran from 12 April 1862 to 10 May 1862 stated to be written by "the Editress:" "A Lady's Walk Over the Scheideck and Wengern Alps; or, The Unprotected Females in Switzerland." But there is nothing personal or individual in the text to indicate who the writer might be. Another new feature introduced in April 1862 was a serial story: the first, on 19 April, "The Three Ladies of Fuddleborough; or, How the election was won and lost, A Tale of Love and Law." The author's name was not given.

Another acquisition occurred later in 1862. *The Lady's Newspaper*, founded in 1847, a rival to *The Queen* by its name alone, was purchased by Cox with effect from 11 November 1862. Cox then did a very odd thing. He did not kill off the paper entirely. *The Lady's Newspaper* continued to come out, but apart from the first and last sheets containing the first two and the last two pages, mainly advertisements and perhaps a fashion engraving, the contents were exactly the same as the corresponding pages of *The Queen*, except that they bore the name of the other paper at the top of each page. The public would buy what they thought was a different paper and find that the whole of the inside was the same as *The Queen*. Thus from 17 January 1863 the readers of both papers got a serialisation of Balzac's *Ursule Mirouet*.

This absurdity, however, only lasted until 27 June 1863, no. 95 of Volume IV. From the next issue, 4 July 1863, the proprietors started a new volume, numbering the issue, 862, and the volume, XXXIV, to harmonise with the numbering of *The Lady's Newspaper*. Thus there are no volumes V to XXXIII of *The Queen* as such. The Title engraving was redesigned to read:

THE LADY'S NEWSPAPER
THE QUEEN
& COURT CHRONICLE.

The design still had Windsor Castle in the background. On page 6 of this issue there was an announcement under the heading "AMALGAMATION:" "THE LADY'S NEWSPAPER, THE QUEEN, and COURT CHRONICLE—this day Amalgamated, and will bear the three titles in future. Established twenty years." I have not found any reference to a paper called *The Court Chronicle* in The British Library.

From 2 January 1864, with the commencement of volume XXXV, the title plate was redrawn much more drastically, the order of the names being reversed to "The Queen, The Lady's Newspaper, & Court Chronicle." Windsor Castle was still in the background, but in the centre of the design there is a pattern of leaves underlying the names of the other two papers. At the bottom right there are the names "Butterworth & Heath S.C." The price for this issue was 1s. but it reverted to 6d. the following week. Inside, the pages were headed simply "The Queen, The Lady's Newspaper." Also from this issue we get references to a Lady editor again, but not of the whole paper. Under the heading "Confidences," this notice is now added: "This department of THE QUEEN is Edited by a Lady; as are also the departments of "Dress and Fashions," "The Work-Table," and "Domestic Economy." Similar notices appear under each of the departments mentioned, until by December 1866 they appear only under the heading, "Our Boudoir." The last such notice was printed on 26 January 1867 (XLI, 72). Thereafter no information of any kind was given about the editorial staff.

The next important change in the paper's fortunes and character arose out of the sudden death of John Crockford, early in 1865. The last issue with his name in the imprint is that for 14 January. The following week his name is replaced by John Pownall Chorley, another member of Cox's managerial staff and at the time publisher of *The Field*. The imprint for 28 January 1865 is "Printed and Published for the proprietors by Horace Cox at 346, Strand." Horace Cox was the nephew of the proprietor, Edward William Cox, and had been with the firm since April 1862. His name stayed on the imprint until he retired over fifty years later in July 1913. His retirement was announced in the issue for 5 July 1913 and the paper paid a fulsome tribute to his long and meritorious service (CXXXIV, 7). In 1865 he was co-manager with Irwin Cox, becoming sole manager when his uncle died in 1879. Seven hundred people attended his jubilee celebrations in 1912, when he was presented with a silver cup. In his time the paper expanded from 16 to 200 pages, but many of its characteristics remained the same throughout his period of service.

There is something very special and distinctive about the contents of *The Queen* from April 1862 to the end of 1866, especially in the first two years. Whether this has anything to do with the influence of Crockford himself or with the alleged Lady editor is impossible to say. Certainly the influence of *The Field* is strong as is the feminine or even feminist flavour of the paper. Contributors write in a vein of spirited whimsicality. It is as if the boys from the men's newspaper had come across to help out the girls, bringing with them an atmosphere of romp and horseplay. In the articles on "Womanly Exercises," the girls are taught, among other things, to ride and drive (not cars, of course, but horse-drawn vehicles), angling, archery and swimming. The articles on swimming led to an instance of what I mean by horseplay. Readers ask about bathing costumes and also about whether a woman can swim in her clothes if she has the misfortune to fall overboard. Nothing loth, the swimming instructor puts it to the test by rowing out in a small boat, putting on the clothes he has borrowed from his sister and jumping into the sea. ("How I swam in petticoats and sank in crinoline" by "Un Giovonotto" in "Answers on Pastimes," 12 September 1863, XXXIV, 181-2)

An example of a lively article is "Suggestions on Female Costume" on 14 November 1863 (XXXIV, 322), in which "J.M." argues that the Bloomer costume was unsuccessful because it was worn with a tight bodice and suggests loose Mamlouk trousers and tunic without a corset as a wholly new costume for women. J.J.B. in the person of Mr. Surly Hardbake denounces this in a letter of 21 November 1863 (XXXIV, 341): "If the ladies take to the breeches—bedad, I forgot they wear them enough already—but I mean if they took to the pillowcases on their legs, we men should have to follow the Turks' example and don the petticoats. Fancy a Peer of Parliament or an admiral in a Turkish bedgown sort of robe! Pooh, the things is absurd—un-English." On the other hand in a previous article (30 August 1862, II, 507), condemning male drapers' assistants for taking employment away from women, J.J.B. would like to thrash one with his yardstick and tell him to be off, "or else put on petticoats and a crinoline." Anson Hartley Turnour also disagrees with "J.M." and in her long reply of 5 December 1863 (XXXIV, 375) expatiates on the feminine delights of wearing skirts: "Only a woman knows what it is to experience a soft feeling of satisfaction in the sound of a dress that rustles like the autumn leaves that 'through the forest-paths come drifting.' The dress must not creak or crackle, it must just rustle like falling leaves as it passes over the floor behind you. . . . Then again, at what perfect ease it puts a woman to have an immense amount of drapery about her that she can arrange and re-arrange, and take up and adjust, and let fall, and still be always sure that it will not look meagre." There were further contributions on this subject including two more from "J.M." On 2 January 1864 (XXXV, 26) she conceded to A.H.T. the charm of rustling skirts, but argued that the inconvenience of long, full skirts outweighed everything else. This is frank and illuminating writing about dress, and of its time unique, with its disclosure of personal attitudes and preferences as compared with contemporaries who wrote in general terms on the Art of dress.

"R.B." contributed many amusing articles. "Turn About" on 6 February 1864 (XXXV, 121) is a brilliant comic exposition of the reversal of male and female clothing and behaviour, already hinted at by J.J.B. "WHY NOT WEAR THEM AT ONCE," be begins in capital letters, "—grossly, openly, palpably? They've been worn figuratively (cynics declare) ever since

Adam and Eve were one." "Petticoats I have seen", on 12 March 1864 (XXXV, 200-1) is a contemporary male view of the fashion of wearing an ornamental petticoat over the crinoline, but showing beneath the over-skirt.

Above all it is the correspondence columns in different parts of the paper which give it such a special favour: contemporary opinion, frankly expressed, on a wide range of subjects. Correspondents, sometimes the authors of the main articles themselves, often wrote at great length. Some letters were included under "Confidences," others under "Dress and Fashion," "Pastimes," or other departments. Many of the letters were concerned with matters of dress and these included the crinoline, spurs for ladies, something already discussed in *The Field*, shaven heads and wigs for women, fainting gentlemen, men who use scent or have their hair curled, women's figures, corsets and figure training, sleeping in gloves (for white hands) and corporal punishment.

The question of wigs was raised in a series of letters, the first on 30 August 1862 (II, 511), from "Mary Blackbraid," a widow, who claimed that she shaved her head and always wore a wig. Several readers disapproved of her and some obviously thought that her whole output should have gone into the editor's waste-paper basket. The editor defended her thus on 22 November 1862 (III, 222) in his (or her) general "Notices to Correspondents:" "We have received numerous inquiries respecting this lady. Some questioners desire to know her address; some if she be a real personage or not. We can only answer that we believe 'Mary' to be a real personage, that she has a residence, that she is a lady, that she is in earnest in her statements and arguments, and that she practises what she preaches." It is very rare to find an editor vouching for his correspondent in such a detailed manner, although most, if challenged, would insist that the letter in question was in fact received as a letter from the public. In the same issue (p. 228) "Isabelle," in criticising "Mary Blackbraid," apparently wondered if it was a man writing the letters: "If indeed (which I could almost doubt) she be one of us."

On 6 September 1862 (III, 11) a light-hearted correspondence began on men who use scent and are subject to fainting fits. One woman stated that she would prefer fainting to smoking men. On 29 November 1862 (III, 250) "Carlos" wrote about "lady-like young men," who have their hair curled, and feared that if this habit were to spread "the position of the sex would become reversed."

Correspondence on the female figure began on 28 June 1862 (II, 330) when "A FATHER" asked for a work on the evils of tight-lacing. It ended on 30 June 1866, after much intimate detail had been supplied together with an anonymous "History of the Corset" (5 December 1863, XXXIV, 375) and learned articles by Frank Buckland on the natural human figure. One of the contributors to this correspondence compiled a little book on the subject: *The Corset Defended* by Mme. de la Santé (T.E. Carler, London, 1865), and it was reviewed in *The Queen* on 25 February 1865 (XXXVII, 127). She gave the historical background, quoting from Strutt, and reproduced several of the letters which had been printed in the paper. Much of her material was incorporated without acknowledgement into W.B.Lord's *The Corset and the Crinoline* of 1868.

A vigorous discussion on corporal punishment took place from 16 December 1865 to 3 February 1866, when it was closed down by the editor, although he did allow a few more in the period September to December 1866.

It is significant that after 1866 the paper ceased to print letters from readers altogether. Answers to correspondents of course continued as before, but no letters as such, on general topics or personal foibles, were reproduced in full. I have found one or two in the early eighties, but generally this policy was maintained. The management quite clearly abandoned this branch of journalism.

By 1866 and even by 1865 nearly all the writers from *The Field* and those who joined at the same time had left the paper. Some of them started new ventures. Frank Buckland founded *Land and Water* as a rival to *The Field* on 27 January 1866 (see *Life of Frank Buckland*, by his Brother-in-Law, George C. Bompas, London, 1885 and *The Curious World of*

D. H. EVANS & COMPANY, LTD., OXFORD STREET, LONDON, W.

No. 577 FB.—**Girl's Costume**, in Pale Blue, Grey, and Biscuit Faced-Cloth, Coat Lined Satin, Collar and Cuffs Trimmed Small Buttons. Fit girl age 6. Price 41/9, rising 2/- each size larger.
No. 577A FB.—**Fancy Straw Hat**, in White, Trimmed Tips and Ribbons. Price 15/9
No. 578 FB.—**Girl's Waist Dress**, in Navy and White Tweed, Deep Collarette round Shoulders, Piped White. Fit girl age 7. Price 23/6, rising 1/6 each size larger.
No. 578A FB.—**White Muslin Hat**, Trimmed Lace and Blue Rosettes. Price 10/11
No. 579 FB.—**Girl's Three-quarter Coat**, in Light Fawn Faced-Cloth, Lined through Polonaise Shoulder Cape, Trimmed Strappings of Cloth and Small Buttons. Fit girl age 7. Price 31/6, rising 2/- each size larger.
No. 579A FB.—**Drawn Jap. Silk Hat**, in White, Trimmed Rosettes. Price 12/6

No. 580 FB.—**Maid's Costume**, in Creme, Navy, and Cardinal Serge, Eton Coat Lined Sateen, Sun-ray Pleated Skirt. Fit girl age 14. Price 42/6, rising 2/- each size larger.
No. 580A FB.—**Tuscan Straw Toreador Hat**, with Feather Pom-pom. Price 14/6
No. 581 FB.—**Maid's Eton Coat and Skirt**, Coat Piped Navy, White, or Orange Cloth, and Lined through Striped Satin. Fit girl age 14. Price 52/6, rising 2/- each size larger.
No. 581A FB.—**Cream Fancy Straw Hat**, Trimmed Muslin and Daisies. Price 6/6

6. Costumes for Girls. *Catalogue Summer 1904, D.H. Evans & Co. Ltd., p.139.*

Frank Buckland by G.H.O. Burgess, London, 1967, although there is no mention at all of Buckland's contributions to *The Queen* in the former and only one brief mention in the latter, on page 86). "R.B." continued to contribute an article most weeks, usually about "Anglicana," until 9 Sept. 1865, on "Croquet" (XXXVII, 173). His last article, printed the following week, was appropriately entitled "Good-bye." Although he does not actually say that he is leaving the paper, this is his whimsical farewell to the readers of *The Queen*.

An aura of decorum and respectability now settles over the paper. Perhaps it is the influence of Horace Cox. The paper withdraws its skirts from too close a contact with its readers. Humorous, whimsical and spirited articles and essays give way to serious disquisitions on topics of general interest. In 1867 the paper prints a series of ten unsigned instalments on "Costumes and Fashions for Olden Times." In 1868 there are four instalments of the "History of Costume." Also in 1868 there are 14 chapters of "Early Education" by Mrs. Frederick Pedley, who wrote *Infant Nursing and the Management of Young Children* (London, 1866) and *Practical Housekeeping—or the Duties of a Home-Wife* (London, 1867).

There was one important exception to the departure of writers from *The Queen*. Eliane de Marsy's first article for the paper, "The Parisian World," dates back to 2 August 1862 (II, 430). She continued with the paper until 1897, her last contribution on "Paris Fashions" appearing on 25 Dec. 1897 (CII, 1217). According to an answer to a correspondent on 26 October 1872 (LI, 332), Eliane de Marsy was a French countess, but I have not been able to find anything more about her. There is no comment in the paper itself on her departure. A new columnist, Ella de Campo Bello, simply replaces her on 1 Jan. 1898 with a new series entitled "Paris Letter" (CIII, 30).

Another contributor of even longer service was Ardern Holt, well known for her books on Fancy Dress. Pat Raine and Anthea Jarvis, in the course of writing their own book, *Fancy Dress* (Shire Publications, 1984), were unable to find anything more about her. Quite recently, just as I was completing this section of the book, Anthea Jarvis, searching in *The Queen* of 1926 for something else, suddenly came across an article celebrating Ardern Holt's 60 years of writing for the paper. I am most grateful to her for finding this and for help in tracking down some of the articles mentioned. Although the article is inaccurate in detail and remains coy about Ardern Holt's true identity, it is of outstanding interest for the history of *The Queen*, for Holt's own career as a journalist and writer, and for the light it throws on the person who read the letters from correspondents and wrote the replies reproduced in this chapter. I am therefore going to reprint it in full with necessary corrections and comments in brackets.

THROUGH SIXTY YEARS
Ardern Holt—A Diamond Jubilee
and a Record.

On February 7th, 1866 [In fact, February 17th], an article signed "Ardern Holt" appeared in the *Queen* [It was signed "HET."]. That was the first of Ardern Holt's contributions to this paper and was indeed the first article she had ever written. Her latest work appears in this very number [That may be so, but no article in this number is actually signed by her; it might be the unsigned "The Gardens at Hinchingbrooke House."] and all who are connected with the paper hope that it will be far from her last. Sixty years of any honest work is a record to be proud of. Sixty years of brilliant work for one paper, and that by a woman writer, is a record which can never have been equalled. It is a unique achievement, and the *Queen* is proud that it plays its share in it.

In these days when women are reaching out into new spheres of work everywhere, we are constantly being reminded that Miss So-and-So is a pioneer, that Mrs. X is filling a position never before held by a woman. When these claims are put forward by the admiring friends of women writers and journalists Ardern Holt must smile to herself. Not long ago we were being told that for the first time a woman was reporting the Opening of Parliament. It was an account of the Opening of Parliament which formed Arden Holt's first contribution to this paper sixty years ago [The article under this heading on 10 February 1866 was the leading article and was unsigned (XXXIX, 103). Holt's first article seems to have been, "Womanhood and Politics," (17 and 24 February 1866, XXXIX, pp. 124-5 and 143-4)], and she continued an annual description of the event from then until Edward the Seventh was on the throne [e.g. "The Opening of Parliament" by HET. on 9 February 1867 (XLI, 104)].

Ardern Holt, it will be gathered, enjoyed many privileges which are denied to the ordinary working journalist. In her case the rare conjunction happened, for with the possession of these privileges was allied the unflagging energy, the devotion to duty, the keen observation and interest, the celerity of thought which marks the good journalist. When to all her work of writing is added that of managing a large establishment, of living a busy social life among troops of friends, and of much public and private entertaining, it becomes a matter for wonder that one woman could successfully cope with activities so many and so varied.

To hear Ardern Holt talk of her work is to enjoy a survey of the social history of the last three reigns. She was present at the wedding of the then Princess Royal, subsequently the Empress Frederick [Chapel Royal, 25.1.1858], and she reported for the *Queen* the weddings of Princess Alice [to Prince Louis of Hesse, Osborne House, 1.7.1862, but the report in the paper on 5.7.1862, (II, 343) was presumably not by her], the present Princess Royal [to Alexander Duff, Earl of Fife, at Buckingham Palace, 27.7.1889)], the Duke of Edinburgh [to the Grand Duchess Marie of Russia in St. Petersburg, 23.1.1874] and Prince Arthur of Connaught [to Louise Margaret of Prussia in St. George's Chapel, Windsor, 13.3.1879]. There were not then, as now, such facilities for members of the press, but Ardern Holt from girlhood was a guest at all the important functions of the year. In 1867 she began her articles "Peeps through the Lattice," a series of parliamentary sketches [In fact, the first, "The Peep through the Lattice, A Gossip on Parliament," signed "HET." was published the week following her previous article on 3 March 1866 (XXXIX, 159-60). There were twelve more such articles in 1866 up to and including 28 July (XL, 56)] . Her father was a Member of Parliament, and he used to take his young daughter to the House, where she listened to the debates from the uncomfortable Ladies' Gallery until he was ready to take her home with him [A quick look at Volume I (1832-1885) of Michael Stenton's *Who's Who of British Members of Parliament* (The Harvester Press Ltd. 1976) confirms that Holt is not Ardern Holt's true surname. No suitable Holt is an M.P. at the right time]. In that year, too, were gay doings when the Sultan, the Shah and other distinguished visitors came. Ardern Holt's account of them will be found in her articles ["The Gay Doings of the Sultan," unsigned, 20 July 1867 (XLII, 43)]. She was at the Guildhall dinner to the Sultan when Madame Mesurus, the wife of the Turkish Ambassador, died at the table ["The Ball at India House," unsigned, 27 July 1867 (XLII, 64)]; she was present at the great Naval Review, at Ascot ["The First Day of the Ascot Races," signed HET., 8 June 1867 (XLI, 448)], the Derby, Sandown and Goodwood, staying with her friends at pleasant houses and writing her chronicles each week.

"In 1867," she tells, "I first wrote about the meeting of the British Association, which I attended for many years later [Either of two unsigned articles: "The Savans at Dundee," or "The British Association at Dundee" on 14 September 1867 (XLII, 203 and 205)]. I went, in addition to the parties at my friends' houses, to most of the London public balls, such as the Caledonian, and those given by the Yorkshire Society and the City Companies. I went to the Hunt Balls, and was at Brighton for the autumn season, when there were great balls and festivities at the Pavilion."

About that time, too, she wrote an account of her yachting trip to the Baltic and through the Eider Canal, and even when her marriage in 1882 took her for a time to America and Jamaica, her flow of weekly articles did not cease. She began to write about Fashion (The interest aroused by her articles may be gauged from the fact that when she mentioned the productions of one firm the proprietor had to engage extra clerks to deal with the enquiries and orders which followed), and, herself a discriminating collector, on Curios.

But it would be difficult to name any woman's subject on which Ardern Holt's lively and industrious pen has not written.

Although her name has not recently appeared among the contributors to the *Queen*, it is no infrequent matter for the Editor's postbag to contain enquiries about her and requests that she should again contribute, the writers, remembering the youthful spirit which marked her work, not realising that Ardern Holt was not now a bright young girl but a worker who has more than earned her rest.

With Ardern Holt, however, rest is a comparative term. It means that she has made a change, and not a cessation of work, and that she now devotes herself entirely to the *Queen* Helping Hand Fund. Until recently, when a cold made the journey inadvisable, she never missed her regular days at the office, when she interviewed pensioners and applicants, packed parcels with the assistance of devoted friends, and attended to her correspondence. The accounts are now kept by the cashier of the Field Press, and a secretary helps her with letters, but the guiding spirit is still Ardern Holt. The administration of the Fund occupies the greater part of her life, and its success is her dearest wish.

To-day Ardern Holt is still the charming companion, the entertaining talker, the shrewd adviser that she was when the *Queen* readers, on opening their paper, first turned to read "the Ardern Holt." Her youthfulness she has retained to a surprising degree, and nobody meeting this bright-eyed, charming lady would guess that she was about to celebrate the passing of sixty years of unceasing work.

Her indignation at being ordered by her doctor to remain indoors and rest was both amusing and characteristic. "Ill!" she exclaimed. "I've never been a day ill in my life!" And no sooner had she been left alone than she was up and at work on the business of her beloved Fund. And to-day, when her persistent cold is troubling her, she may greet a visitor with a shake of the head and "My dear, I'm ill!" but a moment later the spirit bursts through and she is talking away with her old vitality and wit.

Ardern Holt is very proud of her long connection with the *Queen*. The *Queen*, in its turn, is proud to have had so vivid a personality among its contributors, and the Editor knows that in conveying congratulations to her on the sixtieth anniversary of her first contribution to these columns she is also presenting those of the many readers who still recall Ardern Holt's work with enjoyment.

(*The Queen*, 3 Feb. 1926, CLVIII, 4)

There are several curious features about this article. There are the inaccuracies which I have indicated. There is no mention of Holt's first signature, "HET." Nothing is said about her writing apart from her contributions to *The Queen*. Two photographs of Ardern Holt were printed with the article, one showing her "in the Court gown she wore when she was presented by her mother as a debutante of seventeen," the other "At the last Court of 1924." Anthea Jarvis thinks that the Court gown dates to 1859 or 1860, which takes Holt's year of birth back to 1842-43. In 1926 she would be in her early eighties. We learn that her father was an M.P. and that she was married, rather late, in 1882, an event which led to travel abroad. Otherwise her identity remains a mystery. The Ardernes were an old Cheshire family with a country seat south of Stockport (Harden Hall), but the male line had died out earlier in the century (see Volume I of J.P Earwaker's *East Cheshire: Past and Present*, 1877). "Holt" also has Cheshire connections. Perhaps Ardern Holt wished to preserve in her name some memory of such Cheshire families. Research into Victorian Members of Parliament, the weddings of 1882 and obituaries after 1926 may throw further light on the life of Ardern Holt.

Now that we know for the first time the full extent and nature of Holt's earliest, and more about her later, contributions to *The Queen*, we can see that she was one of those who added weight and substance to the character of the paper during and after 1866, which I have already remarked on. She wrote well-informed and sensible articles on politics, supporting women's suffrage, but she was also interested in the costumes of those who frequented the Opening of Parliament and Court functions. Holt mentioned Brighton in the remarks quoted above. It so happens that the first article I have been able to find actually signed "Ardern Holt," rather than "HET.," is "Doings and Fashions at Brighton" on 2 Jan. 1869 (XLV, 5). Then there is "Gossip on Dress and Knicknacks" (24 April 1869, XLV, 255 and 28 Aug. 1869, XLVI, 132-3), "A Gossip on Knicknacks" (30 Oct. 1869, XLVI, 255), "Spring Knicknacks" (30 April 1870, XLVII, 271) and "A Gossip on Dress" (29 April 1871, XLIX, 284). The unsigned, "A Gossip on Knicknacks" on 4 Feb. 1871 and "Dress at Scarborough," on 1 and 15 Oct. 1870 (XLVIII, 220 and 248) are probably also by her.

I have said above that no more letters from readers were published after 1866. This did not apply to the question and answer columns under each department. Readers continued to send in enquiries which were printed in full, and various contributors, some obviously members of the public, submitted replies. Holt's first contribution to "Dress Notes And Queries" was, I believe on 16 March 1872 (LI, 175) and her subject was fancy or historical dress, in particular, Di Vernon's costume in Scott's *Rob Roy*. There was also a column of shorter answers under "Dress and Fashion" headed simply "To Correspondents." In 1893 there are two developments. On 11 March 1893 Ardern Holt begins a new fashion column under the title "Dress Echoes of the Week," which continues until 1903, when it is replaced by "Fashion's Forecast" by Mrs. Jack May. Then from 6 May 1893 Ardern Holt's name appears under the heading "To Correspondents," although she continues occasionally to supply answers in "Dress Notes And Queries." Eventually the latter column is dispensed with and Holt's replies in the former become more expansive.

Meanwhile Holt had started to compile books on these subjects. *Fancy Dresses Described; or, What to Wear at Fancy Balls* was published by *The Queen* itself in 1879. Inside the front cover Debenham & Freebody of Wigmore and Welbeck streets advised readers that they could produce "every Description of FANCY and CHARACTER COSTUME" in connection with their "EVENING DRESS DEPARTMENT" and also that they could make to order any of the "Various Designs described by 'Ardern Holt.'" "Full Information, with Estimates, will be forwarded post-free on application." Ardern Holt's Introduction began, as it did in all later editions, with the words in capital letters: "BUT WHAT ARE WE TO WEAR? As a rule, this is the first idea on receipt of an invitation to a Fancy Ball. . ." From the second edition onwards her Introduction always ended: "There are few occasions when a woman has a better opportunity of showing her charms to advantage than at a Fancy Ball." *Fancy Dresses Described* went into six increasingly larger and better illustrated editions, 1881 (2nd.), 1884 (4th.), 1887 (5th.) and a sixth revised edition in 1896. Debenham and Freebody themselves took over publication of the second edition, in conjunction with Wyman & Sons, Great Queen Street (fourth and fifth),and with Edward Arnold, Strand (sixth). The sixth edition was enlarged and illustrated with sixty new coloured and black and white plates by Miss Lilian Young. This work contained a short appendix, "A Few Dresses Suitable For Boys."

In 1882, however, Wyman & Sons brought out Ardern Holt's *Gentlemen's Fancy Dress: How to Choose it*. This work also went into six editions, although only 3, 4 and 6 (1890, 1898 and 1905) are in The British Library. There were fewer changes to the different editions. The main text is the same throughout, with an appendix on "Fancy Dresses Suitable For Boys" from the third edition and more illustrations, in the form of photographs, in the sixth. The first edition, with minor alterations in subsequent editions, contained this amusing preface:

> The success of my little book on Ladies' Fancy Dresses, entitled, "FANCY DRESSES DESCRIBED; OR, WHAT TO WEAR AT FANCY BALLS," now passing through its third edition, has induced me to prepare an accompanying volume of Gentlemen's Costumes. I trust that the suggestions therein contained may be of some practical usefulness when "buckling shoes, gartering, combing, powdering," "silks,

velvets, calicoes, and the whole lexicon of female fopperies" come under the consideration of the Lords of the Creation.

LONDON, *Christmas*, 1882.   ARDERN HOLT

Ardern Holt's next publication was *Dress Outfits for Abroad* (London, Edward Arnold, 1904), followed by *How to Dance the Revived Ancient Dances* (London, Horace Cox, 1907). According to Holt's 1896 Introduction to *Fancy Dresses Described*, Horace Cox had also published *Cotillon by Ardern Holt*, "a small volume" in which "full particulars of the several figures are given" (p.xii), but this is not included in the British Library Catalogue. An illustrated article entitled "The Jocund Dance" was published in *The Queen* on 20 November 1909 (CXXVI, 944-5).

All these titles reflect some of the most popular subjects in the Question and Answer columns: historical dress, folk costume, fancy dress, costumes for all sorts of dancing, outfits for foreign parts, especially India and The West Indies. In addition readers requested information about a bewildering variety of subjects as well as advice on dressmaking as regards style and fabrics and also with particular ages and situations in mind. There was much about the care and cleaning of clothes, details of shoes, types of corset for different figures and ages, questions on jewellery and earrings.

Although Holt wrote in such an arch manner about her book on men's fancy dress and mentions "female fopperies," no such fopperies are suggested for her male clients. Some costumes, such as those for Persians and Sardanapalus (as in Byron's verse drama) involve gowns, but they are in no way feminine gowns. She has no liking for cross-dressing for either sex. For her, the only thing remotely acceptable is baby or child costume such as these items in *Gentlemen's Fancy Dress* (the costumes are set out in alphabetical order):

> BABY (to be assumed by a tall man). White muslin dress tucked and trimmed with embroidery, low neck, short sleeves, broad blue sash; coral necklace around the throat; sleeves looped up with coral armlets; white socks; blue kid shoes, with straps buttoned round ankles; rattle in hand.
>
> FATHER'S DARLING. To be worn by a grown man. Child's tunic; frilled trousers; sandalled shoes, with socks; the skin covered with tights; a hoop in hand; large pinafore.

There are also costumes for "schoolboy" (for a tall man) and "Tommy Tucker." The acceptability of these presumably lies in the fact that they are male costumes at different ages. They represent a reduction in age, rather than a change of sex. That frequenters of "Fancy Balls" used this sort of costume is proved by the following extract from *The Queen* of 14 February 1891. It shows that "baby parties" were popular long before the antics of the twenties as described by Evelyn Waugh in *Vile Bodies*:

> The FANCY BALL of the HAYDN MUSICAL SOCIETY was held at the Portman Rooms, Baker-street, on Monday evening. Coote and Tinney's band occupied the orchestra. Only fancy dresses were admitted, the term including boating, tennis, cycling, and Windsor uniforms. The prevailing idea, carried out in a variety of ways, was the representation by adults of juvenile costumes. A gentleman appeared as a baby in a long muslin infant's robe, low bodice, and short sleeves, a close-fitting cap, blue sash, with a baby's bottle and a rattle tied to the waistband. Two young ladies had short tucked muslin frocks, wide sashes, and poke sun bonnets; and another little girl, as portrayed by a grown-up person, wore a gold curling wig, a mob cap, large muslin pinafore, a large red sash below the hips, red shoes and stockings. (LXXXIX, 252)

For boys who were still in petticoats, there was a FLY COSTUME FOR BOY OF FOUR, consisting of a "Golden yellow satin skirt, ornamented with black braid, and studded with small gauze flies." Under the heading REYNOLDS, SIR JOSHUA she writes:

> There are many costumes, peculiarly well suited to boys, which this celebrated artist has made famous by his portraits. For example, in "Feeding the Chickens," black

shoes with black bows; red stockings; blue petticoat, with blue band; white high pinafore, with red sash, made with a wide falling collar, bordered with frill; sleeves to elbow; a red bow at throat. In "Doubtful Security," the child wears shoes with straps; also a yellow and blue skirt; low white pinafore, with pink sash. "The Affectionate Brothers" . . . . . the baby all in white, with a gaily trimmed Gainsborough hat in miniature, and a cherry-coloured sash round its tiny waist. (*Gentlemen's Fancy Dress*, 3rd. edition, 1890, p.53, but the first two items were included at page 66 of the first edition of *Fancy Dresses Described*, 1879)

The last is "The Lamb Children" of 1783 (Royal Academy Exhibition Catalogue, 1986, pp. 153 and 305), but I have not been able to identify the other two with any certainty. Such fanciful titles, popular with the Victorians, have gone out of fashion. I presume that by "Feeding the Chickens" she means the portrait of Lady Catherine Pelham Clinton at the age of five painted in 1781 (R.A. Cat. pp. 152 and 297), although the little girl has pink shoes and a white petticoat. Perhaps Holt is suggesting that black shoes and a blue petticoat are more suitable for a boy. "Doubtful Security" I can only guess is Master Philip Yorke painted in 1787 at the age of two-and-a-half years. A robin is perched on his left arm. To the left a seated dog looks up at the boy. An engraving of it was entitled "Anne and her Friends," wrongly identifying the boy as a girl. The painting is now part of the Iveagh bequest, Kenwood (A. Graves and W.V. Cronin, *A History of the Works of Sir Joshua Reynolds*, 1899, III, 1085 and Ellis Waterhouse, *Reynolds*, 1941, p. 279).

Some boys, however, did go to fancy dress parties in the garb of the opposite sex, as can be shown from other newspaper reports. At the Bicycle Gymkhana in the Warren, Donaghadee on Saturday, 24 Aug. 1901, "two prizes for gentlemen were awarded. Master Willy Turtle winning that for style and appearance as Britannia" (*Irish Society and Social Review*, 7 Sept. 1901, p. 2713). At the Children's Fancy Ball at the Pillar Room for the Aidus fete, "Master Irwin was a handsome toreador, in a dress beautifully made by his mother; his brother went as "WHICH?" half as a boy and half as a little girl" (*The Figaro and Irish Gentlewoman*, 29 Nov. 1902, p. 815). While at the Mansion House Ball for children in 1909, "Master Maurice Brough was a suffragette, attired in a plaid dress and a poke bonnet" (*Modern Society*, 16 January 1909). These examples illustrate the point that cross-dressing in fancy dress for the male sex is acceptable where the costume is not the ordinary wear of a girl or a woman of the same age and class as the boy or man, but something quite different and distinctive. After all, a youth convincingly got up in a fashionable woman's evening gown would appear not to be in fancy dress at all, and therefore not qualify for admittance. In this connection Ardern Holt seems somewhat out of touch or old-fashioned. She was equally opposed to men's dress for her lady clients and is in fact puzzled by it. "Why does your daughter want to dress as a boy?" she asked plaintively of one mother, but still gave details of costumes for Aladdin and Dick Whittington. To "Cymric" she replied on 13 February 1909: "What an altogether extraordinary party! Certainly let her wear the golf knickers if it is a dance; otherwise it would be most objectionable, unless she had the usual underskirts and drawers in one sold for girls who are learning dancing. . . . The son would have as underwear with kilts tight short drawers of the same tartan as the kilt" (CXXV, 286). On 14 May 1910, however, she was quite happy to advise "Patricia" about Shakespearian dress: "As you want to go as a boy and to look girlish, choose Viola" (CXXVII, 895). But she does not approve of Dollie Effie's ideas of "Dress for Daughter:" "England is a free country, and provided the costume is decent no one will interfere; but it is not usual for a girl of thirteen to go about in the suburbs in kilt and sporran. There are many 'cranks' about, and no doubt her appearance will come under that head, especially if she indulges in all those jewels you mention—quite unsuitable to a young girl. You seem to exercise much ingenuity in the matter of costume" (7 Sept. 1912, CXXXII, 446).

On the other hand the first reply in this selection consists of advice to a man on the correct riding dress for women. Why he needs it is not explained. She is also quite happy to advise a man on a suitable corset and gown in which to appear as a lady in a play. Earrings for men, however, she found distasteful.

By 1900, there was just one column of answers to questions on dress. It was headed "Dress and the Toilette," with underneath that, "To Correspondents by Ardern Holt." The procedure was that the questioner's pseudonym was printed on the left in capitals, then the question or topic in italics, then Holt's reply. The reader's original letter was not reproduced, so it is not always possible fully to understand the reply. Sometimes Holt replies at such length that the nature of the question can be inferred with some certainty. At other times, one is left in tantalising bafflement.

From 1901 (I have not checked earlier years in detail) we find Holt answering questions of ever greater variety and strangeness. Her readers show an interest not just in the best or cheapest corsets, but in the practice of tight lacing, not just in shoes, but in specifically high-heeled shoes. Men write in about stays for themselves and some want women's stays. There is a great deal of interest in the clothing of the small boy, not just contemporary wear for day or evening, but in the skirted costumes of mid-century and the underwear worn then. There are also questions about what a boy should wear under the kilt. Some readers seem to think that it is a good idea to dress boys as girls. Two or three men seek advice on costumes for female impersonation, while others are interested in earrings and jewellery for themselves.

I have therefore made a selection of Holt's replies on these topics, in so far as boys and men are concerned. Normally in these selections I have not included letters about men's stays, as that is really a matter of men's dress, but Holt's replies on these points are so informative that I have included them. She provides, for example, names of suppliers that I have not seen mentioned elsewhere. Holt did not agree that boys should be dressed as girls for any reason, except the very small boy in fancy dress as we have seen above, and she gave her views forcefully whenever she disagreed. But she had some strange ideas. She seemed to think that long hair weakened a boy, and that if a mother did dress her son as a girl, the police would intervene, and restore the lad to trousers. Perhaps she was influenced in this by her memories of the press reports of the Boulton and Park case of 1870-71 (see *Men in Petticoats*).

It is noticeable that interest in these topics increased during and after 1909, just as it did in the other papers included in this collection. It is as if, just when Fashion decreed the end of it, a nostalgic passion for, and interest in, the wasp waist, was suddenly awakened in the public mind. Similarly, just as small boys were beginning to be dressed in a less girlish way, so a sudden interest arose in the period when feminine influence over boys' dress as at its height, the eighteen-fifties. The idea that boys wearing a kilted costume could or should wear petticoats under their kilts also found favour in some quarters.

Ardern Holt continued to answer readers' questions until January 1914. Her last signed column appeared on 10 Jan. 1914 (CXXXV, 66). On 17 Jan. 1914, p. 124, there were only three replies, with no name under the heading, "To Correspondents." A full, but unsigned, column reappeared on 24 Jan. (p. 168). Before the discovery of the 1926 article I had supposed that Holt died, fell ill, but certainly left the paper, at this point. But we have seen that she continued to make contributions until at least 1926. Nevertheless she does seem to have relinquished this column early in 1914. Over the years her replies represent a fascinating body of evidence about the dress and manners of the time, and about the foibles and idiosyncrasies of her correspondents.

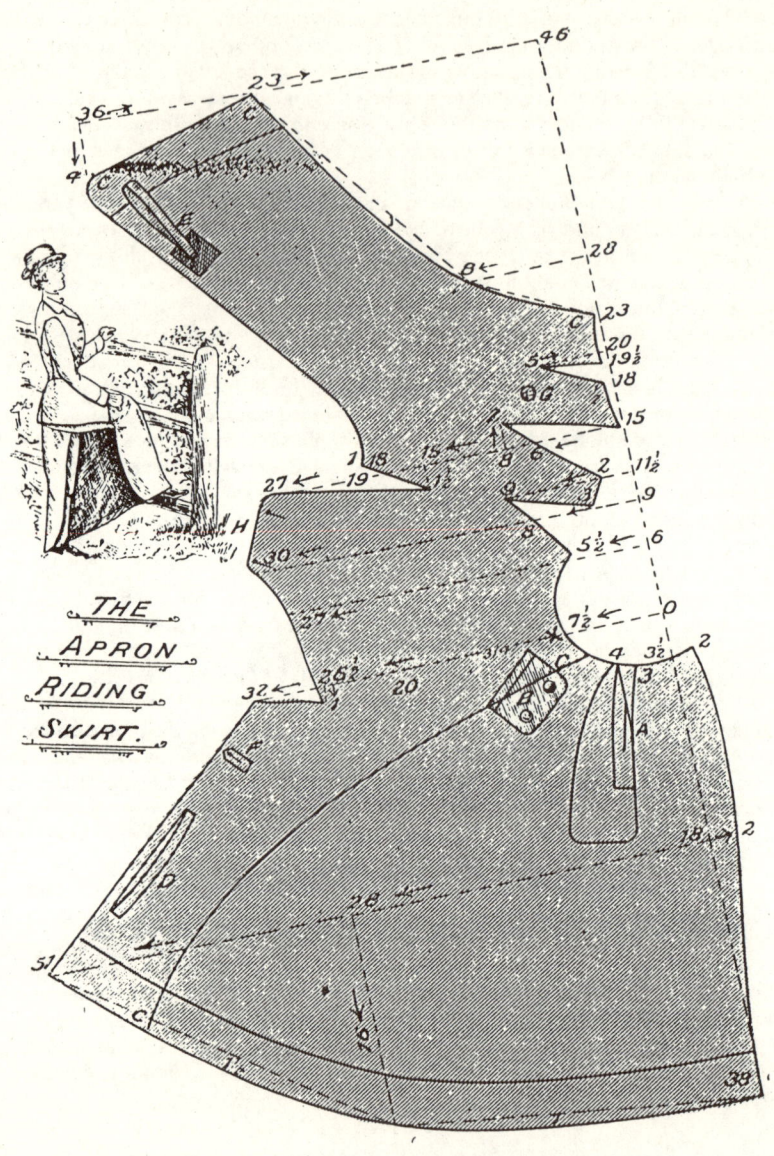

7. The Apron Riding Skirt. *The Ladies' Tailor*, September 1906, p.197.
(*By Courtesy of Janet Kent*)

i. Ardern Holt in the Court gown she wore when she was presented by her mother as a debutante of 17.
The Queen, 3rd February 1926, p.4.
© Manchester City Art Galleries.

ii. Toilettes de Casino pour Villes d'eaux.

The Queen, 3rd April 1909.
© Manchester City Art Galleries.

THE QUEEN, THE LADY'S NEWSPAPER

DRESS AND THE TOILETTE
ANSWERS TO CORRESPONDENTS by ARDERN HOLT

4th January 1902 (CXI, 25)

SNOWDROP.–No coupon is necessary for the dress department. I am very happy to give information to a "Mere Man."
The Complete Outfit for Riding.
A habit with basque bodice and skirt, breeches (generally wash-leather or cloth), high boots. Breeches are better than knitted or woven pantaloons. You had better put yourself in the hands of such a firm as Tautz (Oxford-street). The first habit is not the kind of thing to intrust to a country tradesman. The best breeches are either all cloth or all wash-leather. Shoes are utterly out of the question; high boots are the proper thing. Ordinary walking boots are also impossible. The length of the riding habit entirely depends on the cut, and each good tailor has his special one. Busvine, in Brook-street, W.; Tautz, in Oxford-street; Simmons, Coventry House, Haymarket; Hart, in Regent-street; and Thomas, in Brook-street, W., are all to be depended on. It would be quite impossible to give you a pattern of a good riding habit; you should certainly have a safety habit, and the skirt should be just long enough to cover the foot. The present style of habit is with a basque to reach to the saddle at the back and to the waist in front, worn with a vest, but some people wear covert coats, and in the summer sailor hats and even loose skirts. A felt hat is the best all the year round. Dark blue, dark green, and dark brown habits are worn, but dark blue would be more generally useful. The high hats are said to be coming in, but at present they are mostly confined to certain hunts. It is not usual to wear a veil now unless it is to protect the face in case of heat. Doeskin and chevrette gloves are worn. A small light riding whip should be carried, but it would be quite worth your while to go to a good house and be well turned out. Riding gear that is not up to date and correct in every detail is a solecism.

[This riding outfit seems to be destined for the man himself, but no hint is given of the reason behind the enquiry. The costume described is of course for riding side-saddle and the "safety" skirt, which was slit up the back and fastened with hooks or press studs when dismounted, was designed to prevent accidents when the rider was thrown from her saddle (see Phillis Cunnington & Alan Mansfield, *English Costume for Sports and Recreation*, Adam & Charles Black, 1969, pp. 121-125; Sarah Levitt, *Victorians Unbuttoned*, George Allen & Unwin, 1986, pp.193-199; and, for more detail, contemporary volumes of *The Ladies' Tailor* and Part V of *Vincent's Systems of Cutting all Kinds of Tailor-Made Garments* by W.D.F. Vincent, The John Williamson Co. Ltd., 1903). A detailed description of what was then the latest safety skirt supplied by Messrs. Thomas and Sons, of 32, Brook street, who are mentioned above, was given in *The Queen* of 14 Feb. 1891, (LXXXIX, 265), and by another firm on 2 May 1891, (LXXXIX, 691).]

SNOWDROP
Handkerchiefs.

11th January 1902 (CXI, 59)

You are certainly wise in getting really good handkerchiefs; they look so much better and are so much more pleasant to use. If you go next week to John Wilson's Successors Ltd., 188, Regent-street you will find Irish linen cambric hemstitched handkerchiefs very low in price, as are the real French cambric, and they have what they call a glove handkerchief, very small in size, which will get over your difficulty when wearing a pocketless dress, as they are easily slipped into the opening of the glove.

[Is this further advice to the same man?]

MICHAEL 30th April 1904 (CXV, 738)
A Good French Corset Maker in London who would Copy My Own Pattern, and Make Stays to my Measurements.

Mme Zilva at Debenham & Freebody's Cavendish House, Wigmore-street would reproduce any design desired.

FANNY 10th September 1904 (CXVI, 406)
Can a Boy of Twelve be Dressed as a Girl?

You give no address, and the rules for correspondents are clearly set forth on the last page of the *Queen* each week as follows: "Every communication must be dated, and bear the name and address of the writer." When you have conformed to these regulations I will consider your communication seriously, and give you the legal as well as the commonplace view of the subject.

["Fanny" apparently never did comply with the rules as no further reply is addressed to her. She may well have been put off by this response. We shall see from a later reply that Holt believes that there is some legal bar to what "Fanny" suggests.]

NON-EFFEMINATE 14th April 1906 (CXIX, 632)
Men's Stays.

I have had many queries from men on this subject. The firms that seem to give most satisfaction are Ruben & Co., 15, Sloane-street; Mme. Land, Rostrevor-road, Fulham, S.W.; Ford and Parr, Electric Parade, Brixton, S.W. and Mey & Co., 116, Newgate-street. I give you all these addresses because each has a *specialité*, and I strongly advise you to write to all and see which best suits your ideas.

[Since January 1901 similar lists were provided on 30 May 1903 (p.862) and 21 October 1905 (p.686). In both those lists the name of Mme. Dowding, 8, Charing Cross-road was also included. She is however mentioned with approval on 2 Nov. 1907]

PREVIOUS CORRESPONDENT 12th May 1906 (CXIX, 806)
Stays to be Worn by a Man, but not Stays Usually Sold as Men's Stays.

You had better go to Sykes, Josephine and Co., Regent-street, and be fitted, and have a pair made for you.

[This is the first definite request from a man for women's stays, presumably from "Non-Effeminate." The firm mentioned was a well known ladies' outfitters.]

ELLALINE 4th May 1907 (CXXI, 826)
Corsetière Wanted to Make Stays for Two Gentlemen Who are to Take Ladies' Parts in Private Theatricals.
Mrs. George Sykes, 24, Hanover-square will do this very well for you.

ANGLO-INDIAN 2nd November 1907 (CXXII, 928)
Where Gentlemen's Stays Can be Had.
You would get these from Dowding, 8, Charing Cross-road. I have received both your letters, the last one enclosing a card. I often have similar enquiries, and I find when I have recommended this firm it has always given satisfaction.

[Curiously Dowding was not mentioned in the reply to "Non-effeminate" on 14 April 1906, but she now gets this whole-hearted tribute, which is useful evidence of her standing in the trade. An article about her was printed in *Modern Society* on 15 Aug. 1908, p. 28, entitled "A Famous Corset Artist."]

DIAMOND 22nd February 1908 (CXXIII, 329)
Stays for Boys of 17 for Reducing Waist Measurements.
From Mrs. Sykes, 24, Hanover-square.
What Underclothing for a Boy of Fifteen to Wear with a Kilt Costume Who is to Dance a Pas Seul.
Lace underclothing would certainly be quite out of place; close-fitting drawers and an under petticoat are the only alternatives.
Are Ladies' Shoes Made with 5-inch Heels? If so, Where can They be Had?
You can get shoes with heels of any height from J. Box, Regent-street.

[As I interpret the lay-out of the text, these are three questions from "Diamond." The correspondent is apparently contemplating putting a boy of seventeen into stays, and making a boy of fifteen wear a lace-trimmed petticoat under a kilt. Even Holt allows a petticoat of some sort, but she is criticised for this by a later reader. It is not clear who is going to wear the shoes.]

ZNYIGUA 22nd February 1908 (CXXIII, 329)
Costumes for Children After Styles Worn About 1855 to 1860.
I have before me at this moment a coloured fashion plate of a small boy in red trousers that come just below the knee, not drawn in knickerbocker fashion, and with stripes outside. He wears white stockings and blue, low buttoned boots, a blue-banded paletot, with a red band down the front, large sleeves, with turn-back cuffs, and white full undersleeves, a straw hat and black ribbons. These little trousers were certainly buttoned on to stays, but a boy of six nowadays would be too big for this, and would need braces.

Another little boy about the same date wears a short, plaid kilted frock, with white trousers, cut much as the red ones were, appearing below, and a short blue jacket opening over a shirt, the sleeves also made with under muslin sleeves. In 1863 knickerbockers for boys were just coming in. In 1850 boys wore trousers, edged with vandyked embroidery, appearing below their frocks. For women combinations were unheard of in those days, and the drawers were buttoned on to bodices or stays. The lace-trimmed petticoats were made with a deep flounce, which, like the hem, was edged with lace, and set into a band fastened round the waist with a button.

[The name of the correspondent may be Czech, as some of their words begin with "Zn."

Although Holt refers to fashion plates, she may to some extent be writing from memory, having probably been born well before 1850, as I have suggested above.]

ENQUIRER   7 March 1908 (CXXIII, 426)
Underdress for a Highlander in Kilts.
A Highland lady has written that a Highlander would never wear a petticoat under a kilt. The pipers who dance on platforms at concerts or competitions all wear tight short drawers of the same tartan as their kilts. Gentlemen at balls or on any other occasion never wear anything but white woollen or spun silk tights under their drawers and so do all big boys.

QUEENSLANDS   4th April 1908 (CXXIII, 588)
Where Can Two Boys Coming from the Colonies, where They Were Allowed to Run Wild, Procure Stays to Improve Their Figure?
Mrs. George Sykes, 24, Hanover-square is very clever at making them.
Gauntlet Gloves With Gauntlets that Would Pull up over the Sleeves.
These you could get at Penberthy's, Oxford-street. The stays for a youth of eighteen you could also get from Mrs. George Sykes. Ordinary ladies' stays would not do. You need quite a different cut for the male figure.

QUEENSLAND   25th April 1908 (CXXIII, 719)
Clothing for Boy in Kilt.
It would be more consistent with Scotch custom to wear tight short drawers of the same tartan as the kilt, as the pipers do when they dance on platforms. Gentlemen mostly wear white woollen or spun silk tights over their usual drawers. The tartan drawers will be far better than what you suggest for a boy of fifteen. At balls gentlemen wear white gloves with kilts, but it is quite unusual to wear any gloves with a kilt out of doors.
Stays for Gentlemen.
These can be had from Mrs. George Sykes, 20, Hanover-sq.
[Holt has learnt the correct underwear for kilts, since her reply to "Diamond" (22-2-1908), after taking note of "Enquirer's" letter (7.3.1908). Obviously the correspondent had something more feminine in mind.]

MOME   13 June 1908 (CXXIII, 1012)
How Long Should Boys be Clothed in Corsets and Petticoats?
It is quite unusual for a boy to wear corsets after he is three or at most four years old. Seven years of age is very unusual, and it would be wiser to have his hair cut, as it is probably sapping his strength. In England you would expose your son to ridicule if you kept him so late in life thus clothed. Possibly in South Africa it would not be so remarkable. It is a case where you are the best judge. I can only tell you what is the ordinary idea on the subject.
[Holt reveals here a very curious, old fashioned prejudice about the effect on boys of having long hair. The age given by her for a boy to leave off petticoats is two years younger than would have been normal fifty years before. This may well be the advice remembered by "Ino," writing in *London Life* on 2 Aug. 1941:
"I quote (from memory) some details from the correspondence column of a ladies'

magazine published about thirty-five years ago:

> BOY'S SCOTCH DRESS. Your boy of eleven could not be clothed as you suggest whilst living in the British isles. You say, however, that you are shortly leaving this country to reside for several years in a remote Continental country. As foreigners do not usually understand the intricacies of Scotch dress, and consider it to be a feminine affair, we think that there would be no harm in your boy wearing white frilled petticoats, etc., under his kilt, whilst he is abroad."

The dates are close: 35 years before 1941 is 1906, compared with the actual year, 1908. But in the writer's mind the boy's age has been increased by four years, from seven to eleven, while South Africa has become a remote Continental country. The question has also become one about Scottish costume, instead of just underwear, but then, as we have seen, Holt had recently answered questions about the correct underwear to be worn with kilts. Another point is that it is not clear whether Holt's boy is actually about to visit South Africa, has just returned from there, or is already living there. "Ino" has taken it that the boy concerned is going abroad. Her letter is important and interesting for two reasons. If the paragraph in *The Queen* is not what she remembered, then her letter is evidence for a similar piece of advice from another source. If it is the original source of her "memory," then we can see how she has elaborated Holt's answer in the way she wants, to conjure up a picture of a boy of eleven wearing frilled petticoats and knickers (the "etc.") under his kilt, in short virtually dressed as a girl.]

X.Y.Z.   26th September 1908 (CXXIV, 552)
What Kind of Stays are Best for a Boy of Eighteen, Whose Figure is Very Bad?
    You should have them specially made by Mrs. George Sykes, 24, Hanover-square.

H.R.   10th October 1908 (CXXIV, 649)
Wanted, a Corsetière Who Makes for Gentlemen as Well as Ladies.
    Mrs. Steele, 38, Upper Berkeley-street, Portman-square, makes excellent stays for both sexes, and has scored special success with gentlemen's stays. You may rely on getting a pair there, made and well fitted to the figure. A great many men do now undoubtedly wear stays, and find their many advantages as you are anxious to do.

PERALIA   10th October 1908 (CXXIV, 649)
Stays for Boys.
    At any outfitter's where boys' underclothes are sold you can get such stays as boys of tender years wear, but they do not have any when they don anything approaching virile habiliments. Mrs. George Sykes, 24, Hanover-square, makes excellent stays for youths, and could, of course make them for boys, but you would not find them ready made on anything like the same plan and range as for girls, the boys you speak of abroad this year owe their trimness to wide tight leather belts.

MENTONE   5th December 1908 (CXXIV, 1028)
How Boys Some Fifty Years Ago Were Dressed When about Four to Six Years Old as to Underclothing.
    The drawers were then made to fasten at each side, and were buttoned on to the stays,

D. H. EVANS & COMPANY, LTD.,   OXFORD STREET, LONDON, W.

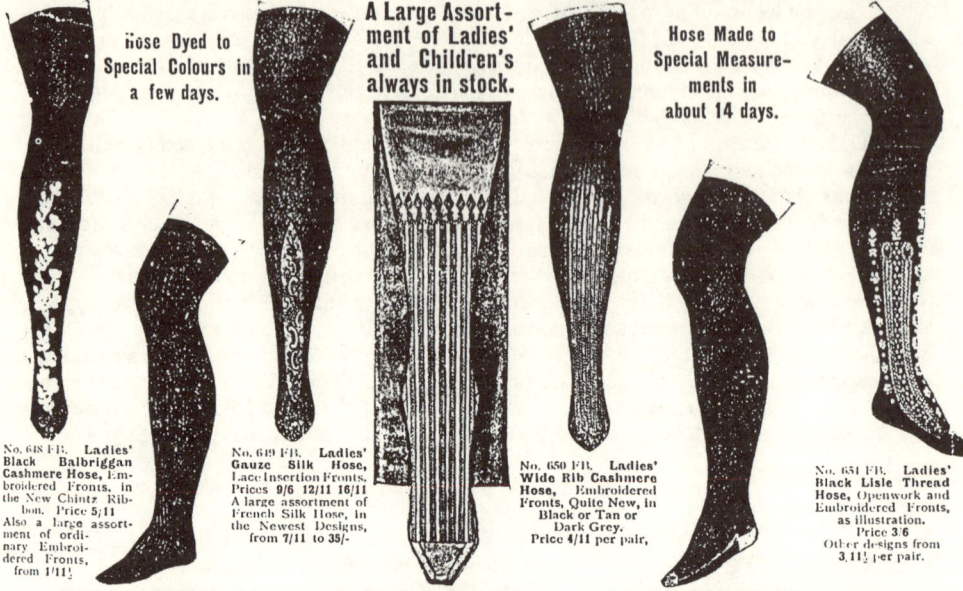

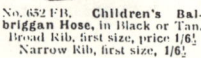

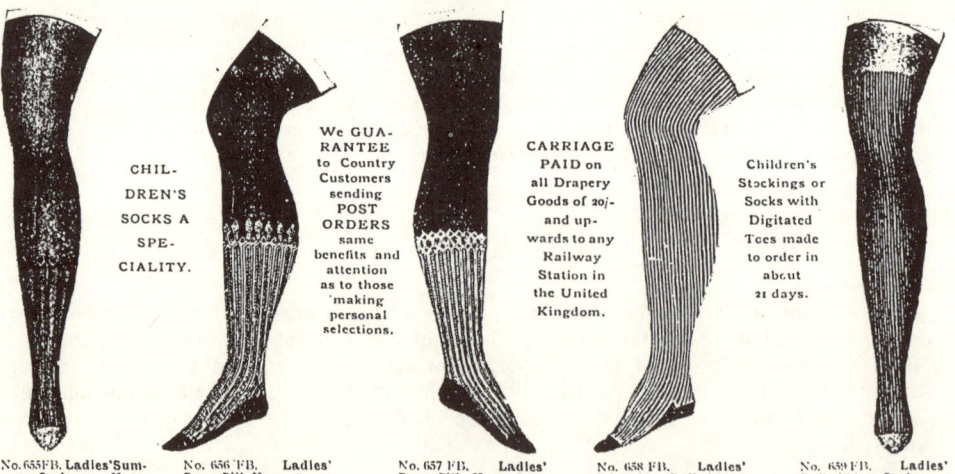

Catalogue Summer 1904, D.H. Evans & Co. Ltd., p.169.

with a flannel vest beneath; combinations were unknown. The little white petticoats were very much starched, and socks were worn with shoes with straps round the ankle.

L.M.   19th December 1908 (CXXIV, 1118)
Gentlemen's Corsets.

Mrs. Steele, 38, Upper Berkeley-street, Portman-square could make them for you without seeing you by means of self-measurement. You could have one pair for day wear of fine broché, one for evening of silk batiste, and a linen broché for hunting corsets, with a porous elastic, for which Mrs. Steele is noted, slip gores, and chamois padding. I do not think this clever *corsetière* makes shirts or underlinen for gentlemen, but she has a choice collection of underclothing and hosiery of every description and quality for ladies in the way of combinations, chemises, nightdresses, knickers, in longcloth, cambric, wool, silk (spun and pure), and silk and wool combined; the stockings of cotton, lisle, and embroidery are particularly good. She does sell gentlemen's handkerchiefs as well as ladies', and makes anything needed to order in this, including petticoats.

STAY LACE   23rd January 1909 (CXXV, 143)
Corsets for Men.

A correspondent says he has worn them for some time, and speaks warmly in praise of the ordinary woman's corset, which, properly fitted, are the acme of comfort. He always wears those which are much the same as are worn by ladies, and goes to the best *corsetière* obtainable.

CORSETED   27th February 1909 (CXXV, 374)
Gentlemen's Stays.

We are very glad that you are so extremely satisfied with the corsets you have had from Mrs. Steele, 38, Upper Berkeley-street, W. made from measurement when in India, and another comfortable pair made when in England, and that you can confidently recommend any gentleman who wished to try wearing corsets to go to this firm.

A.S.   27th March 1909 (CXXV, 546)
Wanted, a Pair of Corsets at Birmingham, to be Worn by a Gentleman, but Such as Ladies Wear.

Staymakers at Birmingham are as follows: Mme. Rosa Shelley, 14, City Arcades; Miss Nellie Blant, 60, Ryland-street; Mrs. Frances Helen Kniff, 39, Horse Fair; Mme Walker, 31, Parade, but you would best get what you want at a draper's, such as Newbury or Lewis, Bull-street; Rogerson & Co., New-street; Holiday, Long & Co. in the same street. Your best plan would be to write for some to be sent on approval, and make your selection.

[All the names cited can be identified in Kelly's *Directory* for 1908, although there are some errors in Holt's spelling: "Shelley" should be "Melley" and "Kniff," "Knibb." There are 32 staymakers in the list and over 100 drapers. Only Melley paid for heavy type, and in view of her prospective male customers, her entry deserves to be reproduced in full:

> Melley Madame Rosa (court corsetière) (corsets modelled and fitted to the figure before completion; fashion agents engaged in Paris and Vienna; figures perfected), 14 City Arcades.]

A.S.   10th April 1909 (CXXV, 618)
Gentlemen's Corsets.

You can obtain from Rosenbaum, 115, Westbourne-grove, the exact kind of ordinary ladies' corsets required, which, a correspondent writes, are far more comfortable than so-called gentlemen's stays.

17th April 1909 (CXXV, 679)
What Corset and Dress Should a man wear to Look Nice as a Fashionable Lady for Theatricals?

As far as the corsets are concerned, you should have the corset novelty of the century, C.B. Royaliste Shield Suspender Corset. The C.B. Corset Company, 31, London Wall, will tell you where to get them if you consult them. In the Supplement to the *Queen* newspaper of April 3 the coloured plate Toilettes de Casino pour Villes D'eaux you will see exactly how the tight dresses are made. I should say the last figure in green, with a very notable hat, would suit you, or the blue at the opposite end of the picture, or the red one in the centre. In ordering the stays you must give your measurements. You do not say whether you need evening dresses. For the day gowns satin delaine or satin souple would be best, for the evening satin charmeuse. Consult the *Queen*, numbers of March 6 and 13 [pp.392-3 and 438-40], where you will see a large choice of the Court dresses represented.

[I have been unable to find an illustration of this particular corset, but "C.B." was a well-known firm, the letters standing for Charles Bayer. By courtesy of The Gallery of English Costume, Platt Hall, Manchester I reproduce the relevant parts of the coloured plate. The court dresses mentioned are shown in photographs of ladies wearing them. With their court trains they go beyond what would be required by "X."]

INSISTENCE   24th April 1909 (CXXV, 720)
Gentlemen's Stays.

Yes, many men now wear them. There is nothing necessarily effeminate in so doing. Stays are no modern inventions either for men or women: on the contrary, they figure in some of the drawings and statuary of ancient Aztec cities. You could get most admirable stays for gentlemen at Mrs. Steele's, 38, Upper Berkeley-street. It is not at all necessary for you to come to town. Just write to her for a self-measurement form. Her stays are made of the very best materials, firm and yet malleable. Mrs. Steele has secured much success for this class of stays, and has made a reputation for them second to none.

LISA   1st May 1909 (CXXV, 770)
Stays for Gentlemen.

These are being very successfully made by Mrs. Steele, 38, Upper Berkeley-street, W. She has specially good materials, and is having a very great success; the gentlemen she has made them for all bearing testimony to her skill. It is not necessary, as you say, to have them so firm that they resemble a vice, but to support the waist, and yet allow of freedom of movement.

FIGURES   1st May 1909 (CXXV, 770)
Tight Lacing.
   We thank you for your letter, but you have not in any way engaged our sympathy for your cause. Tight lacing for girls is objectionable enough, but for boys should be altogether out of the question. Boys in good health who cannot take part in sports and active amusements will grow up the most detestable of human products—effeminate men. To say that the wearing of tight stays should convert a rough unmannerly boy into one noted for good breeding is an absurdity. There are, happily, very few English mothers who would dress up their sons during the holidays in girls' clothes, and probably, if they did, the police would interfere.
   [Again we have the erroneous and comic idea of the police intervening. Perhaps Holt got this idea from the Boulton and Park case of 1870 and 1871, which received a lot of publicity in her youth (see my *Men in Petticoats*, 1987)]

LUCKY   8th May 1909 (CXXV, 796)
Gentlemen's Corsets.
   These can be obtained from Mrs. Steele,. . . who has made such a success with them that many men who had not thought of wearing stays are now adopting them, and with a marked improvement to the set of the coat. Some men wear ladies' stays, but there are many drawbacks to this plan, and they look ever so much better made of good strong material and cut exactly to suit the requirements of the masculine figure.

BORAX   12th June 1909 (CXXV, 1028)
Dress for Little Boys.
   It was the fashion years ago in France for boys and girls of tender age to sometimes wear the same style of dress, and even in the early years of the last century in England boys wore a much more feminine style of garment than they do now, but even now it is not a general plan for boys of two to have cloth knickerbockers like their fathers'. In the early part of the nineteenth century little boys wore jackets with long trousers to the ankle, where they tapered a little. These were buttoned over the jacket at the waist. French boys under the Directory wore the same long trousers with double-breasted waistcoats, white full sleeves beneath. Under the Restoration the boys wore sandalled shoes, tapering but somewhat close-fitting trousers, and full skirts, quite short, forming part of a habit, that fastened in front, was rounded at the neck, and had Bishop sleeves to the wrist. In 1844 boys of twelve wore coloured bodices like a shirt, with long trousers over them. These paletots with tight waistbands worn with long trousers were seen in France from 1840 to 1850, and these short skirts and full bodices were equally adopted by the girls. I hardly see where the advantage comes in of dressing boys and girls alike up to ten or eleven years of age. The boys' companions would probably deride them as mollycoddles.

CONFORT   19th June 1909 (CXXV, 1065)
Drawbacks to Men Wearing Stays.
   I remember some months ago your seeking my advice on the subject of men's corsets. Since then you tell me that you have worn the two pairs you ordered continuously, and that though for some time they were strange and uncomfortable, this soon passed away, and now you would not dispense with them on any account, appreciating the support and comfort derived from their use. Now as to the drawbacks of which you complain. If you have fine silk

vests they will not ruck up in any way, they ought to be comfortable wear; the vests and combinations worn by women are placed under the stays, and you need have no disadvantage of the kind. If the bands of the pants are too large it is perfectly easy to have them taken in, and if the corsets work up they do not fit you properly. Suspenders tend to keep the stays down, but they must be ill-fitting stays that depend on the suspenders to keep them in place. The bands of men's under garments are made of cotton or twill or kindred stuff, which permit of side seams or any other alteration that is needed when garments are too big and require alterations. Your difficulties admit of easy solution, you have but to consult your stay maker and hosier. Mrs. Steele, . . . who has had a great success in the making of men's corsets, would give you practical advice. She makes such stays of strong fabrics and many of her customers give her testimonials for her handiwork. Send to her for a price list and self-measurement form.

[I have included this item because of the details about underwear, but I am not quite sure what she means. Do the man's vest and pants go under or over the stays?]

INQUISITIVE   10th July 1909 (CXXVI, 82)
Wanted Two or Three Addresses of Men Staymakers, Also Where to Get Silk Combinations for Men to Wear Under Stays?

Writing from Italy, as you do, I can assure you Mrs. Steele, . . has had a great success with men's stays, which any number of testimonials from grateful customers will show. Mme. Sykes, in Hanover-square, also makes them well, and Rosenbaum, 115, Westbourne Grove and 298, Regent-street. Silk combinations for men you would certainly obtain, or they could be prepared for you, at any of the leading hosiers. F. Penberthy, Oxford-street; Skidmore, Matlock Bath, Derbyshire; or such houses as Hummels, Old Bond-street, Holbrook and Walker, opposite the Burlington Arcade; Poole and Lord, Oxford-street and City; or Beale and Inman, New Bond-street.

Is There a Men's Staymaker in Paris?

Doubtless Leoty would make men's stays as well as women's. The address is 8, Place de la Madeleine, Paris.

A.T.   17th July 1909 (CXXVI, 116)
A Man Fond of Pretty Things.

It would be wiser to let your artistic tastes take some other channel. The dress as worn by gentlemen in this century does not admit of much artistic development. You should have lived in the Georgian era, when satin breeches, velvet, satin and brocade coats, lace ruffles, and bag wigs were in vogue. Now if you indulged in lace-edged ties, etc., you would be looked upon as a "bounder." Your only outlet for expansion of this sort is in waistcoats, which are worn in fancy materials, but you can very easily step from the sublime to the ridiculous even here. It is unusual for men to wear bracelets.

YANK   16 October 1909 (CXXVI, 692)
Where to Get a Kilt Made for a 14-Year Old Son.

Go to a tailor, certainly, or one who makes a speciality of Scotch garbs, such as Rowan and Co., 104 Argyle-street, Glasgow. At Scott Adie's, Regent-street you could get an excellent one. They would not encourage the wearing of the undergarments you suggest, which, forgive me saying, would make your son of fourteen ridiculous.

[Presumably the writer suggested petticoats.]

QUINTO   29 January 1910 (CXXVII, 202)
Boys' Smart and Neat Figures.

Boys do sometimes wear stays, which gives them a smart, trim appearance. Possibly this is the best plan, unless they are drilled and go through a system of gymnastics, which probably would be far more efficacious. If you go to Mrs. George Sykes, . . .you will find she has been very successful in making stays for young men. They could be worn with any of the suits you mention. Sometimes only a belt suffices, and in all cases the stays are very shallow.

ST. LUC   26th February 1910 (CXXVII, 379)
Corsets for Gentlemen.

These are to had from Mrs. Steele, . . . They can be made without coming to London by means of self-measurement. You could have them in linen broché or of silk batiste. Many men wear them for hunting, of linen, broché, with porous elastic hips and chamois padding.
Can Empire Corsets be Had in London?

Any kind of stays you may want can be had for ladies from this firm. There appear to be no chance of stays being superseded, though they are altering their appearance, and are made lower in the bust and longer in the bodice, keeping the hips in. Suspendors [*sic*] certainly are not uncomfortable to wear, and they help to keep the stays firmly down in their place.

EFFEMINATE   19th March 1910 (CXXVII, 520)
Earrings.

Being a young fellow of effeminate appearance and ways, you should be the last in the world to do anything so silly as to wear earrings, and make yourself ridiculous and conspicuous. Natives in India, certainly some of them, do wear earrings, but that is no criterion for an Englishman. If they were worn in the time of Elizabeth, Charles I and Charles II, they are not worn in England by men now, and it would not only seem but be absurd for you to adopt them. The operation of having your ears pierced is so painless that the weakest specimen of manhood might undergo it. It is carried out with a sharp pointed instrument not unlike a stiletto. Sometimes the ears are numbed first. It is necessary to have the usual gold sleepers inserted. You cannot wear the other pair of earrings till the ears have healed.

[Although very critical of "Effeminate," with the hint that he himself is perhaps a "weak specimen of manhood," Holt does not refuse to provide some helpful information.]

EARRINGS   30th April 1910 (CXXVII, 783)
Earrings for Men.

You ask for my advice with regard to earrings, viz., as to wearing them yourself. As a young man of twenty years you have not much experience, and if you are so silly as to have your ears pierced I am sure you will regret it all your life, or till the holes have filled up and disappeared, as they might perhaps in the lapse of years. You must confine your admiration of earrings to those you see in the shops, at exhibitions, and in the ears of your lady friends. There are many things that women wear which would be ridiculous for men, and earrings are among the number. Fairholt tells us that men wore these effeminate articles during the reign of Elizabeth and James I. You ask me if I do not think that men are prevented from having their ears pierced by the universal dread of appearing different to anyone else. I imagine it never enters into the mind of the average man to make himself an object of ridicule.

DRESSY   25th June 1910 (CXXVII, 1142)
The Wearing of Earrings by Men.
   If you are determined to wear them, there is nothing in a free country to prevent you, if you do not think you will look ridiculous, only conspicuous, and do not mind, that is well. It is to be hoped your sister will use all precautions in piercing, as I conclude she is not experienced or at all events has not the experience which a professional accustomed to piercing many ears would have. You date from Australia, and may not be near a town. I fear you will regret wearing ear-studs at first; the reason rings are worn is that they can be turned round in the ear, and so heal healthily and quickly. In a stud you have nothing to revolve, and if your blood was not in a good state you might have trouble. You say they can be rotated in the healing process, but surely not in the same way as a ring, and not, I should say, so painlessly. Your sister, in my judgement, is perfectly right.

A VICTIM OF EAR PIERCING   8th October 1910 (CXXVIII, 642)
Earrings.
   You ask me to take your letter seriously, but it is very difficult to think that any sensible man could write such absurdity. I know of no publisher of books on the subject. There was an article in the *Queen* of August 13, profusely illustrated, which entered on the subject fully.
   [The article referred to, on the history of, or types of, earrings was apparently by Holt herself (CXXVIII, 304)]

EARRINGS-FOR-ME   29th October 1910 (CXXVIII, 780)
On the Subject of Earrings.
   I told you all that was necessary some months ago, and, as far as the wearing of earrings by men are concerned, the subject in this column is closed.
Kid Gloves to Lace.
   These are kept by Hope Brothers at their various establishments all over London. Many thanks for the information.

WEST MELBOURNE   29th March 1913 (CXXXIII, 572)
Advice as to Dress.
   Your question is indeed, a difficult one. It would evidently be quite wise to continue as things are till you return to England, and then abandon such an impossible situation. It could not be continued there being contrary to law. You could put him into under knickerbockers such as are worn by both sexes. You would, of course, be guided by your medical man, who must know best, as he says his final recovery is only a matter of time. The point will be to endeavour in every possible way to let that time coincide with your return to England. There are, of course, certain styles of dress now which women wear that are very masculine, and by degrees you could get him into these to start with.
   [This last reply of Ardern Holt's that I am including in this selection is even more intriguing than the first, the unexplained riding habit for the mere man. It seems to be clear that some male person in Australia has been wearing female clothes, but it is not explained why. Again we have Holt's misapprehension that it would be illegal in England. The person concerned would appear not to be a child since it is suggested he might wear ordinary women's clothes, albeit of a masculine style. But in what relationship does he stand to "West Melbourne," who seems to be a woman, and someone who may decide on his mode of dress? His mother? His

wife? Some other female relative? From what sort of ailment or condition is he on the way to recovery? How is a doctor involved? Was he brought up as, or deemed to be, a girl, and now it is desired that he should return to England and adopt the clothes of his true sex? I am afraid we are just left with an enigma.]

———————

9. Bridesmaids and Attendants.   *The Designer*, June 1902, p.183.

EXQUISITE FRENCH LINGERIE ASSORTIS, of Finest Nainsook and Lace.

No. 10.—The **Charming Neglige Cap,** so desirable for popping on the head for Ladies in morning deshabille, is composed of Fine Muslin and Lace, trimmed Soft Rosettes of Ribbon, price 18/9.
No. 10.—The **French Boudoir Nightgown** of Empire Design, is charmingly arranged with Embroidered Muslin and Ribbon entre-deux, 9½ **Guineas.**

Nos. 11 & 12.—**Chemise and Pantalon** corresponding, price 4½ **Gns.** each Price for Copies of same:—
Nightgown from 5½ **Guineas. Chemise** from 65/9.
Pantalon from 79/6.

Special Full Detailed Lists For Trousseaux sent on application.

10. Exquisite French Lingerie.

Catalogue Autumn & Winter 1904,
Wooland Brothers, p.121.

III

THE DAILY MIRROR

The Daily Mirror was founded as a penny daily for women on 2 November 1903. It was not a success and Lord Northcliffe quickly realized that there was no public demand for such a paper. Refusing to accept defeat, he converted it in twenty-four hours into an illustrated newspaper. In its new form it was soon firmly established.

In 1906 the paper printed some letters on tight lacing. At first these were contributed by women readers, but soon men joined in the correspondence. On 17 September "Bank Clerk" of London, E.C. claimed that men also wore corsets and laced tight "on account of the delightful sensation." Other male readers confirmed this. I reproduce those letters where something more than just stays is involved.

HEREDITARY SMALL WAISTS   24th September 1906

"Squeezable" and "Squeezed" are quite right.

Tight-lacing is not only useful in producing the tiny waist so much admired by the male sex, but it is a delightful sensation.

I commenced to wear corsets about twenty year ago, when as a lad I took part in private theatricals dressed as a girl, and I had to be very considerably tightened in to produce the necessary figure. I was so delighted with the feeling of wearing them that I have stuck to corsets ever since.

I was first attracted to my wife by her small waist, and although she is now the mother of two little girls, she still retains her dainty figure, and enjoys being laced in as small as well-fitting corsets and a good staylace can make her.

Our little girls will be brought up in the same way, and I shall be much surprised if they do not have even smaller waists than their mother.

MALE CORSET-WEARER.
Dulwich

SCHOOL BOYS IN CORSETS   27th September 1906

Recently, when my young brother was home for the holidays, on his thirteenth birthday, for a joke I laced him into an old pair of corsets of mine, and dressed him in a shirt-blouse and belt. He liked it so much that he asked to be allowed to wear the things all day, and in the evening he himself laced the corsets up to 17in. (I had laced them to 18½in.)

He has just gone back to school laced in to 16in, and with a spare pair in his box. He tells me that the sensation is delightful, and that he would not stop wearing corsets on account of any chaff he gets from his schoolfellows. My other brother, twelve years of age, is now wearing corsets, and laces tightly to please himself.   ALPHA.
Uckfield

FOR AND AGAINST CORSETS

29th September 1906

The man who wears corsets has only to don the kilts also to make him the nineteenth century woman complete.

C. ORAM
Waltham Abbey

Two years ago my wife for a joke laced me tightly into her corsets and put me into one of her tight-fitting dresses, and, like Alpha's brother, I found the sensation so delightful that I have stuck to corsets ever since.

My waist used to be 28in., but I now wear a 20in. corset and feel no inconvenience whatever, but a most pleasing sensation in being tightly laced.

MALE CORSET-WEARER
Leytonstone

It is disgusting that a man should degrade himself so far as to have recourse to the arts and wiles of the modern doll of society to supply him with what he has styled a good figure.

G. FIFIELD
Kentish Town

My friends and I have been simply astounded to see "Alpha's" statement in your columns. That any schoolboy should have the audacity to return to his school bringing corsets with him is perfectly ridiculous!

It would be almost better for him to return in skirts and petticoats, with long hair in curls, than go back thus. He ought to be "ragged" and teased until he throws them into the fire.

SOME ASTOUNDED BOYS
Westgate

iii. Toilettes de Casino pour Villes d'eaux.

The Queen, 3rd April 1909.
© Manchester City Art Galleries.

iv. Ardern Holt at the last Court of 1924. *The Queen*, 3rd February 1926, p.4.
© Manchester City Art Galleries.

IV

MODERN SOCIETY

INTRODUCTION

I discovered *Modern Society* over 40 years ago when I came across this passage in Havelock Ellis's *Studies in the Psychology of Sex*:

> One evening at the tea table my sister read from a periodical called *Modern Society* about a young man dressed as a girl. I at once went rigid with excitement, and I am sure turned pale. Until then I had thought I was unique in my thoughts. Later I had the paper to myself, and enjoying tremendous excitement, read a page or two of readers' correspondence on "effeminate men." My excitement was so great I had sexual sensations almost involuntarily. From that time my inner desire was to live as a girl. No thought of love or affection entered my head. If I had had a supply of lingerie, corsets, and high-heeled footwear I would have been happy. [from Case History of "D.S." *Studies in the Psychology of Sex*, Random House, New York (1936), Vol.III, Part II, Eonism, p.54]

From the context it was possible to date this correspondence to 1910. I consulted the relevant volume of *Modern Society* in the Bodleian and quickly found the letters "D.S." had been reading. I am surprised that no other student of cross-dressing seems to have done the same. They are now reprinted for the first time.

Modern Society was first published on 4 December 1880 at 3, Falcon Court, Fleet Street [*The Newspaper Press Directory*, 1881, published by C. Mitchell & Co., London], but the first issue available in the British Newspaper Library is that for 25 November 1882, when the address is given as 9. Crane Court, Fleet St. According to an article in *Answers* of 14 Sept. 1889, the paper was then edited by a Mr. Lawrence, who had taken it over from a Mr. Kenealy, a son of Dr. Kenealy.It had been a failure when taken over, but "now produces £10,000 per annum." The Bodleian has the volumes from 1905, and there are a number of individual issues and loose sheets in the Liddell Hart collection on Costume belonging to the Art & Design Library of the Liverpool John Moores University. These include one or two sheets which are missing from the relevant volumes in the British Library.

The nature of the paper is well conveyed by this comment of McQueen-Pope:

> Very widely read by women was a pink-coloured little journal called *Modern Society*. Nothing of the lives, doings or relationships of European royalty or the Society of the world was hidden from the editor. Apparently his sleuthlike reporters were everywhere. But women devoured every word—and believed every word too. [W. McQueen-Pope, *Twenty Shillings in the Pound*, London, 1948, p. 346]

Writing of the Queen's jubilee in 1897, he says:

> Elderly ladies, readers of a pink-coloured periodical called *Modern Society*, which enjoyed a tremendous circulation, understood all about her....
> [*op.cit.* p.295]

McQueen-Pope's remarks are born out by references in contemporary novels. This is from Mrs. Frances Hodgson Burnett's *The Making of a Marchioness*, published in London in 1901:

49

Jane Cupp took "Modern Society," and now and then had the pleasure of reading aloud to her young man little incidents concerning some castle or manor in which Miss Fox-Seton's aunt, Lady Malfrey, was staying with earls and special favourites of the Prince's (p.8).

In H.G. Wells' *The History of Mr. Polly* published in 1910, one of Mr. Polly's colleagues is said to keep himself "*au courant*" by a penny paper of infinite suggestion called "Modern Society." (ch. I)

James Joyce was aware of some of the correspondence in this paper. On page 682 of the John Lane 1937 edition of *Ulysees* the description of the contents of the first drawer of Bloom's desk includes "a press cutting from an English weekly periodical *Modern Society*, subject corporal chastisement in girls' schools." It is quite possible that Joyce possessed or had seen such a cutting. There was a correspondence on corporal punishment in September and October 1898, and by an amusing coincidence several of the pages containing correspondence in 1898 have been torn or cut out of the volumes in the British Newspaper Library.

Apart from the foregoing I have found very little mention of, or knowledge of, *Modern Society*. Until recently it was not generally known to historians of costume, society or family life. Only Sir Basil Liddell Hart, who collected copies of, and loose pages from, the paper, recognised the usefulness of its comments on dress and fashion as a supplement to our knowledge of the clothes of the period. After the First Annual Conference of The Costume Society in April 1967, Sir Basil was one of the people who contributed comments on the lectures. Referring to Anne Buck's lecture on the underwear of the period 1890 to 1914, "Foundations of the Active Woman," he wrote:

> It was mentioned that decorative or "frilly" underclothes date from about 1900. But the "gossip" columns of popular weeklies such as the Tatler-type *Modern Society* show that they had become fashionable since 1890, or even before. [Costume Society Publication, *La Belle Epoque*, London, 1968, p. 64]

Since then David Kunzle has mentioned the paper briefly in his *Fashion and Fetishism* [Rowman & Littlefield, Totowa, New Jersey, 1982, p. 231], while Valerie Steele, in *Fashion and Eroticism*, has described and quoted from the articles and correspondence on underwear (pp. 199-200 and 251).

Most of the letters and articles about boys and men in female attire up to 1900 have been reprinted in *Men in Petticoats* and all the short stories in *In Female Disguise*. There were no more stories in *Modern Society* covering this theme after 1900, and not many letters, until 1909. In 1898 and 1899 there were four letters from men who claimed that they had worn corsets as boys, one of which, from "Martyr" (8 July 1899), was included in *Men in Petticoats* (p.30). "Acton" (20 Aug. 1898) enjoyed the stays imposed on him by an eccentric aunt, while "R.B." (8 July 1899), born into a family of corset-makers, happily experimented with the stock-in-trade. "Martyr" and "Tamed" (22 July 1899), however, strongly deprecated the imposition of stays on boys. "Martyr's" aunt hated boys and tried to make him as girlish as possible, even dressing him as a girl in the evenings. When at thirteen "Tamed" returned home from school and found a step-mother, he became a "wild animal." His step-mother "tamed" him by taking him to a ladies' shop and having him fitted with corsets. Here we have corsets used as a disciplinary measure, as a way of controlling and subduing unruly boys, something which correspondents had advocated in the pages of *The Family Doctor* a few years before. A lady correspondent, "White Cat" [*F.D.* 13 Sept. 1890 (XII, 42)] had also taken a youth of fifteen to a ladies' shop for that purpose.

Women readers confirmed that some boys did in fact wear stays. On 13 April 1895 (p.688) a correspondent claimed that "absurd though it may seem, I know two or three families where the boys are made to wear well-laced stiff corsets—their mothers telling me they thought 'it vastly improved their boys' figures and carriage.' Can this fashionable folly go much further than this?" "Trained in Time" (22 July 1899, p.1169) stated "It is almost a tradition in my family that both boys and girls should become accustomed to the stay-lace. The boys have always worn, and worn without reluctance, firmly laced stays."

The paper continued at 9, Crane Court for several years. From April 1905 the paper was printed and published by John Christopher Brock of 18, Kirby Street, Hatton Garden, but this does not seem to have produced any significant change in the paper. There are several references to men wearing stays and to effeminacy of various kinds, whether in the way of gloves, jewellery or cosmetics. Such activity met with both approval and disapproval from correspondents and contributors. On 1 Aug. 1903 (p.1233) the editor printed a piece by the regular contributor called the "Nice Boy," introducing it thus: "The 'Nice Boy' enlarges upon the subject of Vicarious Vanity." He argued that men have had to give up any vanity in dress on their own behalf. The only way for them to satisfy their inborn vanity is through the opposite sex. "And this is where the Vicarious Vanitist comes in. It is not that he abandons his vanity altogether, but he transfers it to some feminine relation (actual or prospective!)" The article ends: "Even the ugliest of us can enjoy the luxury of Vicarious Vanity." A famous prospective feminine relation in literature, though not actual, was Bathsheba Everdene in Thomas Hardy's *Far from the Madding Crowd* (1874). Bathsheba is loved by Gabriel Oak and Farmer Boldwood, but marries Sergeant Troy, who is murdered by Boldwood. The latter, in anticipation of eventually marrying Bathsheba himself, has accumulated women's clothes and jewellery for her future use. Before Boldwood's trial, it is implied that he is mentally deranged:

> In a locked closet was now discovered an extraordinary collection of articles. There were several sets of ladies' dresses in the piece, of sundry expensive materials; silks and satins, poplins and velvets, all of colours which from Bathsheba's style of dress might have been judged to be her favourites. There were two muffs, sable and ermine. Above all there was a case of jewellery, containing four heavy gold bracelets and several lockets and rings, all of fine quality and manufacture. These things had been bought in Bath and other towns from time to time, and brought home by stealth. They were all carefully packed in paper, and each package was labelled "Bathsheba Boldwood," a date being subjoined six years in advance in every instance. (Ch.LV)

Although Hardy calls these items "somewhat pathetic evidences of a mind crazed with care and love," we can perhaps see them as evidence of "vicarious vanity" at work. It has been Boldwood's pleasure to acquire clothes and jewels which he hopes he will see Bathsheba wearing. There is also the implication that the clothes have been carefully chosen in her favourite colours. Many an actual husband has enjoyed buying clothes for his wife. As an example I can cite my wife's great-great-grandfather, Henry Hall of Alton, who was born on 18 Aug. 1814, married on 21 April 1840 and died on 31 Jan. 1899. On Christmas day 1951, his eighth child (of ten), Beatrice, born on 7 June 1854 and married on 27 July 1882, wrote a brief memoir of her family life. It included this statement: "My father was distinctly fond of clothes and he bought yards of lovely silk for dresses for my mother. I distinctly remember one, a lovely shade of blue silk with a pattern of leaves of the same colouring." From the dates given it is likely that this dress dates from the middle of the Victorian period, just as Hardy's novel does. A photograph of their golden wedding in 1890 shows Henry Hall's wife wearing a handsome silk dress for the occasion.

The "Nice Boy's" article is a useful statement of what Flugel called "The Great Masculine Renunciation" (J.C. Flugel, *The Psychology of Clothes*, The Hogarth Press, London 1930, p.110), except that the "Nice Boy" suggests that men may find consolation in the gorgeous apparel of their womenfolk. The phrase "Vicarious Vanity" is also an attractive alternative to the notion of "Conspicuous Consumption," introduced by Thorstein Veblen in his *The Theory of the Leisure Class* published in 1912 and espoused by Quentin Bell in *On Human Finery* (The Hogarth Press, London, 1945 and revised edition 1976). The expenditure by men on female finery is not just a demonstration of wealth for the purposes of display or demarcation of class but sometimes derives from a full appreciation of, and liking for, the garments themselves, as I think is implicit in Boldwood's operations. The article is also interesting as giving a foretaste of the views of "Cosmopolite" in *Photo Bits* which we shall see in the next chapter.

The first letter proper to this post-1900 collection is from "Amethyst" on 2 Nov. 1907, in

11. The Latest Corset and Skirt from Paris. *Lady's Pictorial*, 1st April 1905 (Page 125)

A Novelty for the Coming Season

The *dernier cri* from Paris is to be found at Messrs. Peter Robinson's, of Oxford-street, in the shape of a perfect fitting corset combined with a smart underskirt, which enables the wearer to avoid any risk of a ridge from wearing a petticoat outside the corset. The material of which the corset is made extends to the knees, and a fascinating flounce is attached to it there by a simple arrangement of threaded ribbon, so that it may easily and quickly be detached when the flounce needs cleaning or it is desirable to change it for another one. The flounces are made in silk or *lingerie*, and this "Princess" corset and underskirt, as it is appropriately called, is certain to be a great success, for now that it has been created one wonders why it was never thought of before, because it seems so obviously the very thing that we have all been wanting, especially now that princess dresses and close fitting skirts are fashionable, so Messrs. Peter Robinson are heartily to be congratulated on this charming novelty, which costs, by the way, six guineas complete, with a lace and muslin flounce.

THE LATEST CORSET AND SKIRT FROM PARIS. *(Peter Robinson, Oxford-street, W.)*

which she states that her twin brother's figure was trained in the same way as hers. In April and May 1908 there were several letters from men who wore stays and from April to September 1909 several about figure training for boys. Of special interest is the letter from "M.M." on 17 July 1909, who delighted in "the mothers' darlings" of the past, who wore frocks until they were ten.

By 1905 *Modern Society* was printed and published by John Christopher Brock, 18, Kirby Street, Hatton Garden. From 1909 onwards the ownership and management of the paper changed hands at frequent intervals. How far this was due to a decline in its popularity generally or to disputes about the subject matter covered is impossible to say. First, a private limited company, Modern Society Ltd., was formed and took over publication from 18 September 1909, but the address remained the same. There was now a slight change of policy and rearrangement of contents. The editor outlined his proposals for the paper on 16th October 1909. One of the changes was to put all the miscellaneous comments on fashion in a new series of articles signed by "Suzanne," under the heading, "Woman and her World." This was in addition to the existing column "Woman's Mirror" contributed by "Lily." "Suzanne" invited readers to send in enquiries and, as we shall see, very surprising some of these enquiries were. Another change was to place greater emphasis on readers' letters by having a special correspondence column with a heading for the subject discussed.

The first topic, on 30 Oct. 1909, was "Are Women More Cruel Than Men?" and a woman wrote in favour of spurs for women. The following week Edwin Dawson argued that women were cruel to tight lace their daughters. On 13 Nov. 1909 (p. 12), the editor welcomed the response from readers to the letter published the previous week. He printed four letters on tight-lacing under the heading: "Should Girls Tight Lace?" and invited more letters. This, together with a similar one in *Photo Bits* in the same year, was the first invitation of its kind since Samuel Beeton's in *The Englishwoman's Domestic Magazine* of 1867, and there followed a full scale debate on tight-lacing, much after the manner of that journal from 1867 to 1874 to which one reader compared it. At first the heading was "Should Girls Tight Lace?" then "Slaves of the Stay Lace." For a period of nine weeks several dozen letters were printed, with strong views expressed on either side. Particularly vehement in his opposition to tight-lacing was "A Middle-aged Bachelor" on 27 Nov. 1909 (p. 21). Those in favour were curiously unaware that the shape of the fashionable corset was in the process of change.

At first the correspondents selected for this collection are concerned with the boy in stays or girl's dress. Alan Brewster (27.11.09) mentions a French boy who was brought up as a girl. On 11 Dec. 1909 he wrote again with advice to "Retired Colonel" on corsets for his nephew. He himself now wears the new directoire type which he finds the most suitable of ladies' corsets for the masculine figure. In saying this he is one of the few correspondents to mention the change in fashion. Y.S. de Frayne (4.12.09) describes his life as a boy female impersonator in New Orleans. Alec A. Northwick (11.12.09) was dressed as a girl until he was fourteen. Geoffrey (11.12.09) was "rough, clumsy and troublesome," and like "Tamed" (22 July 1899) was put into girls' corsets, boots and gloves. The brother of a friend of A.I. (1.1.10) was adopted by two maiden ladies at the age of thirteen. "For any exhibition of boyish spirits" he was dressed as a girl by his nurse. This is the first mention in *Modern Society* of a complete change into female clothes being used as a punishment. Unfortunately no hint is given as to how long ago that took place.

The series of letters, "Slaves of the Stay-Lace," closed on 8 Jan. 1910 with three letters. The editor made this final comment: "We have received a very large number of other letters upon this interesting subject. As, however, these cover substantially the same ground that has been traversed by the communications already published, no good purpose would be served by publishing them. This correspondence must, therefore, now cease." (p.22)

In the same issue the editor printed a letter which he perhaps hoped would give rise to a similarly interesting debate. Under the heading "The Modern English Girl" (p.18), "Colonial" described his disappointment on coming to England in search of a wife only to find mannish women who rode astride, played men's games and smoked. "Fancy marrying a woman who smokes!" The following week (15 Jan. 1910) "An English Girl" defended her class, while "A Convert" raised the question of the effeminacy of English young men. The latter were denounced with scorn by "A Bachelor Girl" on 29 Jan. 1910. This, however, produced a reaction in favour of men with some appreciation of female attire, but who are not unmanly. "Modern Matron" (5.2.10) approved of corsets and "dainty underwear" for her husband. In February 1910 several very interesting correspondents write with approval of youths and young men dressing up as women. "A Happy Sister" (12.2.10) dressed her thirteen year old brother in her clothes, and is happy that this continues now that he is at university. His dressing in her clothes had removed a barrier between them, but he is still masculine. "Jupon" (19.2.10), however, after a similar experience at the age of fourteen, admits that he is now quite effeminate. This is the first letter in the whole run of the paper in which a man has made a confession of this kind. Previously, in the nineties, the accounts of female disguise and impersonation were in the third person. Marion Inglis of New Brunswick (26.2.10) brought up her boys and girls to share their interests and clothes. "Bachelor Uncle" (26.2.10) approved of dressing boys in girls' clothes for their moral improvement. Putting a boy into dainty underwear and petticoats inculcated a sympathy with the feminine point of view and removed antagonistic instincts. But "Bachelor Uncle" warned of the dangers. The occasional "petticoating" of his sister's elder boy was very successful, but the younger boy now prefers to wear female dress. "C.U.A.C." (5.3.10) was persuaded by his wife to try on her clothes, while "Talon" (5.3.10) describes the joys of dressing up in female attire in the privacy of his bachelor flat.

Some of these letters must be the ones which the sister of Havelock Ellis's "D.S." read out at the tea table. "D.S." was born in 1896, the son of a sea-captain, and the youngest child of five. After service in the army, i.e. in the First World War, "D.S." met a girl and decided to get married, and Ellis did not hear further from him. What is so interesting is the situation in the home with one of the boy's sisters reading out the letters. "D.S." himself does not seem to have looked at the paper before, otherwise he would have noticed earlier letters. This confirms the status of *Modern Society* as a woman's paper, purchased and read by the female members of the household, which a boy would not normally read or even see. His sister must also have found the letters amusing or surprising, to make her want to read them out to her family.

"Suzanne's" advice on boys' costume, which began on 15 Jan. 1910 (p.26) is intriguing. Her readers seem to want to dress their sons in corsets and kilts, with petticoats under their kilts, or even as girls entirely. These enquiries are similar to those answered by Ardern Holt in *The Queen*, and "Suzanne" also had to dampen the enthusiasm of readers who wished to feminise their sons, although "Suzanne," unlike Ardern Holt, did allow petticoats under the kilt, at least for dancing.

Towards the end of 1910, the paper was apparently in difficulties, some light on which is thrown by the liquidation papers of Modern Society (1911) Ltd. in the Public Record Office (BT3-20301-118573). A journalist, E. Huskinson, was appointed receiver for the Debenture holder, Charles Percival, on 16 December 1910 and he is shown as publisher from 21 January to 9 December 1911. Again, changes were made in the paper. "Suzanne," was replaced by "Mondaine" after 25 February 1911, and the letter page ceased abruptly on 18 March 1911 and never reappeared. Then a new company, Modern Society (1911) Ltd., registered on 14 November 1911, with the same Registered Office, 18, Kirby Street, took over publication from 16 December 1911. On 13 June 1913 the Registered Office was changed to 55a, Shaftesbury Avenue.

In that year there was a further change we actually know something about from another source. The playwright, the late Enid Bagnold, worked on the paper as a young woman. "Soon Frank Harris had slipped out of his editorship of *Hearth and Home* and bought a tainted little property called *Modern Society*. . . . Harris took on Hugh Lunn (later Hugh Kingsmill). We were the staff. We filled the paper (except for the scandal page which was the paper's claim to fame).... There was also a slim girl who worked outside getting advertisements." (Enid Bagnold, *Autobiography*, London, 1969, p. 90). I wrote to Enid Bagnold to see if she knew anything about the previous history of the paper and its contributors. She replied that she had put all she knew in her book. She had never heard of "Suzanne," and knew nothing about the tight-lacing correspondence. In her letter to me she called the paper "a dirty little rag." She was thinking of its reputation as a scandal sheet.

From the liquidation papers we know that Frank Harris acquired the position of Managing Director to serve for five years from 22 September 1913 and he was issued with 20418 ordinary shares, although their effective value depended entirely on the future success of the paper. The Registered Office was changed to 16, King Street, Covent Garden on 18 October 1913. Frank Harris's first article for the paper was "How I began Journalism in London" on 13 September 1913. Thereafter he printed several articles over his name, but his reign was even shorter than those of his predecessors, his last contribution being on 11 April 1914. According to Enid Bagnold, Harris was sent to prison in 1914 for contempt of court for commenting on the Fitzwilliam divorce case and she had to run the paper on her own. She does not say in her book exactly when she ceased working for the paper, but it would have been later in 1914. A receiver was again appointed, Joseph Thomson, and he took possession of the assets on 25 April 1914. According to his accounts, he produced two issues, which must be those of the odd days, Thursday, 30 April and Tuesday, 12 May 1914. In a final note in the liquidation papers, he recorded: "Assets passed into hands of Receiver for Debenture-Holders April 1914. The company has therefore ceased to exist. Two of the Directors went to the U.S.A. Signed by J. Thomson, late receiver, 7.12.1916." The company was dissolved on 7 November 1917. It is interesting that, a few years before, several private individuals had been prepared to invest in the future of the paper, holding ordinary shares in the 1911 company and probably in its predecessor. Their names and addresses are available in the liquidation papers. Could some of them have been suppliers of the gossip and society news? They certainly lost their money.

After presiding over the issue of the two numbers already mentioned, Thomson apparently got rid of the paper itself very quickly. By the end of May, he seems to have sold or transferred it to the owners of *London Life*, The Milford Press, who continued to bring the paper out until 3 March 1917, when it finally closed down. *London Life* began publication as *The Penny Illustrated Paper* in 1861, changing its name to *London Life* on 2 June 1913 and to *London Society* on 10 March 1917. From 25 Aug. 1917 to 25 May 1918 the paper was known as *London Life and Modern Society*, and thereafter, as *London Life* again. On 30 Dec. 1940 the premises of *London Life* were bombed and in the next issue the editor lamented that the files of the paper for the past fifty years, including those of the papers which had been merged with it, had been lost. The whole character and look of the paper was drastically changed on 11 Oct. 1941, in circumstances which I have never seen explained. Certainly the famous correspondence pages disappeared for ever. The paper ceased publication in July 1960.

In 1933 *London Life* printed at random, with one or two small changes to make them fit better into the current letter sequence and without acknowledgement, over a dozen letters which had originally appeared in *Modern Society* in November and December 1909. I used to think that this must have been done by the editorial staff, as they had all the original files, although it was puzzling that only letters from those two months, as far as I could discover, had been reprinted in this way. Furthermore later in the thirties *London Life* reprinted whole series of letters from past issues with full details of the dates of original publication. When, however, I came to examine the sheets from and copies of *Modern Society* in the Liddell Hart Collection mentioned above, I made an amazing discovery. The last items in the collection in point of date are the twelve complete issues from 30 Oct. 1909 to 15 Jan. 1910 inclusive, starting with the correspondence on "Are Women More Cruel than Men?" on 30 Oct and including all the letters in the series "Should Girls Tight Lace? and "Slaves of the Stay Lace." There is thus a possibility that the collector who owned the copies before they came into the possession

55

of Capt. Liddell Hart fed the newspaper throughout the year 1933 with carefully edited versions of the original letters. Oddly enough a few of the letters were reprinted again in 1939. If this is so it exonerates the paper from the charge of inserting dud letters. On the other hand it weakens the authority of *London Life* as a source of genuine first hand communications.

The modern sea nymph's toilet is a very winsome affair, of which the piquant little cap forms an important detail

12. Bathing Outfit. *Every Woman's Encyclopædia*, Vol. VIII (1912), p.5380.

MODERN SOCIETY – The Correspondence

20th August 1898 (p. 1296)

Perhaps some of your readers would like to hear the experience of a member of the male sex who knows something of tight lacing. When I was a boy of thirteen, I came under the care of a rich, but eccentric maiden aunt, who in spite of my remonstrances, insisted on my wearing stays. I was taken to a first-class Parisian corsetière and measured for a pair of 23 in. satin corsets, the natural size of my waist being twenty-five inches. So exquisitely did these fit, that though I wore them continuously night and day, to my surprise I found from the first that the sensation of wearing well-boned, firmly-laced stays was an extremely delightful one. At the end of every month I was fitted into a new pair of corsets exactly a quarter of an inch smaller in the waist than the previous pair, until in two and a half years, when I was fifteen and a half years old, my waist only measured sixteen inches. I never felt the slightest discomfort or suffered at all in health, owing, no doubt, to the gradual way in which my figure was trained, and I always derived great pleasure from the feeling of my tightly-laced corsets.   ACTON.

8th July 1899 (p. 1105)

My parents were fashionable corset-makers, and when I was a small boy, I had frequent opportunities of trying on corsets of all kinds, and knew that even tightly-laced stays were by no means the hardship they are generally said to be. In two or three years I began to suffer much from indigestion, and upon the urgent advice of my doctor, reluctantly gave up my satin "armour." There is no doubt that all who have tried it agree that the sensation of wearing firmly laced corsets is pleasant, and that when not too tight they are not harmful; but as one gets used to them there is an inevitable tendency to lace them more and more and more tightly, and to have them still more stiffly boned. The digestion is then, as in my case, sure to suffer, and on this account, and also the amount of ridicule they must incur, I think no sensible mother will make her boys wear stays.   R.B.

8th July 1899 (p.1105)

I cannot agree with your correspondents who advise that boys also should be laced into stays. I am sure the result would be prejudicial to both their health and manliness. I had the misfortune to be brought up by an aunt who had a strong prejudice against boys. She therefore tried to make me as girlish and effeminate as possible. Every morning and evening I was tightly laced into dainty satin corsets; very great care was taken of my hands and complexion, and my feet were encased in smart pointed high heeled shoes. Indeed when alone, in the evenings, I was sometimes dressed entirely as a girl. In time, I confess, like your other correspondents, I grew to like the sensation of tight lacing but of course, I could never join other boys in athletics of any kind, and my health suffered accordingly. I have at last managed to emancipate myself, and though very reluctantly have given up wearing corsets. I cannot think the beautiful figure, small feet, and soft skin I acquired were any compensation for the many disadvantages entailed by my effeminate education.   MARTYR

22nd July 1899 (p. 1169)

Like your correspondent "Martyr" I strongly object to any system of tight-lacing boys, and like him, I can speak with some experience, though happily mine was shorter than his. When I was thirteen I returned home from school to find a stepmother. I was a wild animal. Even my father complained. My stepmother, who was both young and beautiful, undertook to "tame" me, but refused to say how. One morning when I had been home a week, she took me out for a walk into the town of L-----, where we then lived. She wheeled me suddenly into a ladies' outfitting shop. I was unsuspectingly ushered into a sanctum, and in spite of my protests—and I did protest very vigorously—the proprietress and two slim-waisted assistants laced me into a pair of very strongly boned corsets. They were not extremely tight, but they seemed so; while shoulder straps made stooping impossible. A light but strong little chain and lock made it impossible for me to liberate myself. It was very uncomfortable but as my clothes concealed the new figure I had acquired, I did not mind so much. Until I reached the age of seventeen and left school, my holidays were always spent under the corset *régime* and, though I was never systematically tight-laced (the school terms would have interfered), I went about with a far smaller waist than most girls can boast, for I am naturally of a slim build.   TAMED

2nd November 1907 (p. 15)

The only thing "Distressed" [she wrote about her daughter on 26 Oct. 1907] can do is to persevere. When I was a girl of fourteen I was a terrible tomboy, and almost as athletic as my twin brother. My mother then decided it was high time to train our figures. We were both laced in very tightly; but we were very naughty and rebellious over it. My mother, however, who was kindness itself in other matters, was very strict about our corsets, and laced us in herself every morning. It was about a year before I realised she was right, and from that time I have taken pride in my trim figure and seventeen inch waist.   AMETHYST

25th April 1908 (pp. 14-15)

I desire to give your readers my experience of tight-lacing. I was brought up by an aunt who was an inveterate tight-lacer, and when at the age of thirteen, I came under her care, she laced me up tightly into a pair of fashionable corsets, which being tied in a hard knot at the back, prevented me loosening them. I felt awkward and ill at ease at first owing to the stiffness and tightness of the corset, but that soon wore off. At the age of sixteen, I had a waist measurement of only nineteen inches. I have continued to wear corsets, not from vanity, but because I thoroughly enjoy the sensation of being tightly-laced in an elegant well-made pair of stays. If a corset allows the wearer sufficient room at the chest and hips, the waist may be laced as tightly as desired. I have found no ill effects from their use, am able to walk a ten or fifteen mile stretch and feel no greater fatigue than if I did not wear stays.

A propos of this subject, can any of your older readers inform me what the backboard and stocks so often mentioned in several of our older novelists' works were, and give descriptions of them?   A.G.D.

TIGHT LACING   2nd May 1908 (pp. 15-16)

A propos of the letters which have been appearing lately in your widely-read journal on tight-lacing, I was present at a sort of round table discussion, in which about ten ladies took part. It was commenced by two Americans, whose figures conclusively indicated that they were not votaries of the stay-lace, and who were very loud in their denunciation of that fearful instrument of torture—the corset. The next who took up the argument was a lady who as strongly advocated the training of the figures of both boys and girls yet young, and instanced her own two boys, whom she had always kept carefully corseted—more handsome, well-set-up boys it would be hard to find.

The ultimate decision (except for the two first-mentioned) was that a lady could not be really well-dressed without she wore a well-shaped corset laced moderately tight. Extreme tight-lacing was condemned. For gentlemen the opinion was not quite as unanimous. It was, however, agreed that many—perhaps most—gentlemen would be better for a little lacing in. This opinion was very evidently shared by several gentlemen staying here.

One lady very reasonably asked, if ladies have found such advantage in the corset, why should their husbands and brothers be debarred by a silly old-fashioned prejudice from also obtaining that benefit. To which another lady replied, "Perhaps they are as great sinners as we are, only they call their corsets belts." We know that our own corsetières advertise that inquiries in the gentlemen's department are strictly confidential, so perhaps more than we know of are under the tyranny of the stay-lace.
M.H.

2nd May 1908 (p.16)

Just a word on this much-discussed question of tight-lacing. I have always compelled my boys since they were six years old to wear corsets; and now, at the ages of fifteen and seventeen, I am quite pleased that I have done so. Mothers would be wise if they would keep their boys carefully corsetted when growing. It would certainly prevent the slouching habits some boys get into.
E.C.

3rd October 1908 (p.13)

It was quite a pleasure to read the nice energetic letter of "R.M." in defence of the poor "Snowdon girl" ["P.M.," not "R.M.," wrote on 19 Sept. 1908 (p.13) defending the unsuitable attire worn by a lady observed on Snowdon by a correspondent of 5 Sept. 1908 (p. 13)]. If some of those masculine critics who are so loud in their condemnation of everything that is really pretty and feminine had in boyhood been compelled by their parents to undergo a course of corset discipline along with their sisters they would perhaps not be quite so ready to sneer. Surely a pretty complexioned girl in a muslin frock, with tiny waist trimly belted in, and high-heeled strap shoes buttoned over smart openwork stockings, is a much more acceptable sight than if she had left her stays at home and borrowed her brother's shooting boots for the occasion, as your correspondent evidently considered she ought to. I have no patience with such men.
V.W.G.

1st May 1909 (p.8)

I was very disappointed not to find in your last number any further letters on the stooping, slouching carriage of our young men, for I am sure your widely-read journal would do a great deal to induce them to improve or induce mothers to pay attention to the figures of their boys while growing, or even wives to induce or compel their husbands to stand more erectly and walk more gracefully.

I go further than "M.B." in your previous week's issue [17 April 1909], for I would be unreasonable enough to expect men to wear corsets, if it is unreasonable, which I deny; for I am afraid there are a great many ladies who would not stand as uprightly or walk as gracefully as they do if it were not for their corsets.

Why should it be more unreasonable for a man to wear corsets than for a woman? Women must have found them a great advantage, or so much care would not be exercised in their manufacture. I hope you will use your influence to try and bring about an improvement in our men's appearance. Look what splendid figures you see in Vienna, where corsets are so usually worn by both sexes. I know there is a great prejudice against men wearing corsets in this country, but I for one would gladly see that overcome if thereby we could obtain better set-up, handsomer figures among our young men. I have lately got corsets for my boy nine years old, and they have made a wonderful improvement in his appearance.   A CORRESPONDENT

[Editorial Comment]   29th May 1909 (p. 8)

We have mentioned before in these columns that a large section of the young men of today are becoming more ladylike, an effect which is no doubt largely due to the fact that they are brought up much more by the mother than the father, and kept far longer at the maternal skirts than used to be the case.

"M.M." WRITES FROM SALTBURN:–   17th July 1909 (p.11)

I read with interest a few weeks ago your little paragraph about "ladylike young men," and, again, the letter of your "Guileless Girl" on neckties. Now, I agree with neither. I am an old lady, and I confess I would very much like to see more care among men – and especially the young men – as to their appearance. One occasionally does see a man who gives some thought to his clothes – that they are not a mere covering; and to me they are a pleasure to look upon, and I applaud their courage in braving the sneers of those who only consider themselves manly if they have a careless and slovenly appearance, besides earning the disapproval of your good self and the "Guileless Girl."

Why, I ask, should boys or young men be allowed to lounge about as they do in the presence of ladies? Girls are taught to carry themselves with dignity whether walking or sitting, and mothers are mostly to blame for allowing their boys to grow up with no care for their appearance. If a little lacing in (as many of your correspondents, some little while ago, advocated) is necessary, by all means subject them while yet young to that discipline.

In my young days boys were not "breeched" until they were ten, but wore frocks. This allowed mothers more scope for their taste, and "mother's darlings" – would that they were more of them now! – were frequently most tastefully dressed. I am inspired to write this as there is a lady here who has a boy about ten most beautifully dressed in Highland costume, which is my ideal of what a boy's costume should be.

24th July 1909 (p.14)

. . . about the early training suggested by "M.M" opinions will differ. My boy has to submit to it, and I find it valuable not only physically but as a very effective discipline.   MATER

11th September 1909 (p.13)

. . . I have lately been much interested to see some correspondence on the subject of corsets and prettier clothing generally for boys, and I would like to say I agree with the writer of the letter in your issue of July 17th. If mothers would keep their boys more at home and subject them to a little of the discipline their sisters have to undergo, we should have less slangy conversation and slouching and ungainly habits. Properly fitting, well-laced stays are most desirable for all children, whether boys or girls, and are an excellent means of ensuring an upright carriage.

South Rhodesia   Ex-GOVERNESS

SHOULD GIRLS TIGHT LACE?   13th November 1909 (p. 12)

(As was only to be anticipated, the statement of a correspondent in our columns last week [Edwin Dawson, 6 Nov. 1909] that tight corsets are "cruel" has provoked vigorous criticism on the part of our readers. The four letters we print below [one included here] all show that there is a very considerable difference of opinion on this point. Curiously enough, each of these letters defends the practice of tight lacing. There is, of course, much to be said on both sides, and, since this is a question of more than ordinary interest, we should be glad to receive further opinions on the subject.)

Does not your correspondent get rather away from the point in his letter last week anent the comparative cruelty of the two sexes? This is, of course, the sort of question that could be debated for months, and yet no agreement be arrived at.

When Edwin Dawson comes to speak about compelling girls to "pinch their waists in cruelly tight corsets" one wants to laugh. Has your correspondent, sir, I wonder, ever tried wearing corsets, properly made, and commenced at the right age, certainly not less than twelve in the case of a girl? Corsets cause no more discomfort than do, say, a frock overcoat.

Railing at tight lacing has gone on, I suppose, ever since corsets were first worn, but I greatly doubt if there is one woman who has ever got her waist down to reasonable dimensions who regrets for an hour having done so.

From a man's point of view—and, disguise the fact as they may, women dress entirely for men—a decent waist is a necessity. Personally I would not walk a yard with a daughter or sister whose figure was open to reproach. Venus de Milo may be the ideal type of womanly beauty, but I fancy she would want an eighteen-inch waist today before she walked down Regent-street.

Corsets to fit and mould the figure are a paramount necessity, and if I had a boy, let alone a girl, who was a bad shape, I should not hesitate for a moment to make him wear those "cruel" corsets of which Edwin Dawson writes so pathetically. I shall be greatly interested in watching your columns for further opinions on this question.   COLONEL

                                                                                                     5 Nov. 1909

[The last two paragraphs of this letter were reprinted in *London Life* on 11 March 1933 (p. 24), and again on 8 April 1939 (p. 21), without acknowledgement. "So many of your correspondents write" was substituted for "Edwin Dawson writes."]

SHOULD GIRLS TIGHT LACE?   20th November 1909 (p. 10)

Strong Feeling in Favour.

(As will be seen from the correspondence we print below [two letters included here], very considerable interest has been excited among our readers over the discussion as to the injury, or otherwise, caused by tight-lacing. It is perhaps rather surprising to find that, among the mass of letters we have received on this subject, no one has yet come forward to support the contention of our original correspondent that tight-lacing is "cruel." We should, of course, be glad to receive the views of those who are opposed to the practice. Correspondents would greatly oblige us by writing on one side of the paper only.)

As you have asked for further opinions on the subject of tight-lacing, I, having worn corsets from childhood, am, I think, entitled to speak.

13. Fashions for Cowes Week. *The Lady's Realm*, May 1906, p.125.

Up to the age of about six, I had only worn a stiffened band tied round me; but at that time my mother (who now, in her sixtieth year, still preserves her good figure and tiny waist) took me to her corset-maker and had me fitted with properly stiffened corsets. For the first few days my new corsets were a little irksome. That, however, soon wore off, and, so far from objecting, I quite looked forward to my evenings and Sundays, when I was allowed to be laced in a little tighter than usual. Up to my fifteenth year my mother attended to my corsets, more frequently than otherwise, however, preventing me from lacing as I wished.

From that time I voluntarily continued to wear them, except for the first few months after I was married, when my wife, reading a letter on the subject, suggested my *trying* them. I was only too pleased to again subject myself to the tyranny of the stay-lace. I absolutely deny that there is or can be any cruelty in wearing judiciously laced corsets, and, on the other hand, speaking as one having experience, say that the sensation of being firmly laced in a well-fitting corset is superb. My wife I am pleased to say, although the mother of three fine children, still preserves her eighteen-inch waist.
GEORGE DUNCAN
10 Nov. 1909

[Reprinted by *L.L.* 27 May 1933 (p.53)]

20th November 1909 (p. 11)

I was greatly interested to read the letters from other readers on the subject of tight-lacing. For my own part, I quite agree with "Colonel" as to the necessity of every girl having her figure carefully trained in more or less tight corsets. I would also (as he says too) like to see the same done with boys. In a great many cases (nowadays especially) there is quite as much necessity. I should very much like to know at what age he thinks a boy should start to wear them. I have a nephew who has an absolutely shocking figure, and if I knew of a place where they could be obtained, I would insist on his having well-made corsets, and wearing them; but I do not know of any place in London where men's corsets can be readily obtained. Of course in America they are quite common, and boys wear them the same as girls; hence no doubt the fine carriage of American youths and young men. Perhaps "Colonel" could tell us of a London address? I should be greatly obliged to him myself, and, doubtless so would many others.

I hope to see some further letters on this subject.
RETIRED COLONEL
11 Nov. 1909

SLAVES OF THE STAY LACE   27th November 1909
[Such is the heading of the correspondence until 8th January 1910]

I was particularly interested in the letters you published last week, and although a mere male thing, I am a wearer of corsets myself and so perhaps may be permitted to state my views. I am in complete accord with "Colonel". I unhesitatingly advocate putting both boys and girls into corsets at an early age, and letting them undergo a judicious course of figure culture. The beneficial results, from a disciplinarian point of view, of the stay-lace have only to be tested to be realised.

Personally, I took to corsets, at my wife's request, soon after our marriage, and my only regret is that I had not done so earlier in life. It would be interesting to have Edwin Dawson's views of a case which came to light recently in France. A mother there brought her son up entirely as a girl. Small-waisted corsets, high-heeled shoes, petticoats and lingerie of the daintiest description; and the truth of his real sex was never suspected until he was twenty-five years of age. He was quite happy and contented, and when the case came before a magistrate his trim, shapely figure was the subject of much comment in the Press.

After all, it must be remembered that clothes are entirely a question of convention.
ALAN BREWSTER

27th November 1909 (p. 23)

Your correspondent, "Retired Colonel," inquires in your current issue if I can tell him of a London address where corsets for boys may be purchased. I fancy he will find that any West End tailor can supply these, or, I believe, a first-class corset house, such as Madame Dowding, of 17, Charing Cross-road, would make them. Of course, your correspondent understands that a boy should always have his corsets made for him; and, for the matter of that, so should a girl.

I need hardly say how interested I am in the discussion that is now going forward in your columns, but I must confess that the practical unanimity of opinion in favour of tight-lacing has considerably surprised me. Where are the "anti-corset" advocates in these days? COLONEL

[Some letters opposing tight-lacing appeared in this same issue. Madame Dowding in fact advertised in *Modern Society* (there was one at the end of the letter page the previous week). Men's corsets were advertised as follows, "Gent's Belts from 21/-," and in the next line confidentiality was assured by this statement in italics: "All communications in Belt Department strictly private." Furthermore a complimentary article about her was printed on 15 Aug. 1908 (p. 28) under the title, "A Famous Corset Artist." It included this reference to her male customers: "For some time past ladies have not had the field to themselves in the wearing of corsets. These aids to health and symmetry have been adopted by many of the sterner sex, and the construction of gentlemen's corsets has become a very important and extensive art. Madame Dowding was one of the earliest to introduce and popularise these, and her advice on the matter is daily sought by male clients."]

4th December 1909 (p.22)

As an actor on the vaudeville stage in the U.S.A. who for seven years played a female part, perhaps my views on corsets and figure-training may be of interest. My mother and aunt were the sisters of V---d, noted for their voices, dancing, and their figures in an era when tight-lacing was a necessity to obtain success in all walks of life. At the age of seven I was a healthy lad, with long locks, which were my detestation, and a clear soprano voice.

From my earliest age I had been accustomed to step-dancing and singing. One day I was caught trying to cut off my hair, so as to be able to play with the other boys without being subjected to insult. I announced I would no longer be called a girl. My mother was furious (the agony she suffered from her corsets made her very harsh when in private life), so she measured me for corsets, and in a week I was so closely laced that I had no strength to object to my feet being cramped by high-heeled, narrow shoes.

For three years I endured ever lengthening, ever tightening corsets, and my shoulders and head were strapped back to increase my bust measurement. Then I was – at New Orleans – put upon the stage, and remained there, a mere speaking doll, whose sole ambition was to gain applause and to smile through the agony of my act. In 1886 my aunt died through lacing after a meal, and in 1887 my mother, while forcing me into a tight corset, injured my kidneys so badly that I had to give up female parts. Y.S. de FRAYNE

[This letter appeared twice in London Life without acknowledgement, on 11.3.1933 (p.24) and 8.4.1939 (p.21) with the years changed from 1886 and 1887 to 1906 and 1916 respectively.]

4th December 1909 (pp. 22-23)

I admire small, neat, and trim waists, and have read your correspondence with interest. Small waists might not mean tight corsets, and yet tight-lacing might be indulged in by a woman with a thirty-inch waist. It is all a question of proportion. But when I read of a thirteen-inch, and even a fifteen-inch, waist—the circumference of a saucer and a tea-plate—I ask myself: do not the possessors of small waists imagine they measure less than they really do? I have never seen such small waists, and think them impossibilities.

But as to a tightly-fitting corset, and the delightful sensations the wearers all write to say are to be obtained therefrom, allow me to speak from experience. A week ago—on reading the first lot of letters, which were then interesting my sister very much—I asked her what corset wearing and tight-lacing felt like. Now, my sister has not a small waist—it is twenty-four inches—yet she laces tightly, and indulges in it. She is a big-framed girl, hence the sheer impossibility of a fifteen-inch waist. She suggested I should try a pair of her corsets, and I did so. I measure thirty-four round the waist, and it was only by letting out the laces to their fullest extent that I was able to get the corsets to fasten. It was only when I had got them on—after some difficulty, I'll admit, not being used to them—that I discovered the simply delightful feeling they produced—such support, such a knitting of the body. I cannot wonder at girls coming under the influence of the stay-lace, and wanting to pull the corsets tighter and tighter every time.

Of course, I at once proceeded to pull in the laces. The gentle pressure was most comforting. I was able to lace down to twenty-six inches easily, and now every night since I have had them on, and find I can pull in the laces to their utmost extent, and feel perfectly comfortable with a twenty-four-inch (ten inches below normal). I should like to wear the corsets always (my sister has now given me one of her pairs), but I fear such a thing is impossible with man's present dress, as the waist-line would be so marked. However, I sit at home in them every evening, and take a walk, too, and cannot speak too highly of the invigorating and bracing effect the corsets have upon me.

My sister has a dress pair that measure twenty-two inches. I put them on the other night, and, although we both tried hard to lace them up to their capacity, we were unable. There must be a limit, I suppose; but still, in time, I have no doubt I shall be able to wear that size.

I quite agree with your men correspondents, that many men (specially those, like myself, inclined to *embonpoint*) would be improved by corset wearing. Of course, men's corsets should be cut a little different in the front from women's, otherwise the style is quite the right thing. Do any firm cater specially for men's corsets? Not belts, but proper fitting corsets for the reduction of the waist and lower part of the body.

I advise all your male readers to beg, borrow, or steal a pair of their sister's (or wife's) corsets and put them on. They will agree with me, the sensation is simply superb. It must be tried to be fully appreciated. I am looking forward to other male opinions.   WALTER

4th December 1909 (p. 24)

I am most interested in the correspondence, as I have been staying with an old school friend in Vienna, who was always a most inveterate tight-lacer. She is now married, and has one girl aged fourteen years and a boy fifteen, and they have both worn tight corsets since the age of nine years. The girl's waist is fourteen inches and the boy fifteen-and-a-half inches, and my friend has a fifteen-inch waist. Corset-wearing in Vienna by the male sex is quite common, and I am sure they look smarter for it.   SMALL WAIST

11th December 1909 (p. 20)

[Criticizes the wasp waist: this is his final paragraph.]

Being only a mere male, perhaps I have no right to dictate; but I can assure Evelyn Day and "Tight and Trim" that a man does not admire a girl with a wasp-like waist, but rather pities her. If "Retired Colonel's" nephew has "an absolutely shocking figure" I am afraid corsets will have very little, if any, effect upon it. Perhaps his absolutely shocking figure may be attributed to the fact that he stoops. If so, ordinary corsets will never cure him, but straps for straightening the back can be obtained at any corsetière's. I would advise "Retired Colonel" to purchase a pair for his nephew and give them a trial. Together with the straps, a systematic course of gymnastics might be taken with beneficial results. I am, yours truly, A MERE MAN

[A longer extract from the original letter was reprinted in *L.L.* on 22 April 1933 (p. 22). The name "Retired Colonel" was retained, but the other two in this extract were replaced by "your correspondent." Oddly enough the letter from Evelyn Day (*M.S.* 20 Nov. 1909, p. 11) was also reprinted in *L.L.*, on 25 Feb. 1933 (p.56), so that name could have been left in the extract from "A Mere Man's" letter. On the other hand, while part of "Colonel's" letter appeared in *L.L.* on 11 March 1933 (p. 24), I did not find any trace of "Retired Colonel's." Not everyone may agree, but I suggest that this better suits the view that these copied letters were sent in by a reader and not inserted by the staff.]

11th December 1909 (p.21)

I am astonished, not only at the approving general attitude adopted by some of your male correspondents, but even more by the actual suggestion that boys should be put into corsets. One of your correspondents seems to suggest that it would not be a bad thing if boys were dressed as girls. Speaking from experience, I can only say that I consider corseting or petticoating boys, apart from its palpable unreasonableness, a grave danger. I am a victim of parental vanity in that direction, having been dressed as a girl until I reached the age of fourteen, and well can I remember the reluctance and regret with which I gave it up, or rather was forced to give it up. I should say that the modern way of bringing up girls as uncorsetted, semi-men is just as pernicious as "disciplining" boys by forcing them to wear things which cramp and clog their manhood. We suffer from undisciplined women and over disciplined men nowadays.

ALEC A NORTHWICK

[Reprinted in *London Life* 25.3.1933 (p.53) as from ALEC]

11th December 1909 (p.20)

You do well to call the victims of tight-lacing slaves, and I hope the correspondence in your columns will set many against the practice. As for the mother who brought up her son as a girl, with small-waisted corsets, high-heeled shoes, petticoats and dainty lingerie, one does not know whether to reprobate her the most or her effeminate offspring, who submitted to such humiliating conditions. ANTI-TIGHT-LACE"

[This letter reappeared in *L.L.* 15.4.1933 (p.19) with minor alterations]

11th December 1909 (p. 22)

The letters you publish on the subject of tight-lacing are certainly most interesting, and I find myself looking forward quite eagerly to your next issue. I trust this attractive feature of your journal will be continued for some time to come. "Retired Colonel" has my entire sympathy. With him, I fail to see why boys should be placed at a disadvantage as compared with girls, who, generally speaking, undergo a course of careful corseting from an early age, with the result that nowadays our girls usually possess well set-up, shapely figures, while our boys, as a consequence of early neglect, are often round-shouldered and misshapen. As I have had considerable experience in this direction, perhaps I may be of some assistance to "Retired Colonel" in his efforts to improve his nephew's figure.

Assuming his nephew to be between the ages of twelve and sixteen, he cannot do better than purchase for him a pair of corsets such as a young girl would wear. He should get a "maid's corded bodice, lightly boned," from two to three inches less than his normal waist measurement. It is advisable for his nephew to wear stockings instead of socks, and he should have suspenders attached to his corsets.

"Retired Colonel" should be careful to see that each succeeding pair of corsets is at least an inch smaller than its predecessor. He will find he can obtain all he requires by writing to some reputable ladies' outfitters or drapers, or the stores. Personally, I adopted this course for years before I was married, with the happiest results. My wife now obtains my corsets for me from her corsetière's. For some time I wore straight-fronted ribbon corsets, but latterly I have adopted the new Directoire type that is so fashionable among ladies, and I find them very delightful. They are, I consider, more suitable for the masculine figure than any type of ladies' corsets. "Retired Colonel" should insist upon his nephew wearing his corsets at night; but he can, if he wishes, let him wear them an inch bigger.

I trust the particulars I have given above may prove helpful to "Retired Colonel," and I wish him every success. I am confident that, if he follows my example, both he and his nephew will be delighted with the results.   ALAN BREWSTER

(A large number of interesting letters on this subject are still unavoidably held over. Will correspondents kindly note that all letters must be properly authenticated with full name and address, not, of course, for publication.)

18th December 1909 (p.23)

Dear Sir, – I am much interested in the letters on tight-lacing. As one of the male sex, you might like to hear my experiences. I was rough, clumsy, and troublesome. I was fitted with long corsets, which were tightly laced; had high-heeled, high-leg button boots like a girl's, and wore constantly long, tight kid gloves. I became much improved in figure, carriage and gait. When older I discarded the high-heeled boots, but never have given up the corsets, as I enjoy the feeling they give, and I still wear ladies' gloves in winter, as the extra length in the wrists keeps one's hands much warmer. I am sure discipline such as I had would be good for some boys. I have written without details so as to keep this letter short, and they might not be of interest.

Yours truly,   GEOFFREY

[Reprinted in *L.L.* 17.6.33 (p.23)]

25th December 1909 (pp. 22-23)

[The writer argues against the tight lacing of girls. He continues:]

Another of your correspondents, "Walter," after advising all your male readers to beg, borrow or steal their female relations' corsets, and wear them, remarks that he is looking forward to other male opinions. As he is so anxious for it, I have great pleasure in giving him mine, which is that he should invest in silk and lace petticoats and other articles of feminine attire. I am sure he would feel much more at home in them than in the garb of a man.

MODERATION

(A large number of interesting letters on this subject are still unavoidably held over. With the most interesting of these we hope to deal during the next week or two. Will correspondents kindly note that all letters must be properly authenticated with full name and address, not, of course, for publication, and should be written on one side of the paper only.)

Catalogue Spring and Summer 1906,
Pryce Jones, Ltd., Newtown, p.19.

1st January 1910 (p.23)

On mentioning with incredulity to a friend the references in your columns to boys being corseted and petticoated, she remarked that so far from this being improbable, one of her brothers had been a victim to it himself. Being one of a large family who had experienced financial reverses, he was adopted, at thirteen years of age, by two maiden ladies on condition that his parents should give up all claim to him. When he arrived at their place in the country, which was a large, rambling old-fashioned mansion, surrounded by a huge park, he was treated with the utmost kindness, except that all boyish proclivities were rigidly repressed, and he was expected to sit quietly while they read to him by the hour goody-goody books of a juvenile character. During his leisure time he was placed in charge of a Scotch nurse of forbidding mien and strict ideas, whose principal punishment for any exhibition of boyish spirit was to dress him up in girl's clothes – underclothing, tight corsets, high heeled shoes, and pinafore – from which he could only escape by implicit obedience to her behests. As neither pleading, sulking nor the exhibition of bad temper had any effect upon his gaolers and guardians, and he was not allowed to go beyond the confines of the park, nor receive or write letters, he had no option but to submit with as good a grace as possible. It was only when he got old enough to be a match for this female tyranny that he was able to emancipate himself from their possibly well-meant but eccentric ideas of discipline. A.I.

1st January 1910 (p. 23)

As one who has taken a special interest in the question of corsets for many years, I find it very curious to compare the letters which are now appearing in your columns with those that appeared in the "Englishwoman's Domestic Magazine" and other papers about the year 1860, and at various intervals since. I have a large collection of these, and it seems that, with few exceptions, those who have laced tightly are all in favour, and those who disagree are mostly men who have never worn corsets, and who cannot speak from actual experience. Facts speak for themselves, and the large numbers of old ladies of over seventy who have laced tightly all their lives, and who were brought up under the most severe figure training in their youth, prove that the system cannot be so fatal as many would make out.

All extremes are bad, no doubt; but it is an open question whether those women who have never laced tightly are any more healthy than those who have. I think, however, that there can be no doubt that when lacing is so tight that it makes exercise difficult it must be wrong. I am now nearly fifty, and have worn corsets since I was sixteen [i.e. about 1876], with the exception of three years when I was on active service in South Africa, and have always felt better for it. I have not had a day's illness all those years. Although I lace myself reasonably tight, I take a great deal of hard exercise. I ride, and shoot, and walk on an average ten miles a day. I admit there are occasions, when special exertion is necessary, that I find it wise to discard corsets for the time being, but it is always a pleasure to return to them. Particularly after a hard day.

I notice some male readers have written to ask where gentlemen's corsets can be obtained. Messrs. Worth's Corsets, Limited, 3, Hamsell-street, London, E.C., have for years studied the requirements of men, and have a special department for men's corsets and belts. I had my first pair from them, and have gone to them ever since. Mr. Stanley Dowding, 17, Charing Cross-road, W.C., is in charge of Mde Dowding's gentlemen's department. There are others, no doubt; but both these firms do a large business in gentlemen's corsets and belts, as they are often called.

[The writer mentions two shops where he has seen "The Corset and the Crinoline" and invites readers to supply titles of other books. He also mentions the wasp waists found in Crete by Dr. Evans.]

I think your correspondent "Walter" is wrong in advising your male readers "to beg, borrow, or steal a pair of their sister's (or wife's) corsets." Let them go and be measured by an expert who understands the male requirements. The shape of the female corset is not suitable for a man. I feel sure their they will never regret a well-made corset made to suit their special requirements, and will obtain better health, as well as increased comfort, particularly if they have much office work.

LONG EXPERIENCE

1st January 1910 (p.24)

I am strongly in favour of corsets for boys, only let them be worn young and let the lacing be gradual. It is a fatal mistake for a young man – as indeed for a young woman – to begin to lace tightly without any previous training. There are several firms who supply men's corsets, and there are some kinds of ladies' corsets quite suitable for lads, as they are light and pliant. A boy will naturally complain of some discomfort when he first dons a corset; so will his sister. But in both cases, when the sensation of tightness and support is appreciated, as it most assuredly is sooner or later, the desire to draw in the laces will most certainly supervene. Personally I only indulge in the luxury, as I think it, of being very tightly laced after working hours; but I am always glad of wearing corsets, and would not like to be without them.

MERE MAN

EFFEMINATE MEN 15th January 1910 (p. 25)

Your correspondent, "Colonial," writes very pertinently on the subject of the degeneracy of the present-day English girl; but I am afraid our young men in the Old Country are still more culpable. I speak with considerable knowledge, for I myself was a victim until the perusal, week by week, of the letters in your recent correspondence—avowals made by young men of effeminate tastes—convinced me that I, too, was cutting a ridiculous figure. So I determined to turn over a new leaf, and I will never again look back on what are now closed pages in my life.

Surely this masculinising of our girls, and effeminising of our boys, is an evil which everyone should try to remedy, unless we are prepared to become a degenerate race. Day by day we see ourselves outstripped and beaten by outsiders, and a crisis must inevitably supervene sooner or later. It cannot be possible for our young men to properly acquit themselves if they are the passive victims of effeminate tastes and fancies; and our girls cannot influence them, as they should, if they spend their time unsexing themselves by trying to make manly women of themselves.

A CONVERT

15th January 1910 (p.26)

[Suzanne started her column "Frills and Furbelows", a second feature for women in addition to "Woman's Mirror", on 6th November, 1909. On 20th November, 1909, she invited readers to send in enquiries to her. Many of her replies are on the question of the dress of small boys.]

"LOVELY TWINS" – Personally I do not agree with boys wearing corsets at all. For your little girl it is right enough, but certainly I think the boy should be allowed his freedom. Apart from all questions of health, his lot will be a hard one when he mixes with other boys if you bring him up so effeminately.

SUZANNE

THE MODERN ENGLISH GIRL 29th January 1910 (p. 11)

[The writer approves of the defence of the modern girl by "An English Girl" on 15 Jan. 1910 (p. 26) and continues:] particularly after the very foolish letters—of, should I say *men*? who strive to be as feminine as art will make them. Can we be surprised that girls are masculine in their habits, when we see certain members of the male sex becoming more effeminate every day?

Healthy minded girls admire men who are their opposites, manly in every sense of the word and chivalrous, and not vain effeminate weaklings who think more of their diminutive waists than they do of their country. Until reading the numerous letters in "Modern Society" that have appeared lately, I had no idea that men (unworthy of the name) would make themselves so ridiculous in the eyes of sensible women. And surely they are much more to blame than their masculine and perhaps more healthy-minded sisters.   A BACHELOR GIRL

THE MODERN ENGLISH GIRL 5th February 1910 (p.23)

I entirely differ from the opinion of "Bachelor Girl" in your last number. My first meeting with my husband (over ten years ago) was in the ditch of a dark Devonshire lane, where I was lying with a broken leg, fainting from pain, and loss of blood, on a cold October evening, the result of a bicycle accident. He, returning from a shoot, finding me in this condition, took me in his arms and carried me over a mile, during which we met absolutely no one, to the nearest house – my home. Not much effeminacy about that. He called to enquire for me, and when I was well enough I saw him. He seemed as much attracted to me as I to him. In a few months we were married. At this time he seemed to delight in the very roughest clothes he could obtain. The first evening in our own home, after our honeymoon, I put on one of my prettiest evening dresses, and, although we neither of us said anything, I saw he appreciated what I had done, and seemed sorry he had not changed out of his business suit.

After that he always dressed for the evening. As a reward I gave him some evening stockings I had myself embroidered and these, together with a pair of my grandfather's buckles I had put on his evening shoes, commenced to give him a taste for a little finery. So, gradually adding a little embroidery or lace here and there, I have succeeded in getting him to adopt as dainty underwear as I have myself, to discuss these matters and to interest himself in my dresses. On my last birthday he gave me a lovely diamond bracelet, which I however, absolutely refused to wear without he would allow me to lock one on his wrist also. My most valued piece of jewellery is a medal presented to him two years ago by the French authorities for jumping overboard from a steamer running from Nice to Ajaccio and saving a child which had fallen overboard which shows, although he ruined a new satin corset, that he has not become "effeminate". I have entered into his sports, pastimes, business, dress. He has done the same with mine; and although man and wife, we are chums. I may have become more masculine and he more "effeminate" so that as it should be, we meet on equal terms, and are very happy.

MODERN MATRON

THE MODERN ENGLISH GIRL 12th February 1910 (p.25)

My sympathies are all with "Modern Matron". Surely what is needed today is a strengthening of the bond of sympathy between men and women, and this is only to be attained by encouraging anything that will tend to give each a common ground of interest. To my mind, in the best and truest type of man there is much that is feminine, just as the finest women possess the great masculine qualities. If a husband and wife are endowed with these characteristics an ideally happy union must result.

Let me give my experience. When I was twenty-two, and my only brother thirteen, the death of our father left us alone in the world. Fortunately, we were quite well to do, and I was able to allow my brother to continue at boarding school. But to my sorrow, I found we were drifting apart. Intercourse became increasingly difficult, until one fortunate day, after silently and despondently regarding his handsome face during our most trying meal – luncheon, I suggested to him, for fun, that he should dress himself in my clothes, and see what kind of a girl he could make, and he laughingly assented. I took him up to my room and gave him the run of my entire wardrobe together with much information as to the mysteries of the feminine toilette. I suppose this appealed to some feminine trait in his character, for he seemed quite pleased and proud when I told him later that he made a splendid girl. After that I had no difficulty in persuading him to don petticoats occasionally of an evening during the holidays, and to my delight, the barrier that had arisen between us was shattered. I found I could make a pal and a confidant of him, and he developed quite an intelligent interest in the cult of frocks and frills.

Now this is the important point. His manliness and zest for sport has not suffered in any way. When he left school I sent him up to the "Varsity". He continued to play Rugby football and cricket, and on several occasions he was chosen to play the former for the University team. Now he is reading for the bar, and naturally he has less leisure than of yore; but occasionally, sometimes as often as twice a week, I hear the rustle of a silken petticoat on the stairs and I know that my chum and I are going to spend what he calls a "matey" evening together. My brother may be feminine in some ways, but he is certainly not effeminate; and have not some of our greatest writers declared that it is the feminine in a man that makes him a true gentleman? Anyhow I envy the girl who is fortunate enough to secure him as her husband.

A HAPPY SISTER

EFFEMINATE MEN   19th February 1910 (p.26)

I cannot agree with "Happy Sister" that a young man can be feminine and not effeminate. Like her brother, I was persuaded one day five years ago, when a boy of fourteen, by the two older sisters with whom I lived, to dress as a girl. They were so delighted with my appearance that they insisted on my doing so again and again; and in time it became a custom that I should make a full feminine toilette every afternoon. I disliked it at first, but my prejudices disappeared with experience. Although pretty tightly laced, my corsets were extremely comfortable, and petticoats I found the most enjoyable garments in the world. I do not regret it, but I frankly admit I am thoroughly effeminate. Indeed, one cannot be manly in a dainty prison of lace and silk underskirts; one must bow to one's environment. The petticoat is essentially feminine, and if a man submits to its rule, he must become feminine. I hope that some of your readers, who have probably heard of young men who have adopted feminine attire, will give their opinions on this very interesting subject.

JUPON

26th February 1910 (p.30)

I am a Canadian from St. John, New Brunswick, so perhaps my opinion on the letters from "Modern Matron" and "A Happy Sister" may not be of much interest to you. Nevertheless I wish to put it on record how thoroughly I agree with them. I have four children – a girl 19, two boys 18 and 17, and a girl of 15. I am now in this country to arrange for my elder boy to study medicine. I am sure it would tend to more unity in the family if boys and girls were brought up more on an equality with each other, and not as if they were a different species.

My girls have gone in for all their brothers' sports – hockey, tennis, rowing, fencing, riding and motoring and especially swimming, at which last both girls excel their brothers, and are quite equal to them in nerve when riding or motoring. On the other hand, my boys are adepts at the "feminine" accomplishments of their sisters. Up to the age of fifteen I dressed my boys in kilts for outdoor wear, so that I might approximate their costume as nearly as I could to that of their sisters, their indoor and evening dress resembling it even more. Up to this age I also kept their hair long, coiling it round their heads in tightly-placed small plaits, dressing it like their sisters for the evening when we were alone. At fifteen, when sending them away to school, much to my grief, I had their hair cut short. When they came home at weekends, I was careful to have very pretty evening frocks for them, and I had their own hair worked up into "transformations" for them, so that they were again on equal terms with their sisters during evenings. My girls also wear tailor-mades during the day, and I try to get the same pattern cloth as the boys.

The result: my boys are interested in frocks, and chiffons and lingerie. My girls, in sports. They are never at a loss for conversation, either among themselves or with strangers. We are a most united family, boys and girls on an exact equality, and I congratulate myself on my success. On the much-debated subject of corsets – while, of course, corsets have always been worn, I have firmly checked anything approaching tight-lacing either for the boys or girls.
MARION INGLIS

26th February 1910 (p.30)
I have been greatly interested in the letters of "Modern Matron" and "Happy Sister", with both of whom I am inclined to agree. To my mind it can scarcely be disputed that a judicious upbringing amid the softening influence of feminine surroundings brings out the best points in a boy's character, and eliminates the coarser elements of the brute male. It is unquestionably desirable that men and women should meet on a common plane, and that the antagonistic instincts should be removed. Now, by occasionally disciplining a boy – by putting him into dainty underwear and petticoats – one is able to inculcate in him a sympathy with the feminine point of view, and a knowledge of femininity in general which is valuable.

On the other hand, there are grave dangers; for unless the greatest care is exercised, he may degenerate into a petticoated nincompoop. That is to say he may come to prefer wearing girl's clothes (which should only be administered as a corrective), and indulging in feminine pursuits and occupations, to leading the more strenuous life of a boy. I can speak authoritatively on this point, for my sister, fired by the success that had attended the occasional petticoating of her elder boy, brought her other son up on the same lines, with disastrous results, for now although he is nearly twenty-two years of age, he insists upon wearing dainty underwear and corsets, and to my sister's despair, he prefers to wear petticoats at home, and occupy himself doing needlework: whereas his elder brother is most happily married.

Therefore while agreeing that, under careful supervision, the occasional petticoating of boys is most beneficial, I consider the dangers attendant on the practice too great to admit of its general adoption. BACHELOR UNCLE

EFFEMINATE MEN 26th February 1910 (p.30)
I have read the correspondence on this subject from "Modern Matron" and "Happy Sister". I presume you like to hear all views, so I send you mine. The letters from these two women make me feel sick. To think of a "man" (save the mark!) delighting in wearing "frocks and frills". I should like to kick him. INDIAN ARMY

PRYCE JONES, Ltd., NEWTOWN.

The Rational Corset Bodice

Buttoned back, white or drab Sateen. Childs', 8-in. deep, 2/6; Girls', 9½-in. or 11-in. deep, 2/9, buttoned front, Maids', 11-in. deep, 3/3; 13-in. deep, 3/6; Young Ladies', 14-in. deep, 4/11, waist, 21-in. to 25-in.

Ladies', with suspenders, 12½-in. deep, 6/11; white only, 15-in. deep, removable steels for washing, no suspenders, 5/6, waist, 21-in. to 28-in.

Cycling Corsets, dove Coutil, with suspenders, 10½-in. busk, 5/6, 6/11; fawn Drill, 10-in. busk, no suspenders, 3/6; waist 19 to 25-in.

○○○○○○○○○○○
"OKTIS" CORSET SHIELDS.
1/0½ per pair.
○○○○○○○○○○○
"TITAN" CORSET ATTACHMENT.
black or white, 5/9. In ordering give hip measurement.
○○○○○○○○○○○

"CAMELLIA."
White or dove Coutil, 12-in. busk, prevents stooping, 3/11; white or cream Coutil, for girls 13 to 16 years, 7/11; waist 21 to 24-in.

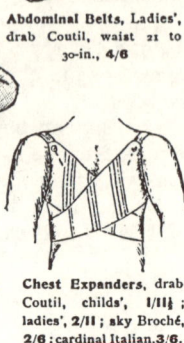

Abdominal Belts, Ladies', drab Coutil, waist 21 to 30-in., 4/6

Chest Expanders, drab Coutil, childs', 1/11½; ladies', 2/11; sky Broché, 2/6; cardinal Italian, 3/6.

Accouchement Belts, white, waist 22, 24, 26, 28, 30-in., 5/11

"Braceline" dove Coutil or black Italian Cloth, 13-in. busk, 4/6, waist 19 to 24-in.

Young Ladies' Corsets, dove Coutil, 12½-in. busk, 3/6; fawn Drill, 11½-in. busk, with shoulder straps, 2/3; suspenders, 7½d. extra; waist, 21 to 25-in.

○○○○○○○○○○○○○
No Order for
CORSETS
can be executed unless waist size required is stated.

"MYOSOTIS."
Dove or white Coutil, 12½-in. busk, 5/11; white Coutil, 14½-in. busk, 3/6; black Italian Cloth, 13½-in. busk, hip suspenders also, 5/11; waist 19 to 25-in.

○○○○○○○○○○○○
"HOOK-ON" SUSPENDERS.
1/0½ per pair.

"HYACINTH."
White Coutil, 13-in. busk, 4/6; sky and white Broché, 5/11; dove Coutil, 11½-in. busk, 6/11; waist 19 to 25-in.

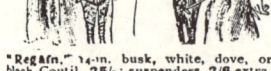

"Regain," 14-in. busk, white, dove, or black Coutil, 25/-; suspenders, 2/6 extra, waist 21 to 29-in.

26th February 1910 (p. 28)

BEATRICE: It seems a pity to have to resort to such severe measures to keep your little boy out of mischief. Boys are bound to get into a certain amount of trouble if they are strong and healthy. It is only the weakly ones who never do wrong. If you think it necessary to put the gloves on, you could sew them securely to his jersey sleeves, then he could not remove them without your knowledge. A far better plan to my idea, would be to get someone to amuse and look after him as you are so much away. SUZANNE

EFFEMINATE MEN   5th March 1910 (p.26)

On casually picking up last week's Modern Society I was immensely interested to read a letter on "Feminine Men", following several upon "earrings". Curiously enough, both these subjects have always had a tremendous interest for me. I am a Varsity man with a fairly good athletic record, and I still keep my muscles fit by some strenuous mountaining [sic] and other severe exercises; but I have with it all two great weaknesses, which do not, I believe, really stand in the way of such real manliness as I am proud to possess. These two weaknesses are earrings, and – at suitable times – woman's dress. Soon after our marriage, my wife – a tall well built woman – said she would like to see me in one of her frocks. I smiled, but consented; but I feel bound to confess that I found something most comforting and seductive in the swish and feel of skirts, and now, continually, in private, dress in feminine fashion for the evening.

She is very fond too of barbaric jewellery, and having dressed me up as I have described, put chains round my neck, rings on every finger, and bracelets and bangles galore. Somehow I liked it all. Then nothing would satisfy her until she made me wear big earrings, of which she is herself intensely fond; and one happy evening she persuaded me to let her pierce my ears and hang in them a pair of her heavy coral earrings. I was a little unwilling at first for her to do it, but I must honestly allow that I have never regretted it. There is not an evening, except when spent in public, in which I do not wear big swinging earrings. The pain was nothing – just a pleasant sensation; and they *do* seem to fill an unexplainable want. And I believe this mysterious bit of femininity to which I give way has been a means of very real happiness, of which others may be glad to know. C.U.A.C
[presumably stands for "Cambridge University Athletic Club"]

5th March 1910 (p.26)

If there are masculine women, there will be effeminate men. I suppose I am one of them; but I am unrepentant. It has always given me a sensation of intoxicating pleasure to wear feminine attire, and some means, and the privacy of a bachelor flat, enable me to let my fancy take its fullest flight. Every evening and many days I don a feminine toilette of the most complete description. Having worn corsets night and day and tight high-heeled boots all night, for five years, I can wear the most extreme fashions, and the daintiest of boots, and my wardrobe is one that any woman might envy. I can certainly understand the pleasure women take in smart dress. As I write I am completely clothed as a woman, wig, Lewis hat, high collared satin sheath gown of white, twenty-inch corsets of the longest and stiffest kind, long black kid gloves, and patent leather boots to knees with five inch heels. Let those that doubt, try the sensation of being imprisoned in clinging silk and lace, corseted as in an iron grasp, and booted so as to walk on tiptoe, and they will endorse every word I say. TALON

19th March 1910 (p.26)

MRS J.F. – I should advise you to have the kilt made by a tailor; a dressmaker, however clever, cannot get a kilt to look or set the same way as one made by a man. I certainly think your son too old to wear petticoats of any kind with the kilt. To my mind it would spoil the effect entirely. I see no harm in boys wearing corsets if made specially for them, but do not consider them necessary. I am in no way in favour of making boys effeminate. SUZANNE

(p.25)

AUDREY D. WILSON – I cannot agree with boys wearing suspenders as well as garters with kilts. I cannot see the necessity for both, especially as you say they have to wear longer kilts in consequence. Kilts, to be correct, should never reach below the bend of the knee. If they do, much of the smartness is lost, and the effect is entirely spoilt. SUZANNE

2nd April 1910 (p.24)

STAY-LACE – If boys are to be brought up to wear stays I think it best that they should do so from babyhood, changing them in style and weight as the child gets older and stronger. I do not think stays should be worn at night by either girl or boy: the restriction is too great.

ALICE VORLEY – I know of no better corset maker than Madame Dowding, who would make just what you require. I have heard of an appliance such as you mention, but cannot recommend it. The best costume for your boys would be suits of the Norfolk type made by a good tailor, in not too heavy a material, explaining to the tailor that you wish the waist well defined. I have no faith in "patent" stays. SUZANNE

9th April 1910 (p.23)

BEATRICE – The underclothing worn with the kilt for dancing should be of the fullest and laciest kind. Two lace frilled petticoats would be best, and side-buttoned knickers with four or five lace frills. Plaid stockings to match the kilt should be folded under the knee and kept up invisibly with garters. The tunic should have long sleeves with gauntlet cuffs and lace frills over the hands, and if liked white kid gloves. No kilt should come below the knees, which should be bare. SUZANNE
[This costume is apparently for a girl – see 11th June, 1910]

16th April 1910 (p.28)

STAYLACE – You might certainly try the plan you speak of with regard to your nephews. I should like to know the result.

ALLISON 1) I think you could find 20in about right. I should not advise smaller at any time, in case it prevents the further development of your son's figure.
        2) Low in the bust and short on the hips; busk and bones about the same as for a girl, but the material should be stouter.
        3) If properly fitted, suspenders will not be necessary; they would only be in the way.
        4) Black or brown velvet suit, with knickers of the ordinary cut, coat well shaped in at the waist, and a white silk or satin fitted waistcoat would be better than the kilt suggestion.
        5) Patent shoes and buckles, but *not* high heels – it would spoil his deportment. SUZANNE

23rd April 1910 (p.28)
IDA D. FOWLER – You will find 20ins quite small enough, and one silk kilted petticoat and plain silk knickers (short) to match the kilt would be best. Lace-trimmed underclothing would only be suitable for a girl's Highland costume.   SUZANNE

30th April 1910 (p.23)
ANNIE HARTMANN – It is not too soon to put your boy into stays if you intend to train his figure; 18ins would be small enough to start with, reducing them gradually to 16ins.

PANTALOON – Let your ward wear kilts by all means and ordinary girls' stays, lightly boned; but unless for special occasions, I think lace-trimmed underclothing quite unsuitable. Boy's combinations and short cloth knickers would be more in keeping.   SUZANNE

7th May 1910 (p.28)
BEATRICE – For dancing, your boy could wear one or two silk petticoats of shades to match the tartan of the kilt; also frilled knickers of the same material. The gloves for day kilt could either be one button cape kid, or tan doeskin; but I do not care for gauntlets for boys, since you would find them very uncomfortable.   SUZANNE

14th May 1910 (p.26)
[The "King's mourning" issue]
A.G. – Surely you have some friends who can advise you better than I can as to the best means to free yourself from your present condition. If not, why not apply to the local clergyman, who would no doubt assist you. I consider your stepmother a very foolish woman.

BIRTCH – The costume you suggest would be quite suitable for day wear, but it is surely imperative that the boy should wear knickers under his kilt. These need only be of thin and plain material.

ELIZABETH – I think feminine influence good for all boys, but cannot see that any benefit can be derived by dressing boys as girls. A blue serge kilt for indoors, and a short serge coat would be more in keeping, and petticoats if you wish them under the kilt.   SUZANNE

11th June 1910 (p.24)
STAGE – I do not think it too soon to have your daughter fitted with good corsets, but should allow the boy his freedom a little longer . . . When you decide to put your boy into corsets, have them made for him, and do not allow him to wear those made for girls. I am glad you appreciate my notes.

CONSTANT READER – I am quite aware that petticoats are not usually worn with kilts. The replies you mention have been with reference to kilts for girls or young boys in the case of fancy or evening dress. With regard to the strap, I maintain that a broad strap (naturally, not buckle end) is preferable to a rod or stick with which to whip an unruly child.   SUZANNE

16th July 1910 (p.28)

A SLAVE – I am afraid the subject is not of sufficient general interest to give much space to. Forty years ago the dress for boys between the ages of, say, three and nine, usually consisted of a black velvet frock, with low neck and short sleeves, plaid sash, petticoats, and lace knickers, and, as a rule, the hair was worn long on the shoulders. SUZANNE

30th July 1910 (p.26)

A SLAVE – The term "lace knickers" for children means, of course, cambrick or nainsook, trimmed with lace at the knees.

G.G. – Your boy could wear kilts for quite another two or three years. It is now time to have corsets made for him, which should not be too heavily boned, and waist about 16 or 17 ins. SUZANNE

3rd September 1910 (p.24)

TIT – The blouse portion of a kilt costume does not want to be tight-fitting, but a good shape. Your nephew should now have specially-made boy's corsets. Underclothing is a matter of taste. SUZANNE

10th September 1910 (p.24)

MAM. (Hull) – Many men nowadays wear corsets, and find them of great benefit, so I see no harm in your son adopting them. I do not, however, approve of extremely small waists for men, as it only makes them appear ridiculous.

E.M. (Kilmocolm) – Your son could wear kilts until he is fourteen easily. I certainly think corsets improve the appearance of a Highland costume. Short plaid knickers of the same material as the kilt should be worn underneath, and if you like, a plaid silk petticoat for best. Two inch heels would be about right for evening wear. SUZANNE

17th September 1910 (p.23)

MRS MALLINSON – For ordinary wear, tweed kilts with coat and vest to match, and underneath short cloth knickers. Heather mixture stockings are best, and patent leather buckle shoes. One petticoat is often worn with kilt, which should come just to the bend of the knee. The accompanying sketch certainly seems rather short. I think a few strokes with a birch would be the best punishment for the boy. You can obtain one from Messrs. Dukas and co. 20, Red Lion Square. SUZANNE

22nd October 1910 (p.24)

J.A. (Glasgow) – Certainly a good corset would help you immensely, and add greatly to your comfort. I should most decidedly allow your boy to remain with his cousins and undergo the same course of training, which in their case has been so successful.

16. Frocks for Girls. *Femina*, 15th October 1906, p.469.

MRS M. (Norwood) – Without doubt your boy and girls should be separately punished, and it it quite time the boy was put into a more manly style of dress. I could judge the costume better from the original photo.   SUZANNE

7th January 1911 (p.28)

NURSE – I should discontinue the corsets altogether for your son, and let him go in for outdoor exercise and sport of all kinds, so that his development should be in proportion, which I do not consider to be the case at the present time.   SUZANNE

28th January 1911 (p.30)

    I wonder why "Observer" did not observe the great increase in tight-lacing among boys and men. Go to any seaside resort and observe the number of boys from say, six to thirteen or fourteen, whose mothers keep them tightly corsetted to give them a figure. I do not deny that in many cases corsets do improve a boy's appearance, and keep him from lolling about. Numbers of our young men are apparently well laced in; while most middle-aged men wear "belts" which in many cases are 14in or even more, in depth, well stiffened, and laced at the back.   ANOTHER OBSERVER

4th February 1911 (p.25)

HELENE – I'm afraid dressing your step-son in girls' clothes would not improve his behaviour. Why not send him to a strict boarding school, under a good master, which is evidently what he requires? This would also break him away from his undesirable companions.   SUZANNE

25th February 1911 (p.23)

Last column signed by *SUZANNE*.

4th March 1911 (p.30)

[Mentions that there were several books on corsets in the sixties]
    . . . I have reason to remember these as my mother was greatly taken with the reasoning and compelled my brother and myself to adopt them, and personally saw that we were properly laced. We rebelled at first, but soon got to enjoy the sensation of being tightly laced. There can be no doubt that there is a great deal of satisfaction in having a small waist. I am now well over sixty, and still delight in being firmly laced into well-fitting corsets.   A.D.M.

4th March 1911 (p. 30)

    While it is undoubtedly a fact that a large number of young men wear corsets, I do not think many are accustomed to them from childhood, as "Another Observer" would seem to imply. School life would mean a serious break of several years in the forming of a boy's figure, and the regime must, for the majority, begin at the age of sixteen or seventeen, whether volun-

v. Fancy Dress Suggestions for Christmas Parties. *The Queen*, 19th November 1910, p.931.

vi. W.A. Bolton as Georgiana Tidman in *Dandy Dick* by Sir Arthur Pinero, Easter 1903.
Courtesy of A.D.C. Theatre Executive Committee, Cambridge.

tarily or under maternal supervision. Girls are more fortunate in this respect, as their waists are looked after at school; but a boy whose education is carried on at home can be subjected to a careful and gradual lacing-in without injury or any but the slightest inconvenience. Once the taste for a neat figure and the pleasurable sensation of being smartly laced-in are awakened most lads will adopt the corset as readily as their sisters and without any surrender of manly dignity.

A MERE MAN.

Parasols are important details in this summer's dress schemes, and are of various quaint shapes

17. Hats and Parasols. *Every Woman's Encyclopædia*, Vol. VIII (1912), p.5501.

A trio of tennis frocks made in a way which gives free scope to the limbs, and at the same time illustrates some of the latest points of fashion. The rucked sleeves in the stooping figure, which come from underneath a very wide arm-hole, are quite correct and distinctly becoming. The skirt of the striped gown with the cross-cut points of the front width running upwards is just what it should be. For tennis all the gowns have low collars.

18. Tennis Frocks. *The Girl's Own Paper*, 31st August 1907, p.761.

V

PHOTO BITS

INTRODUCTION

Immediately following the paragraph about *Modern Society* quoted in the previous chapter, "D.S." continued:

> By the time I was fourteen I had got hold of another periodical, *Photo Bits,* which devoted itself almost entirely to encouraging this trait [i.e. dressing up in women's clothes] and the pleasures of birching. The latter never made the slightest appeal to me. (Havelock Ellis, *Studies in the Psychology of Sex*, Random House, New York, 1936, Vol. III, Part II, p. 54.)

This description of *Photo Bits* is not wholly accurate, and in so far as it is, only applies to the years 1909 to 1912, from which the articles and correspondence in this collection are taken. In this introduction I want to explain briefly how this came about and trace the course of the paper's development into the world's first journalistic vehicle for the exposition and discussion of domestic punishment, clothes fetishism and cross-dressing.

Photo Bits began publication on 9 July 1898 from Temple Chambers, Blackfriars, at the price of one penny. According to the first editorial claim to copyright on 13 July 1901 (p.17), the proprietors were The Brunswick Publishing Company Ltd. The offices of the paper moved to Rosebery House, Bream's Buildings, E.C. on 10 May 1902. With effect from 27 June 1903, The Phoenix Press Ltd. took over the ownership, first at 7, Bolt Court, then at 4, Red Lion Court, and finally, from 1906, at 9, Bolt Court, Fleet Street. This continued at least until the end of 1912. It seems, therefore, that any changes in the character of the paper over the years 1909 to 1912 were not due to changes in ownership.

Classified as a "comic" paper in the Press Directories of the time, *Photo Bits* was in fact Britain's first Pin-Up magazine. MacQueen-Pope said this of it:

> For those who liked spice in their pictures as well as in letterpress there were papers like *Sketchy Bits* and *Photo Bits,* which concentrated on the female form in various states of clothing, and were bought by adolescents. They also were never taken home.
> (W. MacQueen-Pope: *Twenty Shillings in the Pound*, London, 1948, p. 347.)

As one would expect *Photo Bits* was mentioned in *Pin-Up's Progress: an Illustrated History of the Immodest Art* by Richard Wortley assisted by Jeremy Gibson (London: Panther Books, 1971). See pages 17, 19, 21, 26, 32-33, 58 and 167, particularly page 26 for its description of the first issue. Illustrations numbered 3 and 9 are photographs of two front covers, one in 1900 and the other in 1915. Wortley, however, seems to have been wholly unaware of the special character of the paper between the years 1909 and 1912. It is only recently that David Kunzle has thrown some light on this aspect in his *Fashion and Fetishism: A Social History of the Corset, Tight-Lacing and Other Forms of Body-Sculpture in the West* (Totowa, New Jersey: Rowman and Littlefield, 1982, pp. 233-234 and 252).

James Joyce knew of the paper and wished to include it as one of the papers read by Leopold and Molly Bloom in *Ulysses* which describes the fictional events of 16 June 1904. In real life this was the day on which Joyce met his future wife, Nora Barnacle. Joyce left Ireland with Nora on 8 October 1904, returning only in 1909 and 1912 (Richard Ellmann. *James Joyce*.

83

Oxford, O.U.P., New and Revised Edition, 1982). *Photo Bits*, however, ceased publication in 1916, before Joyce started to write his novel. To remedy this, Joyce tried in 1920 to obtain copies of a similar paper through his friend, Frank Budgen (*James Joyce and the Making of Ulysses*. London: 1934, p. 246). The paper that Budgen sent, although he does not mention it by name, was *Bits of Fun*, which was quite different, except for the correspondence page, which did in fact prove of value to Joyce, as I shall show in a future collection of letters from that paper.

It is not surprising, therefore, that the impression given of *Photo Bits* in *Ulysses* is inaccurate, except in the case of the picture over the bed in the Blooms' bedroom: "The *Bath of the Nymph* over the bed. Given away with the Easter number of *Photo Bits:* Splendid masterpiece in art colours" (See page 58 of the 1937 edition published by John Lane, The Bodley Head, London). Coloured plates were issued with special holiday numbers, but, since an extra penny or tuppence was charged, they were not free. There was of course no actual Easter "Nymph" between 1899 and 1904. The nearest example to Joyce's "Nymph" is perhaps the "Splendid Presentation Plate" of "The Wave" by Jan Van Beers issued with "Our Special Summer Number" of 30 June 1900. This showed a woman in a bathing costume sporting in the waves with a man behind on the point of seizing her by the waist. In the brothel scene the "Nymph" comes to life and speaks to Bloom: "Mortal! You found me in evil company, highkickers, coster picnic makers, pugilists, popular generals, immoral panto boys in flesh tights and the nifty shimmy dancers, La Aurora and Karini, musical act, the hit of the century." This and the "Nymph's" next speech about advertisements for "Rubber Goods," etc. convey entirely the wrong impression (pp. 516-18; see also the mention on p. 714). There were highkickers certainly, but only a very few pugilists and no generals or panto boys and no such advertisements in the *Photo Bits* of 1904. Joyce's *Photo Bits* is a literary creation.

In its early years the essential purpose of the paper was the glorification of the clothed woman, especially the high-kicking chorus girl, but not only her. Over the years the paper printed many photographs of society beauties, actresses, singers, dancers, showgirls, male impersonators, circus performers, gymnasts, cyclists and ordinary office and shop girls in every variety of female and sometimes male costume. A special effort was made to capture movement, not just in the high-kicking pose of the chorus girl, but girls walking, running, climbing ladders or gates, girls on swings or having fun on the beach or in shops and offices, with the resultant exposure of ankles and legs, shoes and stockings, frilly petticoats and drawers. These photographs were accompanied by brief captions. The enthusiast of the day could of course see the real thing at the music hall or on the stage, but, although assisting a lady from a carriage or helping her over a style yielded tantalising glimpses of petticoat, such moments were not usually recorded in the family photograph album! To us now, the photographs provide details of historical and theatrical costume; to the callow youth of the day they were an exciting revelation of feminine mysteries.

The body of the paper contained cartoons, jokes, a fairly long short story, and various shorter pieces. From 1903 the number of photographs printed in any one issue grew less, presumably because they were too expensive to produce. In 1904 several photographs on a particular theatrical theme were collected together and made the subject of a two-page article, the first, on 21 May 1904, "Musical Comedy as a Business." Later examples are "High Kicking and Flounced Petticoats" (25 February 1905), "Miss Marie Lloyd, The Fascinating Flutterer of the Frills" (29 April 1905), and, particularly interesting as a contrast to the articles I shall mention later, "Corsets and the Girl" (17 November 1906), in which the use or absence of the corset on the stage is discussed and a Frenchwoman's way of putting on her corsets described. These articles were unsigned. Certain developments also took place in the format of the main short story. These began to be a series of stories about a particular set of characters. Each story was complete in itself, but the same leading personages featured in each one. Later still the stories became serial stories proper, with an underlying plot.

As regards cross-dressing, two aspects were present from the first, photographs and fictional episodes. Male and female impersonation on the stage formed the subject of articles and photographs from time to time as part of the paper's coverage of the whole range of stage and music hall performances, notably, "(?) LIND," in the series "Belles of the Halls of Mirth and Song," on 4 October 1902 (p.7) and "Men Who Wear petticoats " on 7 January 1905 (pp 16-17, 30). Similarly, sexual disguise both ways occurred in short stories and also in serials where a character maintained a disguise over a longer period: e.g. "The Girl From Abroad" from 31 March to 28 April 1906, the "girl" being a man in disguise; and "The Girl Man," by Francis Headley, from 15 September 1906 to 23 February 1907, "the heroine being a courageous young lady who passes herself off as a man in order to conduct a business for the support of the family." Shorter episodes involving disguise either way were also included in the main serial current at the time. Only one of these writers of fiction is recorded in the British Library Catalogue, "Flaneuse," who contributed regularly from 1903 to 1907. The editor described her thus: "a lady writer of light literature, who is a constant contributor to at least a dozen leading weekly periodicals published in London. We first introduced her to the public. She is not willing to disclose her identity" (6 August 1904, p. 6). The B.L. Catalogue lists about twenty novels under her name from 1913 to 1929. There is no information available about her identity.

Although no major changes came into effect during 1908, two men joined the paper who were to play a vital part in later developments, the columnist who signed himself "The Amorist," and the writer, who used various names, but whose real name, we are assured (9 July 1910), was Derk Fortescue. We are also told he came from Florida (4 March 1911). "The Amorist's" first article, "Fairy Feet on Ambition's Ladder," appeared on 11 January 1908. Typical later titles were "The Stage and the Simple Life" (29 February 1908), "Cupid's Archers and the Arrows they use" (11 April 1908) and "French Girls and Fun" (30 May 1908). These articles were inferior in quality to what had gone before and were much less genuinely informative about the world of the theatre and music hall. Four photographs of actresses or showgirls were printed in the two pages and "The Amorist" simply filled up the space available with rambling eulogies of their charms. Derk Fortescue's first serial story was "His Unofficial Wife," from 25 January to 25 April 1908 under the name of Desmond Derrick.

Another important innovation was the creation of an "Answers to Correspondents" column on 1 February 1908. This was announced as follows: "We want our readers to write to us, to tell us where we are wrong and where we are right. This paper is not edited for ourselves; it is edited for our readers. We want to make it what you want, and not what we want. Write to us." At first nothing much came of this, but the column was conveniently in place a year or two later when more readers began to write in. In this column on 2 May 1908 there was an odd reference to a "Lady Editor:" "Phyllis (Dalston): It is not quite nice, dear, for you to engage yourself to four gentlemen at the same time. Our Lady Editor long ago made it a rule never to engage herself to but one at a time, and for many years she has not been engaged at all." It would indeed be interesting if there had been a woman editing this sort of paper at that time but perhaps this curious remark should not be taken seriously. A minor but fraudulent cost-cutting exercise took place early in 1909. The number of pages was surreptitiously reduced. First, on 20 February 1909, the numbers at the top of the pages were omitted and replaced by a succession of descriptive phrases commending the paper: "Bright and Breezy," Comic and Cheerful," up through the alphabet. Then, on 13 March 1909, the number of pages was reduced from 32 to 24 without a word of explanation or apology. The descriptive phrases were dropped from 23 July 1910 and page numbers were reinstated from 6 January 1912.

Nothing out of the ordinary occurred until 29 May 1909, when "The Amorist" adopted an entirely new approach. Setting aside his usual vapid effusions on female beauty, he suddenly focused on the particular theme of tight lacing and wrote an article entitled, "Who Has the Smallest Waist in the World?" I have already mentioned in the Introduction the photograph of Polaire published in *The Tatler* on 30 December 1908 under the heading, "The Smallest Waist in the World" (Kunzle, *op.cit*, pp. 233-4 and 252). This was clearly the source of "The

Amorist's" inspiration and he also printed a photograph of the actress. *The Tatler* did not invite readers to send in photographs of themselves or of others, as stated by Kunzle, but some did, and the paper printed two more photographs of women with tiny waists, on 13 January 1909, "Miss M....." of Kensington, whose waist measured "less than 16 inches over her dress," and on 17 February 1909, "Rose D....." of Paris with a 14 in. waist. I could not find this last item nor the comments quoted by Kunzle in the relevant volume in the British Newspaper Library, but I do possess a scrapbook containing a press-cutting of just the photograph. I presume that it featured in some advertisement page or supplement not bound up with the main body of that issue. I have no doubt that "The Amorist" or the management of *Photo Bits*, after seeing the photographs and captions in *The Tatler*, seized on this theme as one suitable for their own paper. They had staged a Beauty Competition by photograph from June to October 1904. Why not invite readers to send in photographs of their tiny waists? And this is what they did. "The Amorist" finished his article by challenging his girl readers to send in their photographs and prove that they had as tiny a waist as Polaire. He then resumed his usual style ("First Aid to Distressed Beauty," 5.6.1909) and awaited results.

Readers were informed of the progress of this project by means of the "Answers to Correspondents" column. On 24 July 1909 (p. 22) the paper claimed that it had received "dozens of letters on the subject," but no photographs. Readers were advised to paint over their faces with Chinese white. The fact that this was done with the *Tatler's* photograph of "Miss M....." is further evidence that the editor of *Photo Bits* had seen the photographs in *The Tatler*. Incidentally this particular "A. to C." column was signed "Miss 'P.B.,'" which lends support to the idea of a female editor mentioned above, or at least of a woman on the staff. On 11 September 1909 the request for photographs was repeated, together with a statement that the letters they had received could not be printed at any length. At last, on 18 September 1909, a further article was announced on page 4 in these terms: "Since . . . May 29th, we have been simply deluged with letters on the subject. For reasons of space, we have been quite unable to acknowledge the lot; but next week we purpose repeating the article in another form, together with a few photographs we have secured, and "The Amorist" will briefly review the correspondence received and add a few appropriate remarks of his own." Unfortunately, part of the article, which duly appeared the following week, 25 September, is missing from the volume in the British Library. The sheet with pages 7 and 8 on it has been torn out, leaving perhaps a third of the article on pages 9 and 20. Nevertheless it can be seen as the first of the new type of article foreshadowed in the editorial remarks of the previous week. "The Amorist" reviews the correspondence received on a certain subject, quotes from various letters, then adds a few general comments. Appropriate photographs, from readers if possible, are used to illustrate the topic. It is from this article that the first item in the selection is taken.

With this new type of article in place, *Photo Bits* now moves into its most characteristic phase, in which the exposition and discussion of female impersonation is most highly developed. I have already said that there had always been photographs and fiction relating to this subject. Now we have correspondence from readers and comments thereon by a columnist. There were also slight but important changes in the style and presentation of these illustrations and stories. Typical of the old style of photograph are two of Malcolm Scott printed on 6 March 1909 (p. 13) with this caption: "That Inimitable Laugh-Maker In Two Of His Female Creations, As 'Salome' And The Lady In The Directoire Gown." Quite a new note is struck with two photographs printed on 28 Aug. 1909 (p. 4). One is the first of a long series of photographs of the American Impersonator, Julian Eltinge. It is introduced in this way: "You would pardonably be excused if you met this charming young person on the beach and endeavoured to make yourself particularly nice to her. But what a cast iron shock you'd get as soon as you discovered that 'the lady' belonged to your own blameless sex!" The other is a photograph of two young German students in female costume. The paper asks: "Have any of our masculine readers ever appeared in private theatricals as 'real ladies,' painted, powdered and frilled? If so, we should like to have their pictures for reproduction. Surely there's many an English boy who could make a prettier 'lassie' than either an American or a German?" Nothing quite like this frank invitation ever appeared again in an English newspaper. As well as more photographs of Eltinge and of other Americans such as Bothwell Browne, several sets were printed of less well-known English impersonators, but not of amateurs or students. The reason for the absence of amateurs is apparent from a reply to "Clem and Madge (Marylebone, W): "We shall be glad to see your photo, but, as you are an amateur 'Female Impersonator,' we cannot promise to publish it unless you give us your full name and address, not for publication, but as guarantee of good faith" (12 August 1911, p. 21).

A new note was also struck in the story, "Velvet, Female Impersonator," published on 11 Dec. 1909 (pp. 12, 13-17), in which great emphasis is laid on the exquisite femininity of the actor concerned. There is, however, an amusing twist at the end. The handsome gentleman who has an assignation with the charming young lady, still in costume, at the end of the performance, turns out to be the boy's father. This story was very popular and the editor was pestered to produce more stories on this theme. Several instances of men in female disguise figured in the short stories after that, but it was not until 26 Nov. 1910 that a serial devoted to an amateur impersonator, entitled "Amber the Actor," by Derk Fortescue, began.

"This series of charming and fascinating stories—each complete in itself—depicts the life and adventures of the Honourable Clement Dexter, a young scion of the nobility, who has taken up the role of a 'Female Impersonator,' under the stage name of 'Amber,' at a prominent West End music hall. Peggy, Countess of Tanchester, is his patroness, and his remarkable success is owed largely to her influence." So runs the synopsis of the serial at the beginning of each instalment. Dexter is represented as both wholly masculine and wholly devoted to the pleasures of wearing women's clothes. "The sight of a silk or a satin or a velvet gown, worn by those who may wear such things, had always sent me a-quiver to wear them myself, apart from any suggestion of the sinister. . . . It was a caprice that attracted in a manner which absolutely obsessed the quiet, urging voice of what the cynics would call rationality and common sense. . . . I was, in all respects, a healthy-minded young British male article and a perfect athlete into the bargain, but I had a weakness—a passion for 'dressing up'—and I had cultivated that passion so carefully and systematically and studied the sex I was given to impersonating with such cool, calm and calculating thoroughness, that when the chance was given me to show the world my ability as an actor, the fruits of nearly ten years of hard and conscientious work in the training of my waist and figure, etc., rushed me to an instantaneous success" (p. 11). On the last page of the story, 17, there is an advertisement partly in capitals and partly in heavy type surrounded by a border which draws attention to this new serial and invites readers to comment. It illustrates how much importance the paper attached, and how much encouragement it was willing to give, to female impersonation.

WE WANT ALL OF YOU TO TELL YOUR CHUMS ABOUT "AMBER"! WE WANT EVERYBODY TO ENJOY READING ABOUT HIM! WILL YOU HELP US TO MAKE HIM AS POPULAR A CHARACTER AS "PEGGY"? **Viewed from a masculine standpoint, you will find he has much in common with that incomparable lady, who will, in due course of time, share the stage with him, and bring back with her the galaxy and the splendour of her Court.** REMEMBER AND STICK THIS IN YOUR MIND—"AMBER" OWES EVERY-THING TO "PEGGY"! IT WAS SHE WHO FOUND AND MADE HIM! HE BEGINS TO TALK TO YOU TO-DAY! GIVE HIM A HEARING, AND WRITE AND SAY WHAT YOU THINK!

Oddly enough, it was not true that Peggy had "found" Amber; the latter already knew her and asked for her help in his acting venture. The series continued for thirty instalments until 17 June 1911, the hero returning to male costume from time to time and getting in and out of a variety of female clothes, including those of a maid, when, as a punishment for "some foolish behaviour," Peggy condemns him to act temporarily as a maid in her house in Grosvenor Square.

Meanwhile, on 2 December 1909, "The Amorist" had published an article on "Men Who

Garden-party frock of printed Shantung in pale pink with black spots. Belt and buttons of black velvet. Hat of Manila straw, trimmed with deep pink roses and black velvet.

19. A New Garden Party Frock. *The Woman At Home*, May 1908, p.187.

Impersonate Women." He mentioned the Chevalier d'Eon but most of the article was concerned with women who have lived as men. Up to now "The Amorist" had revealed practically nothing about himself. An intriguing exception occurs in an article on "The Classical Girl" on 28 August 1909. He relates how a lady singer came to him for advice as to what part she should take. "We talked it out over tea in my studio, and then an answer to her question came to me, and I climbed into the loft and brought down an old score and a picture of the superb Johann Wagner; and we sat together, and she sang and I played at the piano; and when I have rehearsed her properly, she will be the greatest Romeo since 1856." The singer mentioned is the soprano, Johanna Wagner (1826-1894) and the opera is Bellini's *I Capuleti e i Montecchi*. In the article of 2 December, "The Amorist" mentioned that he knew the old waiter at Morrison's hotel in Dublin who turned out to be a woman. He used to stay at the hotel on his way to school in England. So there is a possibility that "The Amorist" was Irish. George Moore based his short story, "Albert Nobbs" on that same waiter. "The Amorist" went on to deal with the attraction of women's boots and shoes, especially those with high heels. At the end of an article entitled "The Cult of the High Heel" on 26 March 1910 (pp. 8-10), "The Amorist" wondered when the editor would let him get back "to my beautiful poetic studies of the female form divine," which shows what he thought of his previous work and suggests that the initiative to develop these new themes lay with the editor rather than with "The Amorist" himself. This time there is no hint that the editor is a woman.

"The Amorist" returned to the subject of the corset several times, but it was not until 21 May 1910 that he wrote at greater length about the male in female attire, in "Dressing Up." At the end of his article of the previous week he wrote "I think I must start a new hare. I once treated you to a discourse on women who lived as men. I am told there is a great deal of interest in the fact that some parents have a mania for bringing up their sons as women, and that there are actually several supposed young ladies who are actually men, and that this peculiarity is by no means common to any one part of the country or any one particular class." I give the article of 21 May in full, although most of it is an almost word-for-word copy of a letter which first appeared in *Society* on 20 January 1900, and he alludes to two other letters from that paper. It rather looks as if what enabled him "to start a new hare" was the arrival in the office of a small collection of letters from *Society*. The main letter quoted in "The Male Tight-Lacer" of 9 July 1910 was also rather similar to the one contributed by "Acton" to *Modern Society* on 20 August 1898. Thus "The Amorist" had not advanced matters very far, or provided any new information, by the time his last article, "The Tiny Waist," appeared on 16 July 1910. In the article of 21 May 1910, however, he did suggest something of a theory to explain the male desire to dress as a woman: "I can only think that there is a kink in the mind which inculcates masco-feminity—the word is mine, coined on the spot, . . .—and that those so affected were intended by nature for women, but that Nature, according to a woman's prerogative, changed her mind and allowed them to be men without first depriving them of their feminine tastes and instinct." On 25 February 1911 an announcement by the Editor explained the reason for the departure of this columnist: "Our readers will regret to learn that "The Amorist," who delighted them with his articles previous to "Cosmopolite" died after a long, lingering illness at the end of December 1910."

As just indicated, "The Amorist's" replacement was "Cosmopolite," a contributor who was much more communicative about his personal life. Like Derk Fortescue he was an American. As a child he had lived among the cotton plantations of Louisiana (8 July 1911). He was a confirmed bachelor (9 September 1911). He expected to be alive in 1940 (6 May 1911). His first love was Medicine, but circumstances drifted him away (25 November 1911). He had studied the first edition of Krafft-Ebing's *Psychopathia Sexualis* (22 July 1911). The first edition was published in Stuttgart in 1886, but he may mean the first English edition, published by F.A. Davis, Company of Philadelphia and London in 1892, which was a translation of the seventh German edition. He made the interesting comment that English doctors, as compared to German, knew nothing about "fetishism" (13 January 1912). There is another mention of

1892 which also has a possible link with his student days. In an article on "The Lure of Lingerie" (12 August 1911, pp. 8-9), after condemning the hobble skirt as not amenable to lingerie, he goes on: "I am thankful, though, to understand that the flowing skirt—slightly trained or cut an inch or two above the ground for walking purposes, similar to those worn in 1892, the fashions of which year I have cause to remember—is coming into vogue again, and is likely to have a long innings. The longer the better say I! Then again shall our sensitive ears be charmed and soothed by the music of rustling silken petticoats, then again shall our eyes be favoured with twinkling little peeps at ethereal frills and flounces." The fashion change he mentions was only a minor one. Rustling petticoats did not come back into fashion until 1915. What is intriguing is why did he have cause to remember the fashions of 1892. Did he actually wear rustling silken petticoats himself in college theatricals in that year? If he was a student then, perhaps he was about forty in 1910 and would be seventy in 1940. In replying to "Veritas (Stoke Newington, N), who obviously questioned the veracity of some of the articles, the editor vouched for his columnist's integrity: "You are very kind to "push" us so genially. The cases that "Cosmopolite" cites from *his* knowledge are actually authentic, and he has more to give (11 March 1911, pp. 21-22).

The subject of "Cosmopolite's" first article (23 July 1910) was "The Muscular Girl," who dominates and chastises men. He invited "Muscular Girls" to write to him with this revealing glimpse behind the scenes: "Judging from the information that your Editor sent when preparing and instructing me for my new and pleasant weekly task of talking to you about things of moment, I should think there are scores of gymnastic girls who read "P.B." and their opinions and experiences should prove most interesting. So will they respond?" In closing, he introduced himself to his future readers in a way which well illustrates his whole approach:

> I fancy you will find I shall entertain you hugely, and I want to get as close to your hearts and minds as I can. I have no idea of the size of the audience to which I am speaking, except that it's large, diversified and widely scattered, which makes my work all the more responsible. Like your Editor, I shall endeavour my utmost to please everybody; and as I have dipped deeply into books, travelled many a league in heat and cold, and as I know something of the puzzle of human nature, the "kinks" we all have, I don't think you will have any cause to be disappointed with COSMOPOLITE

"Cosmopolite's" next subject was the treatment of grown-up daughters as children under the title, "The Doctrine of Discipline" (30 July 1910). At the end of the article he mentioned that unruly youths had been tamed by being dressed and treated as girls, and he invited readers to send in their opinions and experiences. His first full article on this subject, entitled "The Cultivation of the Cub," immediately followed on 6 August 1910. In the same issue is an episode of Derk Fortescue's series *Peggy the Peerless*, "The Baroness's Bad Boy," in which Peggy uses her hypnotic powers to persuade "Solly," the bad boy concerned, to wear a corset, velvet suit with frilled knickers and high-heeled shoes.

Two weeks later, on 20 August 1910, "Cosmopolite" had further recourse to the collection of letters from *Society* already used or mentioned by "The Amorist." Using the title "The Boy Girl" he copied out with only minor alterations two letters from that paper of 24 March and 21 April 1900. By now, however, genuine, or at least new, letters on these subjects were being received, and were used for quotation or comment by "Cosmopolite." On 26 August 1911 a correspondence column proper was introduced with these words: "COSMOPOLITIANA: Under this heading, we shall from week to week, as space permits, give letters from our readers to our popular contributor concerning his articles and the subjects he has introduced, presenting as much diversity as possible."

At this point the name of the editor is indicated in the paper for the first time. From 3 September 1910 onwards his name is inserted in the "Editorial" statement on page 14 after details of copyright and subscriptions, so that it reads: "EDITORIAL. The Editor (G. Gascoine) does not undertake to return rejected manuscripts or drawings, etc. . . ." There is no further explanation of this, nor is it clear whether Gascoine is a new editor or has simply decided to enter his name. I have no other information about him. There is no change in policy and the character of the paper continued to develop on the lines already described.

"Cosmopolite" gave a sympathetic hearing to all manner of "kinks" and "fetishes," which he regarded as not merely harmless, but positively beneficial and life-enhancing, a modern expression which he would have been happy to accept. Over a period of about two and a half years "The Amorist" and "Cosmopolite" covered the following subjects: Corsets, footwear, gloves, aprons, pinafores, lingerie, tights, satin, jewellery (especially rings—ears, nose, breast), tattooing, bondage (tied-up hands), women wrestlers and even the one-legged woman. In addition they discussed corporal punishment by and of people of different ages and sex. The emphasis was on the sensuality of such articles of dress, the sound, touch and smell of the garments, a delight both in the look of the clothes and in the sensation of wearing them, and the painful envy created in man by the sight and sound of a beautifully dressed woman.

"Cosmopolite" himself was immune to these kinks and fetishes. He was also knowledgeable about dress and fashion. He knew what satin was as a type of weave and he knew that the tiny waist was out of date as a matter of fashion. As early as 1905 a brief article on "Fashions Today" had included this statement on the new princess line in Paris: "The most exquisite princess frocks are made on a strongly boned silk foundation and worn without a corset" (23 September 1905, p. 30). By 1910 things had advanced much further. "Cosmopolite" expressed his awareness of modern fashion in an amusing article entitled "The Vanishing (?) Waist" on 29 October 1910. He asked whether the paper's efforts on behalf of the tiny waist were all in vain. "I am writing the article you are now reading in the early days of September, and I am driven to write it for the earliest possible publication, because I have just read in a weighty contemporary that "there will be no small waists this season, and absolutely no hips. Woman, tired of her resemblance to an animated teetotum, is to reduce herself to the likeness of the nearest pillar-box." "Cosmopolite" did not think that the new fashion would be popular, and, of course, his correspondents ignored it.

The articles about female impersonators and the stories involving men in female disguise are worthy of reproduction in separate future anthologies. What I give here are the articles and letters directly concerned with boys and men being dressed in female attire of some sort. At the ladies' school described in "Should Ladies Teach Boys" (31 December 1910), the writer wore ordinary clothes, but he had experienced "corset discipline." Two more articles appeared on "The Cultivation of the Cub" (28 January 1911 and 22 April 1911, the latter, however, containing no new examples) and two on the similar theme, "The Cub and the Kilt" (8 July and 2 September 1911). Several letters were received on this subject: from "Well-Disciplined" (3 and 10 June 1911), "A Lover of Kilts" (8 July 1911), "Petticoated Male" (7 October 1911), "All White" and "Toga" (18 November 1911) and "H.C.R." (27 January 1912). The letter from "Twice a Child (Liverpool)" was too long to print. "We will, however, keep it by us for the time being." (Answers to Correspondents, 18 November 1911, p. 22). I have included a series called "Dickie's Diary," (five instalments from 21 January to 20 May 1911) which, although written, perhaps, by Derk Fortescue, was alleged to have been based on fact (1 March 1911). It attempted to describe the feelings of a boy compelled by his step-mother to dress as a girl. On 22 July 1911, "A Subscriber (Lark Hill, Salisbury) was told: "Owing to our contributor's illness, the extracts from "Dickie's Diary" have had to stop for a time, but we hope to be able to recommence them in a more elaborate form." As Derk Fortescue was fully active all this time with his serials, perhaps he was not the contributor referred to. What this more elaborate form was to be will appear later.

"Cosmopolite" explored various aspects of cross-dressing in a series of articles. In "The Art of the Female Impersonator" (22 October 1910), he is deceived into thinking a very convincing impersonator is really a woman. He discusses with him his reasons for taking up his craft. "If Men Dressed Like Women" (26 November 1910) is a description of an American base-ball game in which both sides wear women's clothes. In "The Effeminate in Man" (15 April 1911), having seen Eltinge in America, he again discusses why men take up female impersonation on the stage. He praises Derk Fortescue's portrayal of "Amber." Fortescue, who "has no more effeminacy than a billiard ball" attributes the desire to dress as a woman to reincarnation. "Cosmopolite" suggests that the secretly effeminate man derives pleasure from his wife's clothes. In this he echoes the views of "Nice Boy" on "vicarious vanity" in *Modern Society* (1 August 1903). "The Man-Woman" (29 April 1911) he hails as the creator of fashion.

In "The Fascination of the Fetish" (13 May 1911) "Cosmopolite" asks why satin is a fetish and gives the answer, from a reader, in "The Fascination of Satin" (1 July 1911). In "The Kink" (22 July 1911, pp. 8-9 and 15), he denies having an addiction himself to any particular "kink," "being a man practically without a 'kink,' or a turn or a twist in my mental equipment which can lay hold of that peculiar quantity known as the 'fetish.'" On the other hand he expresses perfect sympathy with those who do have "kinks." "There is, candidly, nothing new you can tell me. I know the "kink" from A to Z. I studied each and every one long before I thought I should ever be called upon to write these weekly articles, and I studied them as a man fresh from the first edition of *Psychopathia Sexualis*" (see above: probably the first English edition of 1892). "Cosmopolite" does not convey the full sense of "fetishism" as described by Krafft-Ebing, but that may be because of the limitations of a popular newspaper. That he is aware of this is shown by some revealing comments in "The Call to the Senses" (22 October 1911, pp. 8-9). "You have what is called a 'free press,' but when dealing with psychology in a popular paper, there is a wretchedly circumscribed area to the expression of one's language." Nevertheless it is implicit in his approach that "kinks" are not sexual perversions or anomalies to be cured or controlled. Referring to "the call to the senses" as exemplified by The Tiny Waist, High Heels, Lingerie, even the Art of Female Impersonation, "which gives you its own joy either in private or public," he continues, "well, all these 'kinks' are pleasant, harmless and inductive (*sic*) to as much good as any hard and fast rule laid down for the observance of your sex."

In "A Woman's Slave" (9 September 1911), i.e. one who has married for money, "Cosmopolite" reveals that he is not married: "I am taking the view of a man who has never married and who will never marry, either for love or gold." "Cosmopolite" is for once unsympathetic to a correspondent, "Alec in Petticoats," who claims that his wife insists that he dress as a woman whenever she requires it. He regards the letter as a spoof. For this he is criticized by "Hatine Tie" on the grounds that "Alec's" letter may be fiction, but something like that may well have happened in reality (4 November 1911). Discussing "Why Do Women Dress?"—to please men or themselves?" (4 November 1911) "Cosmopolite" suggests that some men are jealous of the sumptuousness of women's finery, and that this is why they try it on in secret. The great joy of "Pinafore," however, whose letter forms the bulk of the second article on "The Effeminate in Man" (18 November 1911) is to be forced to wear aprons and pinafores, so he spends a lot of his time working as a housemaid under the control of his own housekeeper! An interesting feature of his letter is that he uses the term "feminist" to describe his desire to dress as a woman. "Cosmopolite's last article on this subject was "The Mystery of Sex" (20 January 1912), the mystery being why should a man want to dress as a woman in private. He cites the example of a writer he knew, who, with the full knowledge and support of his wife, did all his best work at home dressed in a complete feminine outfit. "Cosmopolite's" final view is that these urges and feelings are inborn, a view which is not dissimilar to that of "The Amorist."

At the end of the article of 14 October 1911 "Cosmopolite" reflected generally on the correspondence of the past year and mentioned future plans, which were not to be realised as we shall see. "We have opened our columns to a number of opinions, and during the last year we have succeeded in getting some very startling revelations. The pity is that our space is so limited that we cannot do true honour to more than a few of our correspondents; but may I say, on behalf of your Editor and his indefatigable workers, who have done all that human power can do to interest, that several features of unusual attraction have had to be held in abeyance for a time owing to circumstances over which we have had no control." Perhaps these circumstances had something to do with the change in the paper shortly to follow since *Photo Bits* did not last much longer in this style.

After "Amber the Actor," Derk Fortescue gave female impersonation a rest. His next series was entitled "The Island Queen," and again concerned the adventures of "Peggy." On 25 November 1911 he began a new serial, "The Society School," in which gorgeously dressed teenage girls are taught and chastised by glamorous and strict schoolmistresses. In the opening instalment a new girl, Dora Preston, arrives, beautifully dressed. By the end of it, the narrator, one of the girls, confides to her friend that she thinks that Dora is really a boy. Through a number of episodes this is never confirmed, and remains only a hint, but the reader is made aware through the Answers to Correspondents column that Dora is none other than the "Dickie," whose supposed Diary was serialised some months before.

The serial was never completed. On 9 March 1912, in a black-edged square at the top of page 3, the following announcement was made: "We regret exceedingly to have to announce that a serious accident has befallen Mr. Derk Fortescue, which will probably prove fatal; and as he has left no notes or Data of his forthcoming intentions with regard to the development of 'The Society School' we are sorry to have to say that this serial must, for the moment, lapse." The following week, 16 March 1910, his death was reported on page 22, again in a black border: "DEATH OF DERK FORTESCUE. This Sad News Has Come To Us At The Time Of Going To Press. Further Particulars Next Week." No further particulars, however, were ever given. A new serial story, "The Markham Mystery" by Doris Dale, began on 23 March 1912.

Whether Fortescue had really died, or whether this was a way of dropping the serial, is impossible to say. What is certain is that there was an immediate change of policy. The articles of "Cosmopolite" revert to the style of "The Amorist" three years before. "Cosmopolitiana" and "Answers to Correspondents" finish on 20 April 1912 and that is the last date on which G. Gascoine is named as editor. "Cosmopolite's" last article, "The Budding of the Summer Girl" was printed on 1 June 1912. The paper did survive in this emasculated form until 16 Dec. 1916, but it was only in the years from 1909 to 1912 that it became a unique forum for the depiction, description and discussion of cross-dressing.

A Dinner Gown.

Drawn by
K. Pleydel Young.

Dinner gown of supple black moiré with bodice and sleeves of gold and silver embroidered lace; gold and silver tassels. Tucker of pure white tulle.

20. A Dinner Gown. *The Woman At Home*, June 1908, p.281.

PHOTO BITS – The Correspondence

OUR READERS AND THE TINY WAIST   25th September 1909 (p.9)
[Various letters quoted, among them:]
"An Admirer of the Very Tiny Waist" thinks boys and girls alike should be laced, alleging that a fashionable corsetiere has practised what she preaches by having her sons and daughters "stayed" from the age of seven with favourable results.   THE AMORIST

MEN WHO IMPERSONATE WOMEN   2nd October 1909 (pp 8-9)
When Mr. Pinero wrote a play, produced at the Court Theatre, that turned upon a mother, for some reason which I forget, bringing up her daughters as young men, there were certain serious Scotch gentlemen, who take a serious interest in what they love to call The Drama, who protested that such an idea was impossible. I wonder what they would think about a letter I have received from a young man who says that when he was twelve his step sister, much to his chagrin, insisted on dressing him and bringing him up as a girl; and that now she is dead, he is faced by the problem of having to explain to all her friends or remain *en travestie*, as the French call it?

[The play referred to is *The Amazons* produced in 1893. There is a review of it in *Modern Society* 18 March 1893, page 565. The following week the paper printed a letter about the play which is relevant in this context. The writer accepted the idea of the play, but thought the opposite would be impossible. "Had Mr. Pinero described a marquis who desired daughters but had only sons, and brought up those young men as girls, dressing them as such, causing them to ape feminine airs and graces, and having them taught womanish pastimes and accomplishments, by an effeminate man, dressed in a horribly hybrid costume, it would never have been produced. . . . It is certainly a compliment to our sex that a woman is not supposed to disgrace herself when she apes our ways while a man who affects womanish tastes is looked upon by everybody (women and all) with scorn and contempt." [*Modern Society*, 25.3.1893)]

He [the young man] wonders whether this has happened before. Of course everything has happened before. The best known case which comes to my mind is that of the Chevalier d'Eon. [He gives a brief outline of his life.]

There have been many other equally well authenticated cases of men passing as women as there have been many cases of women passing as men. I prefer to dwell on the latter subject, of which there are several famous instances [He mentions briefly Mary Anne Taylor, Christian Davies, Pope Joan, Mary East, Joan of Arc, Mademoiselle de Maupin and Dr. James Barry. His final example was someone known to him personally.]

I knew the old waiter at Morrison's Hotel, Dublin, from the time I was a boy on my way to school in England, and stopping at the place where he was employed. When he died, he, too, was found to be a woman. Taken on the whole, therefore, it seems that more women have impersonated men than men have impersonated women; and it is surely only by stern compulsion, as in the case I has cited at the beginning of this article, that a man would adopt feminine garb.   THE AMORIST

[Another writer who knew that old waiter was George Moore, who used his strange life as the basis for the short story, "Albert Nobbs," which first appeared in the collection: *A Story-Tellers's Holiday (1918), and later in Celibate Lives* (1927). The opening sentence of Moore's story curiously echoes that last paragraph of "The Amorist."

When we went to Dublin in the 'sixties, Alec, we always put up at Morrison's Hotel, a big family hotel at the corner of Dawson Street, one that was well patronised by the gentry from all over Ireland. (p. 44 of the Ebury Edition, 1937)

I am still intrigued by this coincidence, and I used to wonder whether George Moore was "The Amorist" himself. According, however, to an announcement in the paper on 25 Feb. 1911, "The Amorist" died at the end of 1910 "after a long lingering illness." Moore was born in 1852 and did go to school in Birmingham in the sixties, travelling via Dublin from his home in Connemara, so it is perfectly possible that he also was writing from personal knowledge of the waiter. There is no mention of *Photo Bits* or even of the precise origin of this story in Moore's official biography by Joseph Hone (*George Moore*, Victor Gollancz, 1936).]

THE OTHER SIDE OF THE WAIST QUESTION   11th December 1909 (p.11)

[The Amorist reports that he has had many letters on the corset question, all in favour of tight-lacing except one which he quotes at length. It contains this inconsequential and rather obscure comment:]

I have heard that some vaudeville chap was brought up as a girl, but what's the result? Instead of going into the navy, and doing a bit of man's work, he is getting his living as a female impersonator, and I'm told that his early education has not made him any soberer than most of us.   THE AMORIST

THE VIRTUE OF THE STAYLACE   14th May 1910 (p. 20)

[Another article about corsets. Also includes a long letter from "A Lover of High Heels." The article ends:]

So ends my correspondent, and, after such a tornado of eloquence, I am dumb. If one lady can say so much about shoes, what would she say about *hats*? I think I must start a new hare. I once treated you to a discourse on women who lived as men. I am told there is a great deal of interest in the fact that some parents have a mania for bringing up their sons as women, and that there are actually several supposed young ladies who are actually men, and that this peculiarity is by no means common to any one part of the country, or any one particular class. But more anon.   THE AMORIST

DRESSING UP   21st May 1910 (pp 8-9, 20)

The human weakness of desiring to "dress up" is one of the most curious of human frailties. It began in the Garden of Eden, for, I am convinced, the adoption of fig leaves was less inspired by modesty than by the love of adornment, and every primitive people have taken to it naturally without any inspiration from Paris.

The Indian brave and his squaw, the Zulu and his Zuluess in their kraals, and, I doubt not, the Pigmies also take to skins and paint for their bodies and their heads for the reason I have explained, and even the very monkeys have a love for coloured rags and glittering things.

Masquerades and fancy-dress balls we all know of, and private theatricals and the craze for the stage are ever before our eyes, and of late the rural world seems to have gone mad on pageants.

One expects this kind of motley to go with such small fry as mayors and common council men and beadles, and the rest of those who think that disguises make them great, but one is surprised at finding sober-minded and level-headed men of business and position rushing into Masonry so that they may hang brass medals, red ribbons, and tin-pot jewels on their big

vii. G.E. Hubbard as Ida Pinkerton in *Pinkerton's Peerage* by Sir Anthony Hope Hawkins, June 1905. *Courtesy of A.D.C. Theatre Executive Committee, Cambridge.*

viii. M.E. Hawtrey as Belinda Trehearne ("admirable both in gesture and delivery"), G.F. Kidd as Belvawney and Justin Brooke as Minnie Symperson ("extraordinarily graceful and attractive") in *Engaged* by W.S. Gilbert, Easter 1907.
Courtesy of A.D.C. Theatre Executive Committee, Cambridge.

bosoms, and wear gaudy aprons, cheap chains and silk sashes on their otherwise inoffensive persons.

With these facts before one, it would be idle to express surprise on hearing that there is a great tendency in modern times for young men to dress up in women's garb, carrying the disguise as far as wigs, powder, shaped bodices, small waists, high heels, open-work silk stockings and frilled underclothing.

That such disguises are contrary to the law may add a certain spice to the adventure, but, undoubtedly, the taste for this sort of thing is engendered by private theatricals at public schools, and even at Oxford and Cambridge, where one would expect something different.

One looks for an excuse where one finds such proceedings outside the nursery and the school-room, and though one cannot know all the reasons for certain happenings in this queer world of zig-zag minded mortals, yet I am told there are sometimes reasons–if you can call them such–why a boy should be brought up as a girl. Here is one.

[What follows is taken from a letter printed in *Society* on 20 Jan. 1900 from Ellen M.T., who knew the family. The boy's name was Alix/Alec and their home in Germany was Dresden, names which "The Amorist" has omitted. On their return to England they lived in a "Sussex seaside town," not in the north. In two places the phrases "I understand" and "it is said" are inserted which reflect the fact that "The Amorist" is editing what was originally a narrative in the first person. He also omits the best part of the letter, a description of the writer's last visit to Dresden when Alix was eighteen. Only then was she let into the secret, and would never have guessed that the "daintily garbed Alix," with her spotless petticoats, open-work hose and lace-frilled pantalon was not a girl. To enliven the text "the Amorist" has added numerous sets of inverted commas. Ellen M.T.'s original letter can be read in *Men in Petticoats* pp.39-40]

A gentleman obtained an appointment in Germany many years ago, which rendered his naturalisation advisable. A boy was born, and his wife was disappointed in not having a girl. She wished to bring the baby up as a girl, and, to obtain the father's consent, she used the argument that she could never bear to have the child taken for a soldier. As the husband fully intended to return to England in the course of fifteen or sixteen years, when his services would have entitled him to a pension, and the wife consented to allow the boy-girl to become the former when the year ["fear" in the original] of conscription was passed, she was allowed to have her way. The child was brought up as a girl in every respect, and, I understand, you would never have suspected the flaxen-haired, pretty-looking creature, whose well-corseted figure, white hands and beautiful complexion were so well set off by "her" dainty clothes as anything but what "she" really was. As time passed, "she" developed into a stylish looking "daughter," quite pretty, with a waist that could not have been more than eighteen or nineteen inches, a beautiful figure, and a general air of refinement. "She" attended a smart girls' school as a day boarder, and one can imagine how charmed "her" girl confidantes would now be to know that their schoolfellow was identical with the handsome but rather effeminate looking young fellow of two-and-twenty, who lives quietly with his parents in the North of England.

The boy was twenty before his father was able to retire, although he had intended, and hoped to have done so, some years before; and till nearly twenty-one he was garbed as a young lady. Now that he has shed feminine attire, his bust is, though somewhat less pronounced than that of a grown woman, practically that of the sex to which the owner was brought up. The hips are also womanly, and, naturally, the waist. There is the merest appearance of a moustache, hardly more than that of a Spanish woman; and after some months in men's dress, he is awkward and ill at ease. He would, it is said, infinitely prefer *lingerie* and petticoats, and nothing can prevail upon him to give up needlework and the perusal of novels of a feminine sort.

There are several authentic instances of youths and young men who, unable to get employment owing to female competition, have adopted the wearing of girls' attire, and obtained situations as barmaids and waitresses. One would have thought they would have acquitted themselves better and got out of their difficulty by enlisting–it seems a more manly thing to do–but there is no accounting for the cobwebs of the human mind.

["The Amorist" clearly has in mind the letters from C.B. Hugh, "Satin Skin" and "Tablier Blanc" printed in *Society* in March 1900 (see *Men in Petticoats* pp.40-42). Presumably a reader sent him cuttings containing the letters, which he used to construct an article on this new subject, copying the whole letter about Alix. So far he has not provided any new information.]

Who hasn't heard many a girl say, "Oh, I wish I were a *boy*!" But how many have heard a boy say, "Oh, I wish I were a girl!" Yet the latter is an expressed, and equally impossible, desire that is spoken more often than some people imagine, strange as it may sound to a thoughtful few, ludicrous to the majority, in these days when the intensest virility is demanded of the nation. I can only think that there is a kink in the mind which inculcates masco-feminity–the word is mine, coined on the spot, and is open to the discussion and the dissection of philologists–and that those so affected were intended by nature for women, but that Nature, according to a woman's prerogative, changed her mind and allowed them to be men without first depriving them of their feminine tastes and instinct. There can be no other reason, and the same explanation must apply to the masculine women. I know a lady who abhors and detests the rustling of silk, another who hates the sweep of satin and the languorous curl of velvet, and both in their dress are literally tailor-made, stiff and unbending, and as *unfeminine* as you could wish to find.

A large majority of men regard all men as equally ugly, and though the same disregard for feminine beauty does not seem to prevail with women, disregard of natural attributes in one's own sex is a healthy attitude for women as well as men, for a manly woman or an effeminate man is merely a freak of nature bordering on, and often leading to, sex inversion, and is likely to prevail till natural attributes and the simple innocent animal life is encouraged.

THE AMORIST

THE MALE TIGHT-LACER   9th July 1910 (pp 8-9, 16)

If I were to believe each of the letters that are put before me, I should come to the conclusion–not of this correspondence, which is endless–that the world is peopled by young men who wore corsets of abnormally small dimensions and heels of a height that almost entitled them to be called stilts; that they were all brought up by aunts or elder sisters or step-mothers to an acquired taste for these things, and that they have all selected wives or sweethearts who are similarly inclined.

Personally, this is not my experience. I go about in the world, in London, in the country, in provincial towns, in Continental cities and into public places and into society of all sorts in these localities, but I do not meet such people, see such things or hear them spoken of. Still, there are many strange folk in this world, and I do not profess to have met them all, and this brings me to my point.

I am a bit of a Thomas, if not a saint, that is to say, if I am an unbeliever, I am still open to be convinced, and I am not easily frightened or shocked. I therefore propose to accept the invitation of any gentleman who offers to prove to me any of the things which are stated in the following letter, recently received from "Waist" (Transvaal, S.A.), and my offer is a sporting one. I shall respect the confidence of such persons, if such there be, and the appointment can be made at either my house or theirs.

Now for my South African correspondent's letter:

"As a regular reader of your bright and interesting paper for a good many years, and a great admirer of the Tiny Waist and high heel, I should like to tell you how much I have enjoyed reading your articles on these fascinating subjects. Although being of the male sex, I have had considerable experience in the wear of the corset and high heel, so perhaps my early experiences while living in England may interest some of your readers. When twelve years of age, I went to live with a maiden aunt, who was a great advocate of tight-lacing and the proud possessor of a very small waist: she also wore extremely high heels to her boots and shoes.

After I had been with her a few days, I was carefully fitted with a pair of twenty-one inch corsets, my natural waist measurement being twenty-two. I had also to wear high-legged, tight fitting boots with two inch heels. After wearing these for some time, they were changed for others with three inch heels, which caused me some discomfort, but I could soon wear them with ease. At night, I wore a very narrow pair of corsets, one inch larger than those worn during the day. I was never allowed to be without corsets except for the necessary time spent in bathing.

When my corsets were put on, I was always made to stand on my toes with my hands held over my head, to extend my body. The waist was then laced tightly first and then the lower and upper parts fairly so, a separate lace being used to lace the waist.

At first, wearing corsets caused me some discomfort and I was inclined to rebel; but at the slightest sign of mutiny straps were fastened round my wrists and I was helpless. These straps were passed through rings placed in the woodwork of the doorway in my room and pulled tight, drawing my hands above my head till I was standing on my toes and my body extended to the fullest. While in this position, a pair of extra long and tight corsets, which were kept for these occasions, were put on and laced tight, then boots with extremely high heels. I was then released, and my hands strapped behind my back. While thus laced and booted, I was forced to maintain a perfectly exact position; and if I complained, the period of my punishment was only prolonged and I was laced the tighter. To escape this punishment as much as possible, I gave in and resigned myself to my aunt's will. Nevertheless, I often underwent this ordeal, as for any fault, however small, it was the only punishment inflicted.

At the end of three months, I was fitted with corsets half an inch smaller, and at the end of every succeeding three months, my waist measure was reduced by half an inch. This reduction went on till I wore corsets with sixteen inch waist, and I always wore this size up to the age of nineteen. I was then allowed to gradually let the size of my waist increase, but I stopped at twenty-one inches which size I wear now. My costume as a boy while at home was always of black velvet made tight and fitting closely to my figure, the knickers reaching to just above my knees, with very thin black stockings and high heeled boots or shoes.

My health did not suffer in the least, which was, I think, owing to the well-fitting corsets and gradual reductions. After having my figure trained by the constant use of corsets, I came to enjoy the sensation of being tightly laced in well-fitting corsets, and I should not care to give up wearing them now. I may mention that my chest measurement is 34 inches, and my height 5ft.5ins., and I am anything but effeminate, notwithstanding my early training. I enclose snapshots of myself wearing twenty-one inch corsets."

[Two more letters are quoted, one with a bizarre proposal for a club for male tight-lacers called "The Minoan League," and the other some very feeble verses on the beauty of stays.]

THE AMORIST

[Two photographs of the back view of a male figure laced into very narrow corsets are reproduced in the article. The letter is similar to that from "Acton" (*M.S.* 20 Aug. 1898)]

THE DOCTRINE OF DISCIPLINE   30th July 1910 (pp 8-9, 15)

I have had a letter handed to me this week, which, before I answer, I will quote in full. It's signed "H.A.L" and comes from Manchester; and here is what the writer says:

"I was really interested in a recent article in your paper on those peculiar parents who have a mania for bringing up their sons as women. I think equal interest would be found in an article on those parents who have a mania for treating their grown-up daughters as though they were still children. ["H.A.L." continues on this theme and "Cosmopolite" gives further examples of girls being punished or humiliated by their mothers. He continues:]

Unruly youths have been tamed and subjugated and made to see the error of their ways by what is popularly known as corset discipline, by being dressed and treated as girls and kept within the strictest limits until their behaviour and manners improve; and there's considerably more to be said for this kind of treatment than the indiscriminate use of the lash. Personally, I don't believe in it and I never shall. . . .

There may be those of my readers who have had to yield, in spite of themselves, to the most drastic discipline, and I should be glad to hear their opinions and experiences, to be told their views on the subject, and to discuss them in a future article. COSMOPOLITE

ANSWERS TO CORRESPONDENTS 30th July 1910 (p. 22)

G.(A.) J. (Isleworth): This correspondent makes the remarkable statement that in order to avoid conscription in Germany, many hundreds of boys are being brought up as "girls." We wonder if any of our German readers could enlighten us on the subject?

[No German reader did reply to this. The story of "Alix," quoted by "The Amorist" on 21 May is an example of this sort of thing happening, but it was done by an English couple who eventually returned to England.]

THE CULTIVATION OF THE CUB 6th August 1910 (pp 8-9, 16-18)

You will read in Derk Fortescue's story this week of the manner in which the Countess of Tanchester begins the "taming" of an unruly and slovenly boy, by having him corseted and dressed in a *bizarre* fashion.

To some this particular description may read far-fetched, but it is nothing of the kind: cases have been brought under my personal notice where the training – and incidentally the "taming" – of a rebellious youth has been effected in a manner precisely similar to that which is being practised upon the Baroness's step-son, and nearly always with success, but certainly not without "scenes" at the commencement of the "cure", for there was *no* mesmeric influence to aid the operation at the start.

Given a firm hand, and a determined warning that unless he mend his ways a boy shall be forced to adopt the wearing of corsets and such clothes and boots as will materially prevent his following the pursuits of his fellows, a radical change can be effected for which he will live to thank those whom he first regards as his inveterate persecutors; but I must say this radical change is seldom brought into being by a *caution* alone. The things have to be *worn,* the sense of being held in and hampered has to be *realised*, and the imposed indignity of having to yield to humiliation can only be removed by an alteration in manners and behaviour, when, perchance, the edict is cancelled; and there is for the moulding a wiser and a sadder youth, and one who will probably grow up and be a credit to himself and those who knocked him into shape.

Apropos of this subject, a letter has come to me from "Interested" (Oxford Terrace, Hyde Park, W.) who writes as follows:

"As a constant reader of your paper, I send you some further information with regard to a recent article that appeared on the fashion of dressing boys in girls' clothes.

This idea in a modified form is far more common in this country than would be credited at first sight. There are numbers of boys of all ages who, besides undergoing figure training by the wearing of corsets, are made to wear stockings and suspenders, together with embroidered *lingerie* similar to that worn by their sisters. In most cases, these are worn under the suit, but there are some parents who carry the idea further by putting their boys into petticoats and kilts for evening wear.

I myself, when a boy, was dressed in this fashion, wearing an ordinary knickerbocker Norfolk suit during the day, and a kilt and petticoats for evening wear; and I continued this until I was fifteen. My recollections of it are that there was a certain fascination in the wearing of frills, and I certainly took a greater pride in my dress generally than the average boy takes.

I believe it was supposed to have a softening influence upon us, and I think this was so, although as far as myself, it never made me effeminate. Furthermore the evening costume of a kilt lent itself conveniently to the administration of corporal punishment, in which my parents were very firm believers.

At that time, several of my boy friends were decked out in a similar manner, some of them, I remember, with great elaboration, so much so that they were the subjects of great envy on my part. Many of these boys wore petticoats in the evening, and one or two even dresses and high-heeled shoes.

At the present moment, I know of half-a-dozen instances where boys are being dressed in this manner by their parents; and in one case, a boy of nine is wearing a kilt daily with the full underclothing of a little girl underneath. This youngster, unconcerned though he was, created quite a sensation at a popular seaside resort last summer, when paddling on the sands, he exhibited to the gaze of the curious a show of the costliest *lingerie*.

It would be interesting if some of your readers would give their experiences on this subject. I myself cannot see any harm in dressing boys in this manner, and undoubtedly, it gives them a greater pride in matters of dress, which is so sadly lacking in the average boy."

I will not go so far as to say that the only way to encourage a boy's interest in his personal appearance is to rob him of the outward signs of his sex and array him in petticoats, dropping these articles of feminine attire as soon as the lesson has sunk deeply enough into his mind; but I do know that the forced adoption of girl's clothing as a "punishment" has, times without number, proved most efficacious, especially if the wearer is held up to the ridicule of members of the opposite gender about his own age. Years ago, it used to be a moral punishment at "mixed schools" to install the bad boy of the class among the girls, who took a fiendish delight in making him realize the humiliation of his position; and I have been told by a lady teacher, who was in the habit of treating an unruly charge in such a manner that the effect was all that could be desired.

A mother's wish for a girl has often led her to bring up the disappointing boy as a daughter; but supposing, for argument's sake, that the boy yields to her caprice, poses as a girl for a number of years, even as far as his majority, and is then suddenly left to face the world in the garb of a counterfeit sex? The question is not so lunatic as it reads, because I happen to have paper evidence of an identical case, and the writer is now at "her" wits end to know what to do! On the one hand, "she" has not the least desire to shed feminine attire: on the other, there are growing difficulties ahead which are making the position gradually untenable. If the story be true as I understand it, then it forms one of the most remarkable human documents it has ever been my good fortune to have had brought under my notice. The only advice I can give, provided the trouble is genuine and my leg is not being pulled, is a quick severance from all the ties that bind "her" to "her" mother's friends and acquaintances, and the beginning of a new life as a man, and a man only, in a new land. Apparently it is not a question of means, but inclination. Then let commonsense prevail, otherwise exposure is inevitable.

In one of the southern states of North America I once heard of a peculiar case that would have been a delight for a psychologist to handle in his own particular way. Twins were born to a wealthy couple – a boy and a girl. As the children grew up, there was free evidence to prove that in tastes and temperaments the boy was the girl, and the girl was the boy. Both the father and mother were thinkers in the highest sense of that much misused and ill-applied word, and they determined on an experiment as soon as the children were old enough to appreciate and understand atmosphere and environment. Business necessitated the removal of their home to one of the large Canadian cities, and the boy went dressed as a girl, and the girl went dressed as a boy. The result was practically instantaneous: each accepted the outward alteration of sex as to the manner born, and each accepted, in their childish way, the differences that were to follow. It seemed that it was only necessary to put the boy into short skirts to have him speedily reveal his true feminine nature and instincts, and the same fact applied to the girl in a mas-

21. Charming Skirts. *Catalogue Autumn 1908*, Oxendales, Manchester, p.13.

culine sense. Time went on; and as soon as the children could comprehend intelligently, the secret was entrusted to them. Neither evinced the slightest desire to return to knickers or skirts respectively; and with the ending of their schooldays, the girl went into her father's business and the boy remained at home with his mother as a "daughter" should. The father died, and the girl, a strong, virile creature, assumed the control of his factory. The mother died, and the boy kept house for his sister. He was courted, pretty girls flung themselves at her head, and both the men and the women wondered why they were so contemptuously flouted; but naturally neither married. The boy died, and his sister saw to it, that his secret went down into the grave with him, and it is supposed she bought at a heavy price the silence of the doctor who attended him in his final illness. But the truth could no longer be withheld when she happened to be drowned in a boating accident immediately after her brother's death; and from papers found among her belongings, the revelation was complete.

These are the crude facts in a summary, and you may say they probably leave much to be explained; but I have not the least doubt that such an exterior transposition of sex did actually take place, and that the actor and the actress concerned played their parts as represented. Nature had made a mistake somewhere: she is not always infallible, whatever may be claimed to the contrary. The boy was out of his groove, the girl was out of hers, and artificial means had to be employed to effect a change to suit the trend of their lives.

The more I think over this, the more I wonder how often such a drama has been played and worked out to its finish, sometimes to satisfy a caprice, sometimes for the fulfilment of stern purposes? There are considerably upwards of five million people in London. How many women are there masquerading as men, and how many men as women? In the ordinary course of things, the former must be greatly in the majority; and even as I write there comes to me an evening paper with half a column on the front page headed "Masquerading as a Man. Death Reveals a Woman's Secret." Then follows a story of an eccentric old Frenchwoman who had posed as a man for upwards of a quarter of a century–it's quite the usual tale, told in the usual style–and the report ends with a par. about "Previous Cases:"

"Cases of men masquerading as women and women as men have been fairly frequent in recent years, but the affair which perhaps excited the greatest interest was that of a handsome young woman, named Shelton, who was arrested some five years ago for fraud. She jumped from the railway carriage in which she was travelling, and was cut to pieces by another train. Death revealed the secret of her sex, which, as far as was known, had never before been suspected."

Well, it's a funny old orange, this world of ours, and even if I have strayed a bit from my opening subject, "The Cultivation of the Cub" I have at least provided my friends with a chance for a dual discussion in the "P.B." parliament.

Who's going to talk first? The Speaker's eye is caught!

COSMOPOLITE

THE BOY GIRL 20th August 1910 (pp 9, 19-21)

The other week, I talked to you about boys being brought up or dressed as girls, and since then I have heard of a couple of strange cases–somewhat alike, but directly opposite to each other as regards the social standing of the "actresses"–concerning this sex-transposition, which I thought would interest you. So I have gone to some trouble to get as many facts about both as I am able, to probe them as near to the truth as I can, and here they are.

The first deals with a boy fulfilling the situation of a maidservant, and this is how it happened. [Here follows the letter from "Satin Skin" printed in *Society* on 24 March 1900, already referred to by "The Amorist" and included in *Men in Petticoats*, p.41. There are several minor alterations. The opening sentence, referring to a previous letter in *Society*, is omitted as is the Scottish residence of the family. In the original there is no sister. The invalid is the mistress.

They also travelled in Switzerland not "on the Continent." The only trouble "Cosmopolite" has taken is to add lots of inverted commas and make some trivial alterations in order to differentiate his text from that of the press cutting which presumably someone sent to the editor.]

An invalid lady was very much attached to a youth of fifteen, who was employed in light duties about the house in which she lived, and to wait on her and her sister, his elderly mistress. On account of the sex of the invalid, it was thought expedient, when the family changed its abode permanently, for the boy to wear girl's clothes, and behave accordingly; and whilst travelling on the Continent, he began his effeminate life. He was small, slight and fair, so, under the hands of a clever French maid, he soon became as girlish in appearance as could be wished. His hair, which was fine and plentiful, was allowed to grow; his complexion, naturally good, was well looked after; his really very creditable hands, were soon made far better than those of most parlour-maids; and his figure, laced up very tightly, even in the most crowded hotels, passed as an extremely pretty feminine one, his chest being also slightly padded.

His mistress saying that, in a boy's case, tight-lacing could cause no injury, took great pleasure in having him laced and nipped in to the utmost, never thinking his tortured little waist small enough. This was a splendid way to disarm suspicion, if there were any, as his figure was *so* tiny that people turned round in the passages of hotels, when he was sent out to post a letter or perform some errand, and marvelled how the pretty young "girl" could support such extreme pressure, and many a lady asked "her" enviously what means "she" employed to acquire "her" wasp-like appearance.

The boy suffered very much from headaches and impaired digestion, but both the invalid and the mistress were so infatuated with the beauty and the delicious smallness of his waist that they would not listen to any complaints, and each new corset was made to force in the yielding figure still smaller by the strong wrists of one, or even two, housemaids. As his work was very light, and consisted largely in attending the sick-room, or reading ladies' papers to his mistress, his white hands, pretty face and exquisite figure were never suspected by the rest of the household as belonging to a boy; and he was always treated as a superior servant, and even made love to on more than one occasion.

His figure was known to prevent his having much appetite, so he did not spend long in the servants' hall at any time; and his rare walks out-of-doors, when not on duty, were invariably taken–well-gloved, veiled and laced to the verge of faintness–in the company of the lady's maid; so people usually thought "she" was a very smart-looking young governess, whose mistress ought to prevent "her" killing "herself" with tight stays!

You mustn't write and ask me how long he kept his situation as a "maidservant," or what finally happened to him, because I haven't the least idea. I'm only relating to you–as far as I know–a single chapter in his life.

So much for Case Number One, and now for the second, which is related in the first person and between quotation marks as the "history" is taken from a recorded conversation set down in a notebook. [He then gives, almost word for word, the letter from "Martyr", *Society* 21 April 1900 (see *Men in Petticoats*, p.42). The first two sentences are omitted. The boy was "just fourteen," not thirteen. He was put in the care of a "smart French maid," not a valet. Originally he had an "unhealthy" fascination in being tightly laced. "Cosmopolite's" reference to a note book is curious. Perhaps this letter came to him as someone's copy of the letter, rather than in the form of a press-cutting. If so, why the alterations?]

"I was adopted, when young, by a lady of considerable wealth, who was devoted to dress and fashion. I was just thirteen when this lady–who, in a year's time was to travel abroad– decided, partly, I think, out of pure caprice, partly for convenience sake, to take me with her disguised as a girl. I dare say she was influenced in her decision by my effeminate appearance and complexion, and slight, slender figure. A fashionable dressmaker was sworn to secrecy and consulted, and I was furnished with a large outfit of garments of the latest fashion and most dainty cut and material. In particular, great care was taken with my figure. My waist, I think, naturally measured 25 inches. It was decided that, at first, I should wear a pair of 21 inch stays, bound with especial firmness in order to give shape to the figure, and that every month I should be laced into a pair half-an-inch smaller. Henceforward I was dressed as a girl, and underwent a training of the most vigorous severity. I resisted at first, but soon found it was wiser not to do so. My trim little waist was reduced in six months to 18 inches, and I was entrusted to the care of a smart French valet, who took good care that when I went to bed I did not discard the tightly-laced stays, small high-heeled shoes with very pointed toes, and the light kid gloves which I wore during the day. I often had to wear a face-mask for the complexion. The tight-lacing, I confess, I did not mind so much, as there is a sort of fascination in the feeling of support and restriction produced by well-cut corsets, even though very tightly laced. Although my waist was eventually reduced to the tiny size of 16 inches, the reduction was so gradual that I never suffered any great discomfort. I had of course, to wear false hair until my own grew long, and I was most carefully instructed in lady-like manners and deportment. When we went abroad, my dainty complexion and hands, very smartly shod feet, and extremely slim waist and well moulded figure were objects of much admiration and envy. There was not the slightest danger of anybody suspecting that the pretty well-dressed girl of, apparently, about sixteen, was really an unfortunate boy. I had to endure three years of this bondage, and became so soft and effeminate that, when the death of the lady who adopted me made me independent, I went back to the garb and habits of my own sex with reluctance and difficulty."

Yes, but *how* was it done? I will suppose that he was not left penniless, and that he had a circle of friends and acquaintances. Did he, then, vanish from the world in which he had moved for three years, and disappear into the night, so to speak, in order to begin life over again? This is where the weakness of this sort of "confession" comes in, for I would rather believe that a boy placed similarly would prefer to continue the masquerade and "chance things." What say you?

There is a feminine trait in every boy, as there is a masculine in every girl. In some this trait is more pronounced than in others, and, given certain circumstances, is capable of great expansion, the evolving of a truly feminine character, and the thirst for an outward change of sex. It's all very puzzling, but, at the same time, it's deeply interesting to anybody who has a semblance of a thinking brain under his hat.   COSMOPOLITE

THE ART OF THE FEMALE IMPERSONATOR   22nd October 1910 (pp 8-9, 19)

As a regular patron of the music-hall and a lover of all things appertaining to the variety stage, I have often wondered how it is that whilst there are many clever and charming ladies–Miss Vesta Tilley for one–who amuse and delight us with their male impersonations, there are, comparatively speaking, but a few of the opposite gender who retaliate by "taking off" and "reflecting" the girls.

The question arises: after a careful, a really careful and painstaking study of the mannerisms and all the little lights and shades and peculiarities of either sex, which is the easiest–a boy to "make up" as a girl, or a girl as a boy? Whilst leaving this part of the matter open for discussion, which should, judging from some of the letters your Editor has received on the subject, open up a big and wide correspondence, let me tell you of a personal experience I have recently had.

I heard from a friend that somebody he knew was about to go on the music-hall stage. As such an event is chiefly of importance to the person most vitally concerned, you can understand that there was nothing to prompt my asking further questions, but when he stated that this friend was a young fellow of three-and-twenty who had decided to take up the role of a "female impersonator," I was interested. Why? Because with one or two notable exceptions, I had never known a man to make a successful "woman" from amateur theatricals upwards.

I expressed my opinion, and there, for the time being, after a bit of an argument, the matter ended. But the next evening, my friend sent me a cordial invitation to go round to his house for cards, and I went. There were several ladies present, each of them handsomely gowned, and all looking extremely nice. His womenfolk I knew, but there were three strangers to be made acquainted with, and introductions soon followed. One of these strangers, Miss A., struck me especially, both by her good looks and perfect figure. She possessed a brilliant gold-bronze coiffure, and was dressed richly in a tightly fitting black satin gown, which displayed her small waist to the fullest advantage. She had a peculiar cooing, drawling voice, which struck me as a bit of an affectation, and matters so arranged themselves that I found her my partner at Bridge. The game progressed in the usual style, and when it was over, we sat about talking. My friend took up the subject we had dropped the previous evening, the art of female impersonation on the stage, and Miss A. agreed with me fully when I pointed out the difficulties a man had to surmount in order to become a successful masquerader. In the midst of the chatter, when we had nearly all decided our views, for and against, one of the ladies arose and moved behind Miss A.'s chair–and, quickly and dexterously, lifted her beautiful coiffure clean off, revealing a closely-cropped head underneath!

I had had the lie given completely to all I had said, all I had argued, and I don't think I ever felt more thoroughly discomfited and taken down! "Miss A." was the budding "female impersonator," and "she" had deceived me to the top of "her" bent!

I laughed with the rest, the joke had been engineered especially for my benefit, and, as it had been successful, I went to big pains to encourage "Miss A." to talk about "herself." "She" was perfectly candid, and spoke as though nobody else was present, but not in the voice she had "adopted" for the purposes of deception. It was now clearly boyish.

With the re-arrangement of "her" charming coiffure sundry details were pointed out to me. "She" was just the height for a tall well-built girl–5 feet 6 inches; "her" chest measurement was about 36 inches; "her" waist a trifle less than 18 inches; and, at the moment, "she" was wearing 4 inch heeled black satin shoes, and wearing them gracefully too. As a female *tout ensemble*, the creation was perfect and worthy of the highest admiration as a work of art, from the pearl drop ear-rings to the flashing buckle on the shoes.

No perfection of "make-up" can safeguard against those mannerisms of sex which so frequently defeat the best laid plans of deception, but assiduous study and practice has taught "her" more of the graces and charms than are owned by many of the members of the sex "she" counterfeits so cleverly; and when "she" appears on the boards, the male public will have something to stare at and the female something to criticise. Since that evening, I have had the privilege of being present at a private demonstration of "her" ability, and not the least noteworthy feature is the rapidity with which "she" changes her costumes, appearing from a lady dressed for a theatre box to a smart waitress in record time, with four intermediate character studies.

Seeing "her" in the garb of "her" own sex, you have before your eyes a slim, erect, decidedly handsome youth, giving no signs of the corsets he habitually wears, with small, shapely hands and feet, whose only effeminacy lies in his passion for feminine finery and the joy of being arrayed in it.

"That is why I am taking up female impersonation for public appearance," he said, "and I shall stick to it as long as I can. Outwardly, as I am now, I am as manly as any man, ready to take on anybody of my own weight with the gloves, and make him look to himself into the bargain! But once I put on a gown and dress myself as a girl, I sink unconsciously into the ways and manners of the sex I am imitating, and the re- [missing line] in will lay my success if I manage to make a hit.

The songs written around his various characters are all indicative of the person portrayed, and he renders them with a *verve* that is particularly attractive. As for his wardrobe, which is slap up-to-date, to a giant hat-pin, I could understand a girl absolutely crying with envy if she saw it. The *lingerie* might belong to a wedding trousseau for a July bride, but high-heel wearers may note with sorrow that he attempts nothing beyond four inches, which is perhaps owing to the fact that he introduces dancing into his various "acts."

Now, I should like to hear what my lady readers think of a man who elects to dress himself in the habiliments of their sex, whether it be for profit or his own pleasure. I must admit, as I have proofs, that there is to many minds an alluring fascination in rustling silks and shimmering satins and fine laces, which being forbidden to the betrousered fraternity are all the more sought after by them. I have heard it said: "I wish I were a woman for only one reason–that I might dress as a woman dresses!" but that explains nothing: it merely increases the puzzle.

What have *you* to say on the subject?   COSMOPOLITE

IF MEN DRESSED LIKE WOMEN   26th November 1910 (pp 8-9)

At last the question as to what men would do if they were really hampered in women's clothes–hobble skirts, tight waists, high-heeled shoes and all–has been answered–in America!

I have just heard a perfectly delightful description of a "social event" which recently took place at Englewood, New Jersey, and I believe it will interest some of you greatly if I tell you everything about it, especially as Derk Fortescue's "Female Impersonator" story begins in this number, and this article can be read as a comparative note between the exquisite femininity of "Amber" and the rougher doings of a score of Yankees out for fun.

Well, to come to business. The young men of the Englewood Club and the Field Club of Englewood fixed themselves out to play a game of base-ball, and the agreement was that each side should appear in up-to-date female attire–to the veriest stitch, mind you! The teams chose appropriate names: The Englewood Club called themselves the "Englewood Barmaids," and the Field Club masqueraded under the attractive title of the "North Jersey Manicurists."

Under the agreement players could come in any present day fashion, but they had to play in complete costume, wigs, undergarments, everything. It was further agreed that the dresses should be worn until the conclusion of the game. But whether it was ball gown, hobble skirt, promenade costume, bathing suit or what-not, the players had to conform to fashion. And they did.

Each dress had to have its appropriate hat and shoes. No player was allowed to go in to bat who wasn't up to date in every particular. Where the attire demanded it, a veil had to be worn, or hair ribbons or gloves, with the proper stockings and etceteras.

And with these accoutrements the young fellows of the two clubs, all New York businessmen, and most of them college athletes, essayed to play a game of baseball. And, think of it–the score was only 3 to 2 in 5 innings! So much for women's dress!

Many a professional game has gone to higher figures when the players have been togged out in real athletic uniforms. The hobble skirt didn't after all prove such a detriment to good play, and the bathing suit was actually a great help because of its lightness and freedom from stiffness. Of course the pitcher–the man who throws the ball–wore the bathing suit. But the best batsman was dressed in a hobble skirt and ran two bases with ease, though the fielder at the base in walking skirts put him out with equal ease. In fact, the "star" baseman of them all wore a long trained evening gown but he was on his job even then.

"The truth was," laughed a member of the "Barmaids" team, who was hobbled worst of all, "it was too good baseball. We expected a lot of bad plays, but we didn't get them. The costumes didn't seem to bother anybody, as the score of 3 to 2 certainly proves. Both sides could hit just as well, but then both sides seemed to field just as well. The score makes that perfectly plain."

All fashionable Englewood, a thousand strong, saw the game. The grand stand was crowded and motors filled up the spaces. On the verandas of the club house and in the boxes were the young society ladies of Englewood, only too ready to laugh at their brothers, husbands and sweethearts as they went to bat or fielded in their borrowed clothes–oh yes, the garments were genuine and had been temporary loans from the aforesaid sisters, wives and sweethearts. The only thing the players had really to provide were the shoes–no woman in

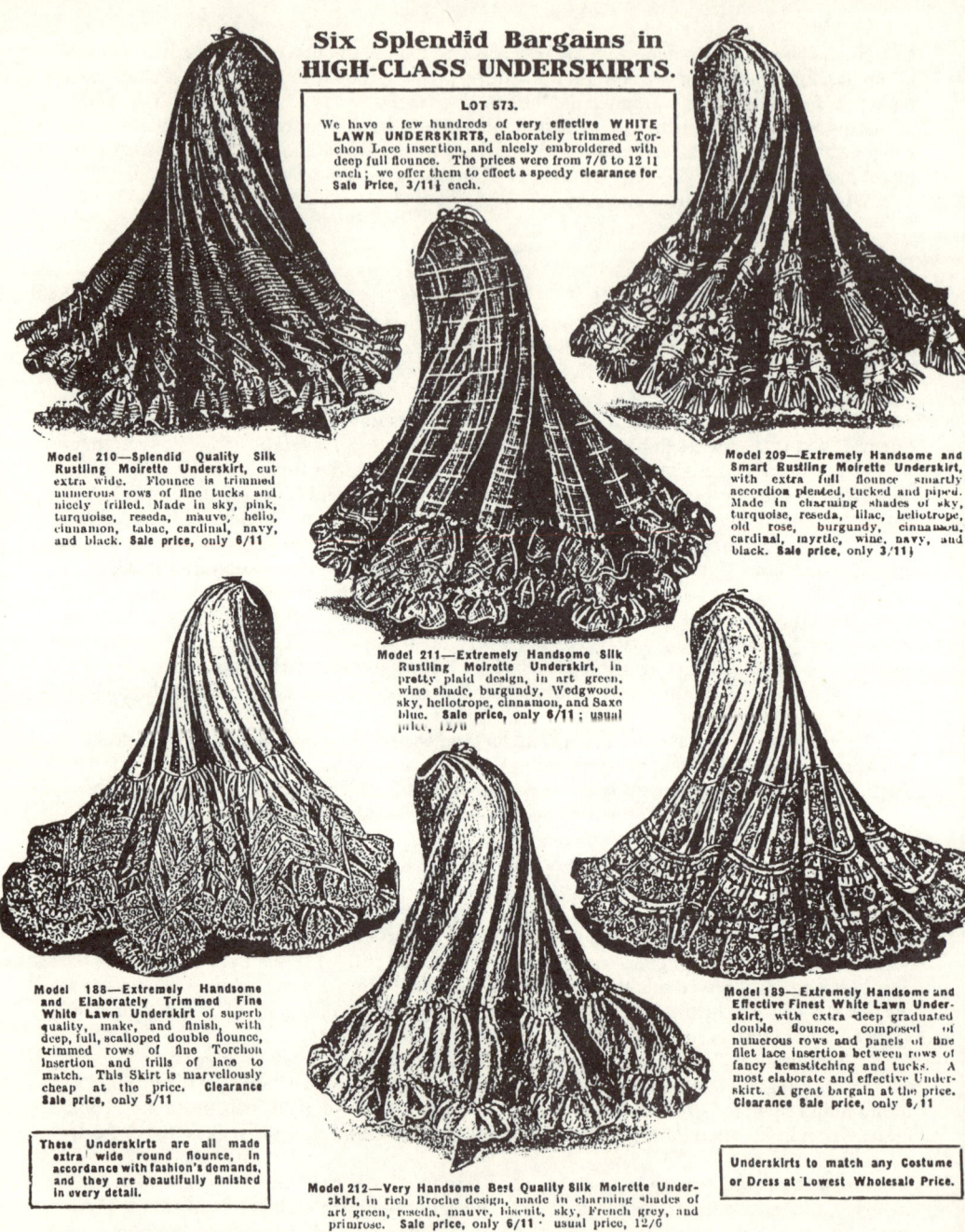

22. High-Class Underskirts. *Catalogue Autumn 1908*, Oxendales, Manchester, p.33.

Englewood would admit owning anything in the line of footwear big enough to fit the men. No heels exceeded three inches, which was a pity, as the sport would have been so much greater if higher "elevators" had been tried.

It must have been worth going miles to see that slide of the player along the ground in his hobble skirt, when he tied the score and made it 2 to 2. And then when another player, togged out in bathing suit and mob cap, put out three batsmen in succession, the cheers that went up could almost have been heard across the Hudson in New York City.

"How did he do it?" went up the cry, when still another player went almost four feet in the air clad in afternoon costume and pulled down a high throw, putting out a man who was coming at him like a young locomotive, pigtails, tam o'shanter, tartan and all.

"Miss Bennett to bat!" called the umpire.

A beautiful young thing in short sleeves, skirts and striped stockings, with a rat in her–beg pardon–in his hair, took up his place, and the catcher, in white silk and a mask, took his position behind the bat. Swat!–a ripping single that looked like a run home. But the right fielder in his matinée negligée got in front of it in time and nailed the runner at second base as he tried to stretch it into a double.

A player in full afternoon costume–big black picture hat drooping with feathers, black satin hobble skirt, and thin black veil–was caught out by an opposing fielder in an evening gown and opera cloak; and then came the queen of them all! He was really pretty and the best athlete, besides. He wore socks and a short skirt of white pique, topped off with a white blouse, cut low in the neck, just to show his bronzed chest. His auburn hair–it was a wig–was nicely bound with ribbon, and on his little feet–number 11's–were tiny white shoes, that is, as tiny as he could wear, with two-and-a-half inch heels!

"Oh!" went up from the men who weren't playing and "Ah!" from the women. "Isn't he just too pretty for anything!" He lined out a swipe that made the hobble-skirted fielder run like anything to stop him from going to the third base. A moment later, however, he stole the base by a mighty slide along the ground, and scored a long fly!

"I'd just like to play baseball myself," remarked a pretty girl in a motor car, "he does it so easily."

But then she didn't reckon on the fact that the young gentleman's collar bone was built on different lines from hers, and she didn't seem to notice that the muscles on his legs and arms quite belied his dainty dress. Could she have done as well if she had been out on the field–even to play croquet–in men's attire? Could she have smoked a cigarette with the same aplomb as he did when he faced the pitcher?

Just suppose that she and the other young ladies who watched the game had donned men's clothes. Could they have played as well? Could they have worn the protectors and the masks and the gloves–not the dainty things from Paris but the big mitts which baseball players wear? Could she–or they–have played any game? Would they have golfed or tennised or croqueted in men's garb as well as the men played baseball in theirs? Is it an open question–or not?

COSMOPOLITE

SHOULD LADIES TEACH BOYS?   31st December 1910 (pp 8-9, 18-20)

Is a boy taught best by a man or a woman?

Well, whilst leaving this question open for your discussion after what follows, and without at present giving my own opinion on the subject, let me tell you a story as 'twas told to me by a man who is now as old as I am, and whose veracity I do not doubt for an instant, as in the way of proofs he has amply convinced me of the truth of his really striking narrative.

When the boy was thirteen, his father–a widower–left England on business and sent him to a boarding-school for lads of from ten to fourteen, conducted by three sisters. The idea was ostensibly to effect a grounding in elementary education, as, since his mother's death, he had been running loose and had become careless and slovenly in his habits, and annoying and tiresome in his behaviour.

"Whatever my father knew about the school," he said, when talking on the subject, "was very carefully kept from me; and I asked for nothing softer than to be sent to a place where women taught, where I might be as unruly and as untractable as I liked with no fear of corporal punishment hanging over my head, for in those days I had all the average cub's contempt for the feminine gender.

The school, situated near a drowsy old town in Devonshire, had once been a mansion of some pretensions, and still wore its stately, old-world air: it stood in extensive timbered grounds, bounded by high and candidly unclimbable walls; and, somehow, as my fly took me up the drive to the front door, I did not altogether feel so comfortably indifferent to the immediate future. The surrounding silence awed and gave me a strange impression; and, suddenly, a turn in the drive allowed a view of an exquisitely kept lawn and two boys in tight black velvet suits walking nicely and prettily beside two elegantly dressed ladies in full afternoon costume. One of the ladies kept dropping a glove, and one of the boys kept picking it up. My fly drove on, and I fell a-wondering. As I learned afterwards, these boys–comparatively new scholars–were being instructed by a couple of the resident governesses in the art of polite manners and attention to ladies.

My introduction to the three Misses Blank will never be effaced from my memory. They received me in state in the drawing-room–a trio of handsome, splendidly gowned women whose only aim seemed to hurt my feelings by making cuttingly sarcastic remarks to one another about my personal appearance, the while they ignored me as though I wasn't present. Unruly and troublesome as I was, I had yet a sensitive nature, and some of the things they said, touched me to the quick. I understood later that this was one of their methods with a new pupil, and it had this certain effect: if a fellow had a single ounce of pride in him, he was taught a salutary lesson to begin with never again to give them cause to utter such bitingly acid and tingling words concerning himself.

I was given into the charge of a haughty young lady in rich black silk, who eyed me disdainfully through her gold-rimmed *pince-nez* and informed me that I could on no account mingle with the rest of the pupils until I had undergone a thorough cleansing process! I was certainly a bit grimy after my train journey, and my hands were sticky with the sweets I'd been eating, but *she* spoke as though I was a verminous tramp! She added other comments, too, upon my general deportment and owlish rural stare; and when a slip of cambric handkerchief fluttered down the front of her shimmering gown to the floor, and I stood stupidly looking at it–well, I never thought that such white little fingers could administer such a box on the ear! I may have reeled a yard: it seemed to me that I reeled a mile! Tears darted into my eyes: one side of my head felt as though it was on fire. She extended her shapely afflicting hand: the rings on it seemed to twinkle at me mockingly. 'You may kiss that!' she said, loftily.

I could only stand and stare at her, thoroughly puzzled. And then a wave of anger dried my tears and swept through me like a hot, searing flame. I had been humiliated–struck by a woman!

'Kiss it yourself!' I exploded, or something boyishly vulgar to that effect. She said nothing: she touched an electric bell on the wall, and a servant appeared–a tall, well-built girl in the daintiest of caps and aprons. The haughty young lady made a gesture, the servant grasped me from behind by the elbows and nearly made them touch, whilst I squeaked unmusically; and before I knew what had happened, I was in a small boudoir-like room. The haughty young lady had followed. Her black silk sleeves were detachable. They came off in a flash, revealing two white rounded, polished arms a-quiver with muscles . . . She held a long, flexible cane with a gilt and tasselled handle. My fate was plain, and the servant, who might have been an expert in the then unknown art in England of ju-jitsu, had me in such a rounded cramped position, that I couldn't budge an inch. At the first stroke, which was like the cut of a scorching, flaming razor, I let out one good, ear-piercing scream, which was the vent, as I only wriggled beneath the remaining nine.

'And now,' she said, majestically, as I stood erect again, flushed and smarting and wondering if I dare express myself, 'you may go and pick up my handkerchief in the hall!'

Needless to say: her steady, searching look almost mesmerised me. I had to give the slip of cambric to her on bended knee, kiss the cane, and thank her for my deserved punishment, in words which she put into my mouth; and mighty meek and humble words they were, too!

Such were my opening minutes at ----- Hall.

I had more than a strong presentiment that I was not going to have it all my own way. I had never been caned before, and I was dazed to think I had been subjected to such humiliation at the hands of a woman. . . . My introduction at tea that evening to the rest of the fellows–there were about twenty altogether–showed me a spruce, dandified, well-set up lot, among whom I felt a *lout!* The smaller boys of ten and eleven wore perfectly fitting black velvet suits, to which were added deep white collars, neat bow ties, black silk stockings and patent leather shoes; the bigger, including myself, wore the correct Eton costume into which I had changed and to which I was quite unaccustomed.

The haughty young lady in black silk, and another equally unbending lady in black satin, presided respectively at each end of the table, whilst half-a-dozen maids fluttered around and attended to our wants. That meal was a misery of miseries. Every instant I feared I should commit a *gaucherie,* and I felt all eyes, especially those of the two governesses, were upon me, eager to detect a fault. . . . At last, in reply to a sharp enquiry from the lady who had chastised me, I pleaded nervously that I had no appetite. . . . .

There were, exclusive of the principals, four resident governesses, each of whom had five boys under her jurisdiction. The instruction was, accordingly, almost individual. I found myself in the class that was in charge of the haughty young lady in black silk, and a more perfect martinet you could not imagine. The boys were taught to understand that the governess they acknowledged was, for the nonce, their undisputed mistress; and the homage and attention we had to pay was at first excessively irksome. It wasn't until I had been severely caned on three further occasions during the first week, that I made up my mind to obey to the letter every whim and caprice of the dictatrix.

Then things went smoother, and I felt happier under her wing; and at last when I was permitted to escort her into the town and play the juvenile cavalier, I knew that I was passing muster and that the strict lessons in dress and manners and deportment to which I had been subjected, had met with their reward, and that I was no longer out in the cold, and looked down upon by the rest of the *trained* fellows as a clumsy boor. But, take my word, I had paid pretty heavily to win that distinction!

I think the ladies thoroughly enjoyed the power they wielded–in fact, I know they did; but, all the same, whilst they imparted to us the soundest of practical educations, they never forgot that whilst they taught us to be *gentlemen*–frequently *very* painfully–we were not to forget we were *men*. We played cricket, tennis and football; an army sergeant instructed us in boxing in the splendid and fully equipped gym; and a Swedish lady put us through our paces twice a week in the same place. It is worthy of note that with the exception of a coachman, a groom, three gardeners and the boxing master, no other men were employed by the Misses Blank or allowed to sleep on the premises. We boys were habitually in a small world of women, and the dozen or more maids were trained to watch us carefully, and to report the slightest misbehaviour.

There was no softening, no pampering, neither were there pets or favourites. The Hall was intended solely as "cure" for the unruly, to tame them and, when the taming process was complete, to make each boy realise the full meaning of the word "chivalry" and a pride of self. I stayed at the place for two years, and went through the hands of the four governesses, and finally served my last term under the private tuition of the eldest Miss Blank, a charming and delightful woman, whose devoted slave I was. I left with the deepest regret–a tall, muscular, thoroughly disciplined fellow, speaking three languages and with the fullest knowledge of social etiquette; and as I thought of the dirty, untidy, slouching lout who had gone there and

438   439   440

Two useful semi-tailored dresses to be made of serge or faced cloth, and a tailored coat and skirt. The first dress is trimmed with braid and buttons, while the second—which shows the new long tight sleeves—has the front opening bound by a bias fold of satin with the loops of the same. The smart coat and skirt may be of cloth or fine serge, its simplicity of line making it becoming.

23. Semi-Tailored Dresses.   *The Girl's Own Paper*, October 1908, p.54.

the alert, smart, spick-and-span youth who departed from its doors, I shuddered at the comparison.

I went straight to a public school, and, for a time, was all at sea. I was nicknamed 'The Dandy,' and the label stuck even after I had put three of my worst tormentors to sleep–the best fighters on the spot. I missed the alluring feminine note, the rustle of silks and the swish of satins–the haughty authority during school hours and the gracious unbending after school hours–the pleasant chats with women of the world who responded so kindly and cleverly–if one were submissive–to the expression of one's ambitions–in a word, I missed discipline.

The fellows at my new academy were the sons of wealthy folk and well connected enough, but they were mainly aristocratic hooligans, and had as much idea of civility to a girl as so many guinea-pigs. They disgusted and nauseated me, and, at the least promise of a fight, I called out my man and did him to a frazzle! And, mark you, I was a chap who'd been schooled by women–severely and mercilessly enough, I grant–women who'd initiated me into the mysteries of corset discipline, and encouraged my personal vanity. As a difference around me, I saw a careless, dilatory headmaster, keen upon nothing but Latin and Greek and nebulous preaching, and equally careless assistant masters–and a total absence of the rod. They worked on what they called 'moral persuasion,' and the effect was just about as good as a flea biting a rhinoceros!

I might have backslided, but I didn't. The two years at ----- Hall were to have a lasting and permanent impression, and they have lasted unto today. The cane in the hand of a woman, makes [a] boy: in the hand of a man it brutalises."

Should ladies teach boys? And Why?   COSMOPOLITE

DICKIE'S DIARY – Being Three Extracts From Its Pages   21st January 1911 (pp 15-16)

Jan. 1st 19–.–Oh, my Diary, what further revelations and degradations have I to impart unto thee–on this New Year's Day! I have told thee already, oh, my cherished book of confidences, of what I have been called upon to suffer so painfully, and how I have had to submit to the Rod and the Rule Absolute; and now, surely, the limit is reached.

I have indeed been tamed and subjugated; and the one thing I am truly thankful for is that we have left A------ and gone to live at B------, a hundred miles away, where nobody knows me, where nobody knows that the richly dressed girl who walks abroad so demurely beside her handsome stepmother is a BOY!

If I had been told twelve months ago that her marriage with my father, who yields in all ways to her every whim and caprice, would have resulted in my obeying her as I do, I would have laughed the suggestion to scorn. But because I am small and slim and quiet and studious, like the author of my being, I have surrendered to her imperial will. She said I would look better, and please her more, if I dressed as a girl; and lo and behold! it has been accomplished after a brief but unavailing spell of mutiny, in which I was sorely scarified where it showed not but tingled.

I have been enclasped in the torture of corsets of the finest make and build, oh, my diary, and every day my waist has been slowly but surely diminished under the eye of the tyrant, whilst she has sat in semi-regal state and watched her servile maids do her bidding. I have been clad in the silkiest and most costly of underwear, laced, flounced and beribboned, and splendid frocks above all–silk, satin, velvet. They are short, and reveal the ends of fussy, bunchy *pantalettes*, which foam milk-white around the tops of cobwebby openwork stockings. I have been mounted on boots and shoes, with heels ascending slowly day by day, and my hands and arms have been imprisoned in the longest and tightest of gloves: the adjustment of a single pair has sometimes taken as long as fifteen minutes.

With my waist laced in so mercilessly that I cannot bend, with heels inches high, with fingers stiffened with the bondage of kid, with "hobble garters" worn in the house to educate and control my already stilted walk, the helplessness of my position breeds merely a spirit of resignation. My hair is growing under a long and exquisitely curled and coiffured flaxen wig, my complexion is a work of art, and my ears have been pierced to admit of the wearing of long and heavy diamond ear-rings.

As a boy, I am fifteen: the mirror reflects an over-dressed "flapper" of thirteen who is being attired out of all proportion to her age.

Jan. 14th, 19–.–How lucky it was that I never cared for sports, that I liked the seclusion of my little study better than to join in the rough games of my fellows! My quiet life in the past has in a way, prepared me for the outward change in sex, and I must confess I do not feel so strange and uncomfortable as I did a fortnight ago. Besides, I find I am getting critical about my things, and have vetoed silk and velvet entirely in favour of satin. My stepmother is young– only seven years older than myself–and if she forces me to grow up as a woman, I shall not wear anything else–morning, noon and night. I expect I shall become what is known as a "sensationalist."

Her severity of rule is as strict as ever, but, now she finds I am amenable and submissive, she makes my life as pleasant as possible, and denies me nothing. But, still, it *is* a bit irksome to have to change one's toilette four times a day, and each changing means the expenditure of an hour, because I am arrayed with such delicate care, and so much talk is passed upon my appearance before the Tyrant is satisfied.

I have learned to love the support and compression of corsets, and this morning was told that my waist measurement was exactly fifteen, which means that several of my finest frocks are now useless. I am sorry, as they happen to be some I like best.

Jan. 21st, 19–.–This afternoon, a great surprise was visited upon me: my stepmother said she thought it advisable, after all, that I should resume my life as a boy; and to effect that end, I had better begin at once. Her change of mind quite staggered me, and I implored her to reconsider her decision.

"Do you *really* want me to?" she asked.

I assured her I did, and she laughed. "Well, it was just a test!" she smiled. "I had no intention of making you return to "Dickie:" you are to be "Dora" as long as *I* live!"

My fate has gone forth! "It was just a test!" But what has it proved? That the lure of lingerie, the cult of the corset and the high heel, the fripperies and the frivolities of the feminine have shackled me in the indescribable pleasures of their fetters, and all within a month!

What mistake did Nature make when she made me a boy? I wonder? And what mistake did Nature make when she made that big, broad-shouldered woman we meet sometimes, a woman–who wears a hard felt hat; a man's tall collar, tie and shirt; short, floppy skirts, and thick-soled lace-up boots; who carries a heavy walking-stick in gloveless hands and who has a voice like a bull? She glares contemptuously at me and my dress when we chance to encounter her, and glares contemptuously at my stepmother–I suppose for attiring me as a doll!

She sniffs audibly at my four-inch heels, she sniffs at my *pantalettes* peeping saucily beneath the hem of my skirt. And, somehow, I feel desperately sorry for her. It may not be right to masquerade as a girl, but the dress of the sexes is custom not law; and if you *are* a woman, why abjure and sneer at those delights which are yours by right of that custom?

THE SLAVE

THE CULTIVATION OF THE CUB　　　　　　　　　28th January 1911 (pp 8-9, 21)
(2nd Article)

Since my first article on the above subject appeared in our issue of 6.8.1910, I have had a letter from "W.H.S.R." (Shanghai) to whom the above subject seems to appeal, as it does to many others.

I can assure him and scores more, as an honest fact, that a refractory boy does not always taste the cane or birch by way of punishment. In a number of instances such treatment is absolutely passed over as tending to brutalize; and then the finer feminine instinct prevails to effect correction. He is tightly corseted, made to experience the "pleasures" of wearing the highest high heels, and generally kept under the strictest restraint.

To cultivate the cub, you have to humiliate him. The most barbarous of thrashings does no good, as dozens of parents have discovered. Instead, other means have been tried, and I don't know of one that has not been successful.

It is, however, useless for a *man* to attempt the job: he must give it unreservedly into female hands, and then the sting is accentuated; for when a cub finds himself faced by the sway of a determined petticoat government, he finds himself faced by something he does not altogether understand: his idea of a woman is a creature who has been taught throughout the ages to recognise his sex as the Aristocracy of creation; and to think that he has to become a useless, helpless pawn under her dictatorial control, weakens for a time his mental balance. And whilst he is waking up from wonderment, she acts.

His attire, suited to the unrestrained freedom of masculinity, is her first point of attack. As long as *that* exists, there is always an incentive to rebellion; so on go tightly enclasping corsets, her own initial acquaintance with the thralldom of her sex; and what more naturally follows than high heels? Before he can turn round, the victim of circumstances has impressed upon him that mutiny is a myth and a fallacy, and a mend in manners imperative.

I shouldn't like to say how often a boy has been compelled to dress as a girl for a lengthy period by way of punishment. These particular treatments observed by certain members of society are not noised abroad and proved to the hilt for a cynical world's edification and satisfaction: they are private to their surroundings, *but they exist*. I have been present when a mother's threat to attire a lad in his sister's clothes for a week and keep him confined to the house for that time, has resulted in a sudden meekness and softening down which has been almost startling! The fear of ridicule may in part have accounted for the change, but the dread of humiliation was greater.

The compulsory tight lacing of boys as a means of discipline is so old that I despair of being able to say how old it is. The instrument as an instrument is distinctly convincing, and if you doubt my words – especially if you have never worn a pair of stays – try it on yourself, *remembering all the time that you can find release from the unusual pressure whenever you like!* Then put books under your heels until you can scarcely stand, and *imagine yourself in the resolute power of others, condemned at their will to exist and walk under such conditions!* Granted the latter position, how soon would it be before your reasonableness was without flaw?

In the course of his letter, "W.H.S.R." writes: "If the stories I have read about this sort of discipline are true, I may congratulate myself that I have not suffered it, for although I am an enthusiastic admirer of a tightly laced waist, high heeled pointed boots and shoes, and a long, tightly fitting kid glove, I would certainly not like to wear all these good things myself, but would prefer to leave them for the adornment of the so-called weaker sex. I would like to know, however, how one of those unfortunate boys, forced to wear a girl's attire, felt when he was trussed up like a fowl".

I am, happily, able to inform him from the lips of one who, as a lad years ago, suffered the ordeal at the hands of a corrective lady relative. "At first, there was such a sense of coercing restraint, that I doubted if I could live for another hour. Anger at my feelings, hot-faced indignation at my personal appearance, so completely transfigured with every artifice to work out to the full the punishment I was supposed to deserve, sent me nearly crazy. But I was both helpless and powerless to resist. After a time, the corsets with which I had been afflicted, and which had been drawn in closely, ceased to give me any pain or discomfort, and, instead, seemed to serve as a support to effect the manipulation of the awful heels on my knee-high buttoned *hautes bottines*. These were my only trouble. The wearing of the feminine garments, unusual as their feeling was at the beginning, neither hampered nor hindered my movements

DICKINS & JONES.
EMBROIDERED SILK & JET ETOLES.

No. 225. Silk Embroidered and Jet Fringed Etole on Net ground. The Bodice forms a complete trimming for Back and Front, with panel, *as illustration*, ready for use on any Dress. Embroidered in bright rich Vegetable Silk, outlined fine Jet Beads and studded large Cabochons. Our own design.
Price **55/6**

No. 226. Richly-Embroidered Etole of Bright Vegetable Silk on Net ground, forming a complete Dress Trimming for Day or Evening Gown. Our own design, not procurable elsewhere.
In Ivory or Black, *as illustration*.
Price **37/6**
Same design, with long Panel at back, to fall on Skirt. Price **3 Gns.**

No. 190. Jet Etole, Handsomely Embroidered, with complete Corsage for Back and Front. Very finely embroidered with Silk Lacet and Jet and Bugle Beads, *as illustration*, ready for wear, a charming finish to any Toilette for either Day or Evening Wear. Our own exclusive design.
Price **4 Guineas.**

ALL PURCHASES of Drapery Goods sent Carriage or Post Free in the United Kingdom or Channel Islands.

24. Embroidered Silk and Jet Stoles.   *Catalogue Summer 1909*, Dickens & Jones, Regent Street, p.47.

– in fact, I experienced a greater freedom of action in short 'flapper' skirts than I had thought would be possible. The heels comprised my only trouble. If I remember rightly, they were four inches in height; and after those attached to my ordinary boots, were tortures *in excelsis*. I could not walk except by pushing and clutching on to a chair in front of me, and even then my equilibrium was perilous to a degree".

The question arises – is all this an efficient scheme of cultivating a cub to come round to your way of thinking? That it is practised, and practised freely and sternly, I know for a positive fact; and the fear of its repetition, after the first sample, has checked and given many a wavering boy cause to think before he again invites its humiliation. I claim that a moral punishment is frequently more lasting in its effects than a physical, and the recollection of ridicule heaped upon one leaves a more permanent impression behind it than the sting of a cane or the combined conviction of birch twigs. I am quite aware that scores will be found to agree and scores to disagree with me on this point, and I should like to hear from the dissentients *why* they think I am wrong.

If you dress a girl in boy's clothes, she is proud of the passing distinction, and cannot be induced to think of anything approaching mortification. So, evidently, as a means to an end, the cultivation of the unruly "flapper" fails in *that* direction. But reverse the act, with all its necessary accompaniments, and the one prayer in the boy's heart will be that the outer world shall never know of his – well, if he can use big and meaning words, he'll call it abasement!

As I pointed out in one of my recent articles "Should Ladies Teach Boys?" the firm – drastic, if you like – influence of a woman is a cub's salvation, if he has a single red corpuscle in his blood. She may have to use a cane or a birch as her emblem of rule and sovereignty, but it is all the time a moral-*cum*-physical correction, owing to the knowledge of her sex and his surrender to alleged weakness. A man wielding the rod would merely breed a panting revenge, an abortive lust to be able to punch his head out of shape. Which is exactly why mothers are the best castigators of their sons.

COSMOPOLITE

DICKIE'S DIARY: Being Another Extract From Its Pages   18th March 1911 (pp 14-15)

Mar. 1st, 19–.–Some weeks have passed in swift activity since I last confided to thee, oh, my Diary, and they have been weeks of much pleasant development. As a "boy-girl," attired in the habiliments of the most exquisite "flapper" creations which the brain of a proud, vain and an ultra-fashionable stepmother can conceive and have made to her order, I have ceased to fret at my fate, and accepted it not so much with resignation as with a decision of sincere gratification. I have lived to learn that a girl's life can be made infinitely more attractive and fascinating than a boy's, if only by reason of the pretty things she has for her personal adornment; and the gentle expression of this philosophy to my stepmother has filled her with delight, and resulted in her being kinder to and dressing me more gorgeously than ever. Yesterday evening, she took me to a juvenile party–*my* first acquaintance with the exclusive social circles of B-----, which soon opened their gates wide to *her* dazzling personality; and, of course, I was "Miss Dora H-----". I had to begin to make my toilette as early as 4 o'clock in the afternoon, as she said she intended me to be a *sensation*! Being so small and slight for my age, and effeminately built withal, no difficulty has been found in the cultivation of my waist, which, on this occasion was rigorously laced into a pair of beautiful fifteen-inch white satin corsets, dotted with golden stars. I experienced no appreciable discomfiture–only a delightful thrill at the rigidity of my gorgeous imprisonment. Two maids, who are in the *secret*, attended to me, whilst *she*, lovely and syren-like beyond description in a superb tea-gown of silver satin, sat negligently in a cushioned chair and looked on and gave instructions. My dreamily scented, fluffy, beribboned silk and lace *lingerie*–fresh from Paris for the event–might have been blown away with a breath, so ethereal and *spirituelle* it seemed; and the maids handled it with almost reverential delicacy. With my long curly flaxen wig adjusted–it was now adorned with large sparkling diamond rosettes on either side, just above my temples, and a brilliant spangled band of pale blue satin ribbon meeting them across the top of my head as a sort of *bandeau*–and two small diamond studs affixed in my ears, the tall triple mirror gave back such a reflection of milk-white dainty wonder that I had perforce to close my eyes to prevent their gushing with tears of ecstasy. . . . My slim legs, clad in their divinely thin openwork white silk stockings, looked very frail and girlish; and who would have thought that a *boy's* feet were shod in those small and miraculous four-inch heeled, diamond buckled, white satin shoes? My thin, white arms, essentially feminine in their slight roundness, added to the delusion. Oh, my Diary, surely there has never been such a person as "Dickie?" Is he not merely a figment of the imagination? Have I not always been *Dora*? . . . I was still dreaming idly when they arrayed me in my silken petticoats and my short "party frock" of rich pale blue satin–so grand, so luscious, so "sensational!"–with short sleeves reaching nearly to my elbows and ending in cascades of costly white bejewelled lace. My *décolletage* was very slight, and almost hidden with six ropes of big pearls, between which there stole fugitive flashes of my tinted and carefully powdered flesh. And then I was ready–an hour-and-a-half had passed in my dressing–my face had been "made up" to soften the least trace of masculinity; and at my stepmother's command, I paraded up and down before her. "Rustle, Dora!" she ordered, sharply. "Rustle all you can! I want to hear *that* tonight!"

There was small need for such a bidding, as I wore four stiff silk petticoats of varying lengths under my satin, and each shivered noisily on the other with the least movement, and gave forth the enthralling sound which I have ever associated with resplendent riches. I pleased her hugely, and, by way of reward, she allowed me to go to my little study, where I placed down my long white kid gloves, my white feather fan, and my thin, beringed hands dallied with the books I love so well until, flashing and gorgeous and awe-inspiring, she swept in upon me at seven o'clock; and my time of privacy was o'er. She herself drew on my gloves; she herself wrapped me within the cosiness and softness of furs worth their weight in sovereigns, for the night was cold; she herself placed my fan within my tightly gloved fingers; and she herself, imperious and magnificent in a glowing, glittering cloak of cloth of gold covering a gown that haunted the memory, was my veritable shadow to the luxurious waiting brougham. I was her toy–the toy she loved to see petted and pampered and reduced well-nigh to helplessness. A gay, fleecy shawl was wrapped carefully around my head, a slip of perfumed cambric was given to me to hold over my mouth and nostrils as I passed from the warmth of the hall and down the few steps under the glass awning to the carriage. A giant footman lifted me tenderly to my seat, and stood aside slavishly for his mistress to follow. She sat beside me, hiding me completely in my corner, and her full, languorous voice spoke as the wheels moved, and I reclined in languid dalliance with my fate. "Dora, I am immensely proud of you! Tell me truly–have I not given you all your heart's desire?"

I could not answer, oh, my Diary, for I trembled to give a reply! But one day, oh, my Cherished Book, I will tell you more, and write what happened at the party in the great, splendid mansion to which I was being driven. THE SLAVE

ANSWERS TO CORRESPONDENTS 1st April 1911 (p. 21)

B.R. (Dublin): Thanks for your experiences as a "Dickie." They will be of assistance to the author of that production, who, by the way, is more of an "editor" than an "author," as the extracts he treats are authentic.

DICKIE'S DIARY: Being Another Extract From Its Pages. 8th April 1911 (pp 16-17)

April 8th, 19–.–Oh, my cherished Diary, now that my beating heart allows me to write again in thy pages, when will the memory of that juvenile evening party at Lady -----'s great mansion fade from my memory? Never, I think–never, I hope!

It was my initial introduction as little "Miss Dora" H----- to the exclusive circles of B----- society; and although I was dreadfully nervous and self-conscious at first, the personal magnetism of my adored but feared stepmother soon pulled me to a sense of repose. She fussed over me charmingly and lingeringly in the cloak-room before my appearance among the young guests, and would not let a maid as much as *touch* my glittering, shimmering gorgeousness. A final kiss from her full red lips, and I was more than ready for the ordeal.

Lady B-----, a big, splendidly handsome blonde woman, went into raptures over me and my tiny waist and my high heels, and called me "*ma petite!*" She told my stepmother that she envied her such a delectable possession, and said laughingly that I might rival *her* before she was half aware of the possibility!

The children present ranged in ages from about thirteen to sixteen; and although all the girls were beautifully dressed, I cannot tell you, oh my Diary, with what superb satisfaction I realised how easily I outshone them! And, suddenly, oh my Diary, I knew that they *hated* me because of my magnificence; and with true "feminine" spite I played back to them; and *felt* my mistress's dark, passionate eyes glowing with pride and exultance wherever I moved and minced and perked and preened.

I was a stranger, and I was freely criticised. There were mothers present, and I heard one say to Lady B----- that I was abominably vain and conceited; another, that I was far too over-dressed and over-powdered and over-rouged for my age; and still another that I was almost too proud to walk, which was true!

The elder men present eyed me curiously; my waist and my heels were the attraction, and one said I should grow up a cruel, selfish, heart-breaking *diablesse*. Another gave it as his opinion that he wouldn't like to be in my power by the time I was thirty! Which set me wondering what I should be doing when I had reached that age–and I began to feel miserable, because I supposed *then* that I should have been a man for ever so long.

The boys–all smartly-groomed, gentlemanly fellows–were a bit afraid of me, I think; and in the dances and the games that we had, they handled me with almost reverential respect and delicacy, as though I were made of sugar and might melt or break at any minute! One, especially, Archie-----, was most funnily attentive. He was a thin, pale, thoughtful looking boy of about fifteen, very quiet, quite good-looking, and very deferential; and when it came to breaking-up, he bade me good bye in such a strange way. We were standing alone near the conservatory, and I was feeling very happy and contented, because I had been a success and a triumph.

"Good night, Miss H-----," he whispered. "I hope we shall meet again." I hoped so too, for, somehow, I was drawn to him: there seemed an affinity between us. "Yes, I hope we shall meet again," he repeated. "And oh!" he blurted, suddenly, "*I do wish I were you!*"

The secret was out! he dropped my gloved hand as though it was red-hot, and almost ran from before me, with eyes that gushed tears and a face that burned red.

Poor Archie! . . . And I would not change places with him for a billion pounds!

He wished he were me! . . . Poor Archie!

As I drove homewards with my delighted stepmother, whom I thought would never cease kissing and fondling and praising me for the perfection of my behaviour and deportment that evening, I told her of the incident. She laughed sarcastically.

"Poor little boy!" she said. "What a confession–on the spur of the moment! Another of Dame Nature's mistakes!"

Another? Yes, and how many of those same mistakes remain ever hidden, and break hearts, and crush souls?

THE SLAVE

THE EFFEMINATE IN MAN
15th April 1911 (pp 8-9, 20)

When I first saw Julian Eltinge, the famous American "Female Impersonator," some time ago, I was surprised at the perfection of his performance and equally surprised at the perfection of his "make-up;" but since those days he has "gone some more," and I should dearly like to see him in the title-role of the "Fascinating Widow," which is portrayed on this page, his new—and his first—musical play. From the beginning, he has been the impersonator only of good-looking, voluptuous girls; and his success has been as startling as it has been deserved. And when I inform those folk who are acquainted with the States that straight-laced, "culchawed" Boston, the alleged Hub of the Universe, has received him with quite open arms, then you may form some idea of the artistic essence of his work. *Bostonians are supposed to be particular.*

Last week, you had a photo of him as a Yankee bathing girl, the type with which we have made you familiar but which some of you may not have seen in actual existence. This week, if you will deign to view him on this page, you will find him in a distinctly different character. Candidly, what do you think of him? Would you, if the picture were given with no caption, take him for a woman? There's no tiny waist, no ostentatiously exposed high heels—just a feminine figure, I assert, that could deceive a Mayfair drawing-room. Do you agree, or don't you? Mind you, I hold no brief for Mr. Julian Eltinge, nor am I his advance agent: I don't know whether he has ever appeared in London, or whether he ever will. But what I want to say is this—with all due respect to the gentleman who has given me a subject for an article—what first actuates a fellow to take up "Female Impersonation" on the stage? Derk Fortescue in his introductory chapters of "Amber," made his creation confess wholeheartedly as to the why and the wherefore of the thusness; but was that confession entirely imaginative and floridly far-fetched? Derk Fortescue himself, as I know, has no more effeminacy than a billiard ball, yet he can lay bare the soul of a man with a "kink" in a manner that makes me think he could take up this department and handle it in a far better way than I can.

I asked him one day—several questions. He was both evasive and candid. "Reincarnation!" he explained. "The secret of the thing from A to Z! Your man of today with the taint of effeminacy, more or less developed, was a woman once—can't say how long ago!—and the threads of the distant past life have never left, or been entirely obliterated from his mental equipment! They asserted themselves as soon as he could understand—*and wish!*"

Hum! A plausible enough explanation on the surface, but, nevertheless, difficult to swallow in these material days. Still, the mind curious wonders reflectively why a man in ordinary life, sane and level-headed in all other respects, should seek a consolation and a satisfaction in attiring himself in the garb of the opposite sex; and strictly *in camera*. And that same man, when seen in every day, matter-of-fact existence, reveals not a fraction of a suspicion of the effeminate in his masculine garb! No, he hides his idiosyncrasy unconsciously, scarcely ever with intent, and his secret is his own.

The fop, as we know him, has nothing of this hidden peculiarity: he is far too intent upon outward display to attract the feminine, or to make it talk, than to think of unwitting subtlety. But, let me tell you this—and it is a straightforwardly proved truth—the girl who marries a man with a love—nay, a passion!—for female attire will never have cause to complain of his generosity in the matter of dressmakers' and milliners' bills as far as his purse will allow him to go. His effeminacy, acknowledged by himself to himself, or vaguely dormant, will be appeased by the decoration of his wife. He will like to see her "smartly-gowned," as the saying goes. And he will love her no end, and despair tragically when he is unable to attire her as he wishes—to satisfy his worship of his fetish.

A secretly effeminate man—by which I mean a man who would never be induced to speak his mind openly for the ribald and the scoffer to work off their gibes against—when he falls in love is more often influenced by the lady's dress than he is by her beauty or other etceteras. He sees something he may have liked to wear himself had a transposition of sex been possible, and the lure is fatal—well, not exactly *that,* but extremely likely to have a big influence on his subsequent advances, if not his future life.

A woman may cheat herself into believing that she dresses herself either to please herself alone or to cause envy and anger to smoulder and burst forth in the breasts of her less favourably bedecked sisters; but, really, she does nothing of the sort: she just lays herself out to attract the effeminate in man, be the object a prize-fighter or an artist. Certainly the devotion of the artist will last the longer.

To a large extent, and coming back to a sense of my opening paragraph, I think the man who is enabled by Nature and ability to take up the art of "Female Impersonation" is a "sensationalist" in the highest degree. And, in the same breath, what am I to say of "Male Impersonators?"–those ladies who give interviews freely and elaborate the delights of masquerading as the "betrousered!" Has a "Female Impersonator" ever been so fluent and candid in confession? Not one! And I defy you to send me authentic details!

Why?   COSMOPOLITE

ANSWERS TO CORRESPONDENTS   15th April 1911 (p. 22))

Resignus (Liverpool)–You must cultivate the spirit of "Dickie," as set forth in his "Diary," and then you will be quite happy.

DICKIE'S DIARY: Being Another Extract From Its Pages.   22nd April 1911 (p. 15)

April 15th, 19–. –Oh, my Diary, once again am I in cloistral quietude with thee in my little study, apart from the select world of B-----, which is now *so* interested in me.

It is my first Easter as a girl-boy, and it has marked many things. My stepmother has come into a big, big fortune; and my father's means as compared with hers is as a farthing ranks beside a sovereign.

Her jubilation at the unexpected news of this massing of worldly riches was *not* exactly jubilation; and that is what I want you to understand. She was quiet, and still and severe, and kept my gaze fastened to hers when, *en famille,* the news was made known. "Now," she said, "I am Supreme Ruler, indeed!" and my father nodded his perfect understanding–and went back to his books! By his action he dumbly confessed his absolute carelessness!

So, now I am left wholly for *her* moulding–and the artificial transposition of sex is complete. Shall I ever again *dare* to think that I am–what I am!

* * * * *

My tutors have told me that I am clever, but I am not clever enough to convey to your intelligence the ecstatic joy I now experience! . . . This Easter Day, after three hours of dressing, I was paraded before the innermost circle of feminine B----- Society, attired in a manner that cannot be described. Great ladies–some of the highest in the county–kissed and caressed me; some took me on their knees, and hugged me to their scented silks and satins; and one, a devilishly lovely woman, with eyes of topaz and lips of blood-red coral, said she would give her soul for the possession of such a "daughter." . . .

As long as I am perfectly tractable and obedient, there is not the slightest restraint placed upon me; but I know I am watched with never-failing vigilance, for often, during my own sweet leisure, I am called suddenly to my stepmother's presence; and after eyeing me with a relentless scrutiny, and satisfying herself that I am exactly as she saw me last, with not a flounce awry, she dismisses me with a smile; and all a-tremble, with my heart beating furiously, I steal back to my little study.

How she glories in her power! . . .

How will it all end? I wonder. Supposing she were to die suddenly, what should I do? There would be no clever brain to advise, no strong hand to guide me–and flight from B----- would be imperative, as would be the resumption of my masculine clothes.

TWO LATE SUMMER COSTUMES.

No. 1 is made in black silk cashmere trimmed with heavy black silk braid. The collar is trimmed with blue and yellow Chinese embroidery on an old-rose background.
The second costume is of black and white checked cloth, made very simply, with a large double pleat in front and back of skirt.

25. Two Late Summer Costumes.   *The Lady's Realm*, September 1910, p.555.

Oh, my Diary . . .,if that happened . . . I think I should follow her . . . very soon! THE SLAVE

THE MAN WOMAN 29th April 1911 (pp 8-9)

It has never been altogether satisfactorily explained to my mind why a man elects to change his sex outwardly, and live either temporarily or permanently in the garments of the opposite gender. I have probed the matter pretty deeply, too, but I have not, so far, come to any really logical conclusion to account for the departure from the conventional. Presently, though, I shall arrange a mass of notes in something like order–and present you with a rather startling result.

[He goes on to discuss Bram Stoker's presentation of the theory that Queen Elizabeth was a man and suggests that] what was possible in those same spacious days is equally possible in these still more spacious: a man, naturally proportioned to the case, can masquerade as a woman until death reveals his secret. Derk Fortescue has been told by a contemptuous masculine minority that his creation of "Amber" is the dream of a fool; hundreds of others have revelled in it–but never given the reason why! No matter! None of you shall suffer by their silence, for, as I have said, presently I will lay bare the whole revelation. Meanwhile, look back at our numbers which contained the photographs of Julian Eltinge, the great American "Female Impersonator," and tell me whether he could not if he so desired, live openly the life of a "lady?" And defy detection? [He recommends readers to consult Stoker's book, *Famous Impostors*, in the free libraries.]

In my recent article on "The Effeminate in Man," I tried to hint at the lurking sense of the "kink" that obsesses more than one of my sex. It has often no deeper an existence than "thought," which may account for some of the truly remarkable letters I have received from those boys and men who allege to have been brought up to relegate their true sex to oblivion. Imagination is a wonderful factor, but I do hold that Nature and *not* will is wholly responsible for the wish for reversion and therein lies the mystery of the "kink."

Analyse a bit. How many *women* create women's fashions? How many *women* create gowns and millinery? Very few. The *woman* costumier and milliner is a mere *copyist;* the *inspiration* came from a *man,* and the world of fashion has cause to be thankful for the existence of the man-woman. He may present himself commercially in the faultless habiliments of his sex, but he's a man-woman all the time, and his true nature is revealed by the art he inspires from beginning to end. In secret, as a consolation, he may transpose his gender outwardly. If so, the Belles of Belgravia and the Maidens of Mayfair may have good reason to give thanks to "Madame La Mode" for this esoteric idiosyncrasy. He'll conceive something they couldn't think about if they tried for a month of Sundays!

Who but a *man* could have thought out the hobble and the harem skirt? Despairing of a new sensation to catch the frail and gauzy multitude of the beskirted, didn't his own personal trousers give forth an idea that appealed to his growing staleness of invention? Of course they did.

Ladies! don't scoff at the being of the man-woman! He can tell you far better how to dress yourselves than you know. Why, when Eve thought out the scheme of the fig-leaf, it was only at Adam's prompting! Otherwise–well, otherwise!

I am as certain as I sit writing that if the average "Female Impersonator" gave his full and candid confessions as to why he ever elected to take up such a *rôle,* they would comprise reading more suitable for the student than the ordinary purchaser of a penny paper, because you can't get away from the fact that the outspoken truth of that weary old tangle, the human mind, is often best expressed between the covers of a text-book. Which is a distinct and quite annoying pity.

Still *you* can write what you like to your Father Confessor.

COSMOPOLITE

THE FASCINATION OF THE FETISH
13th May 1911 (pp 8-9)

There are few men living who can stand up and say truly and honestly that nothing in the form of a fetish appeals to their mental equipment—and accounts for the "kink" they seek to disguise.

Admirers of the Tiny Waist, the High Heel, the Ear-Ring, and any number of other immaterial objects, are fetishists—and each and every one belongs to a high intellectual order, which may or may not be developed: its fire is, however, present for cultivation. The ordinary voluptuary, as we understand him, is right outside the class, although he will claim to be included. But, for reasons too evident to be mentioned, we will place him beyond the pale. You ask for the meaning of poetry, not the gross figuration of the flesh.

The Fascination of the Fetish, whatever it may be, is, I think, at once a comfort and a blessing to those—well, afflicted will have to be the word for want of a better, although to use it seems a trifle unkind and inconsiderate of the vagaries of the human mind, to which I am very sensible.

For the moment, I want to get away from the peculiar influence the Tiny Waist, etc., has upon members of the masculine gender, and touch a fetishistic subject I have not handled before. In a word, it is—satin. The strange and mysterious attraction this material, with the overshot woof and the highly finished surface, has for the most virile and clean-minded of men, is an unfathomable puzzle; and the deeper I dig for an answer, the more mystified I become. Can any of you help me out?

"A woman, be she plain or pretty, is to me an object of mad but respectful adoration," writes "W.B.H." (Ilfracombe), if she is wearing a satin gown, let the colour be what it will. . . . From my earliest boyhood, the wondrous, haunting, shimmering material has appealed to me in a manner I cannot hope to describe: I wish I could. . . . I am poor and unmarried . . . and if I could tell you how I envy a man who is escorting a lady so attired, knowing all the time that I can never hope to occupy such a position as is his by grace of Destiny, you would just write me down as being irredeemably crazy."

I'll do nothing of the sort, because "ENCHANTED" (Baron's Court, S.W.), who is a self-confessed fetishist of the most extravagant kind, assists me in a way to deal with "W.B.H." The former correspondent owns to the possession of money—lucky man!—and the fact that he dresses his wife in nothing but satin—morning, noon and night—surely there's a suspicion of vulgarity here?—and the lady yields to his whim, probably knowing the reason why. "If I saw her in anything else," he writes, "I believe I should hate her!" Which is such a sudden and startling and spasmodic confession that I feel inclined to ask a whole list of questions that would be considered more than personal.

Before I wrote this article, I went out into the street, and looked around for the wearer of a satin gown. It was the Sabbath, and I managed to see one or two. But no appreciable excitement or exhilaration was my portion, and I fell a-wondering. A new fetish had been presented for my consideration, but what on earth did it mean? What was the matter with silk, with velvet, with any material you like to name or imagine? No! it had to be satin—rich, costly, shimmering satin! And there were, apparently, not to be Tiny Waists, High Heels, etc., in conjunction with it! Funny!

Like your luckless Editor, I'm out on the trail to please everybody; but it's a mighty hard job to ring the changes and find something sensational to serve up each week, and so retain the interest of my readers who are pleasantly scattered from China to Peru; yet I guess I've got a "sensational" subject here, and the trouble is to know how to deal with and expand it. Can any lady, right apart from the gentlemen, give me a hint? I've laid hold of a fetish all right, but I can't explain it!

Do *you*, fair dame, wear satin, often or occasionally? And do you think the lures of your exquisite femininity are enhanced by it? If so, have you ever divined, or tried to divine, the logic of cause and effect? A crumb of explanation might enable me to manufacture a loaf.

That the Fascination of Satin is a Fetish, and a thoroughgoing one at that, I will not attempt to abuse or doubt or question. This is not the first time I have been inclined to open the subject, just to see where it leads and how and in what manner you will respond. An appeal to the eye, a fugitive, lurking call to the senses, and thereinafter, as the intelligence dictates, to the inner soul and instinct of the person concerned, must necessarily result in comprehensible explanation, be it written ever so awkwardly or ambiguously.

I can only hope that Tiny Waisters, High Heelers, etc., will give this article as much attention as though it was conceived and devoted whole-heartedly to their favourite subjects, because, surely, I must have touched a line in sympathy with their own pet ideals? I don't want to cry aloud for help, but if this catches the eyes of "J.B.B." (London) or "H.E.G." (Leeds), can they, either of them, find something to say? Or "Mrs.D.?" Or "Jersey Lily?" Or any of those "regulars" who follow my efforts with such interest and kindly criticism?

COSMOPOLITE

DICKIE'S DIARY [The last Extract] 20th May 1911 (pp 14-15)

May 10th, 19–.–Oh, my Diary, can you tell me what slow and subtle change is making itself insidiously manifest in my nature? Has the outward transposition of sex anything to do with it? Is the wearing of silks and satins and velvets, and the gossamer of the most delicate *lingerie* a brain could invent, responsible for what I know is now taking place? Am I so completely a girl-boy, with a combination of the two sexes struggling within me, that a sense of the exterior change is creeping surely to do its certain work?

I am callous, and heartless; I am ineffably vain and conceited; I am cruel in thought and in action: I hate and despise my own sex, because, as *I* stand revealed to them, *they* reveal their contemptible weaknesses. A brilliantly dressed *girl* is something to sport with so they think, and I have proved that truth.

My feared and revered stepmother has me now so entirely in her power that I have no thought of ever trying to escape her magnetic influence. Her wealth is stupendous, and my life is one glorified exaltation. I yield submissively to her every whim and caprice, and wonder if one of her extravagant fancies can possibly be capped by another? This afternoon, she took me out visiting with her, and paraded me with almost maniacal joyousness. The day was clear and warm, and she had had me arrayed in a confection of bright pearl satin, tasselled with scores and scores and scores of tiny pearls. The frock was short–almost too short, I thought–because, for the first time for many weeks I felt sadly self-conscious. The men looked at me with too great an interest: the women tried to seem shocked.

My hat, a fairy-like creation of chiffon and ribbon, was huge. My stockings were white and transparent, and the heels of my little pearl satin shoes were cruelly high. My hands were useless, for they were imprisoned within long pearl kid gloves so tight that it was nigh impossible to bend a single finger. They had taken twenty minutes to fix and straighten!

I was just an exquisite "dollie," the plaything of a Tyrant, corseted so tightly that I could not bend, and arrayed with such a magnificence that I shuddered when a current of air passed me, and I thought of the invisible dust within its atmosphere. *She* has whipped me before now for the presence of a smudge no mortal being could have avoided falling on a film of lace!

I saw Archie----- at one of the houses to which we went, the boy who paid me such funny attention at Lady-----'s juvenile party that evening at the end of March, the boy who "wished he were me!" We had not met since then, and, for quite a while, he avoided me studiously. Then the "attraction" could no longer be withstood, and he crept to where I sat–a captive imprisoned in gorgeousness. His coming removed the presence of a red-haired hobbledehoy of seventeen, who had been trying to "mash" me vulgarly; and for that mercy, I was inclined to give him my most gracious consideration. But, after greeting me politely, and running hungry and envious eyes over my superb toilette, he stammered himself away. I suppose he still "wished he were me!" When we left, I saw him again, and I smiled sarcastically at his earnest

WILLIAM WHITELEY, Ltd.,
LADIES' OUTFITTING DEPT.
FASHIONABLE UNDERSKIRTS IN GREAT VARIETY.

L 57. Effective Underskirt in Alpaca, with pleated Satin Flounce. All new colours, Black and Cream ... ... Price **8/11**

L 58. French Hand-Embroidered Petticoat, daintily finished with Ribbon. Price **12/9**

L 59. Dainty Princess Petticoat, prettily trimmed with soft Lace and Insertions. Price **15/9**; Outsize, **18/9**

L. 48. Dainty Underskirt in British Silk, well cut and finished with Fancy Tucking and new Box Pleat. All latest shades, also Black ... ... Price **12/9**

L. 49. Cambric Petticoat, with newest Flounce, trimmed Val. Lace and Insertions ... ... Price **9/11**

L. 50. Useful Underskirt in Linen-back Satin, with newest pleated Flounce. All new shades and Black ... Price **9/11**

L. 51. Cambric Petticoat, with newest Flounce of Embroidery. Price **5/11**; Outsize, **7/11**

L. 52. Satin Petticoat, with latest pleated Flounce. All fashionable shades, also Black and Ivory ... Price **21/9**

L 54. Underskirt, specially designed for wearing with closely fitting gown, made in best quality Silk Moirette. A splendid selection of colours. Also Black ... ... Price **12/9**; Outsize, **15/9**

L 55. Cambric Petticoat, with handsome embroidered Flounce. Price **9/11**

L 56. Princess Petticoat, with newest Flounce, trimmed Embroidery. Price **10/9**

QUEEN'S ROAD, LONDON, W.

26. Fashionable Underskirts.   *Catalogue*, c. 1910, William Whiteley Ltd., Queen's Road, p.43.

look which caused him to flush hotly and look intensely unhappy. He doesn't want me to be his "sweetheart," as some of the other clumsy egotistical beasts infer: he merely envies me– that's all!

I wonder what he would think and say if he knew the truth? I almost wish he did, that he could be sworn to absolute secrecy, and that we might be able to exchange confidences. I hear he is "booky," as I am and over clever for his age. Physically, he is not strong and seldom mingles with other fellows. I am yearning for a companion, but I fear dreadfully to breach the subject to *her! She* would forbid any friendship, I know!

I am guided day and night like a princess, and my stepmother is acquainted with my every movement. I am, yet I am not, isolated from all contact with the outer world. I dare not stir abroad unless *she* is with me. The feeling of this restraint is dead, though I am resigned, and she is aware of it.

My figure training is getting daily more severe, so is my "heel drill," and my quiet little study does not see me for longer than two or three hours each day. The Tyrant is for ever making me change my gorgeous frocks, to drive with her, to walk beside her in the grounds of the great house to which we have recently removed, to sit where she can feast her eyes upon me, to be ready to respond to her every whim. I think she revels in my powerlessness. She is a woman born to subjugate a man, and to do it in a way that shall prove to him how poor and weak he is beneath her authority. My own father is permitted to see her only at stated times. And as he has just lost all the money he had in a bank crash, and is practically a pauper, I suppose he lives here more or less on sufferance. There was never much in common between him and myself and now I seldom have a chance of a word with him. The servants ignore his presence, my stepmother's friends ignore his existence, and all he does is to browse harmlessly on his books and live the life of a recluse.

But I care for nothing so long as I please my mistress, and win her smiles.

THE SLAVE

PETTICOAT GOVERNMENT   3rd June 1911 (pp 16-18)

The following very interesting and informative letter has been received by "Cosmopolite", from "Well-Disciplined" (Clapham, S.W.) and may serve to prove that one half the juvenile world doesn't know how the other half lives in days of adolescence:

"I have been reading some of your articles in 'Photo Bits' with great interest, as I was when a boy put through a prolonged course of 'Petticoat Discipline', and have fully appreciated the extracts from the correspondence you have reproduced.

My father married a second time, when I was fourteen, and my stepmother was an ultra-fashionable young lady, who from the first insisted on an entire change in our previously somewhat homely life. My father gave way to her in all things, and I was placed, at her request, under her entire control. I objected at once, as she insisted upon my wearing in the evenings a velvet knickerbocker suit, silk stockings, patent shoes and white kid gloves, whereas I had been accustomed to wear my ordinary clothes, and do pretty much as I pleased; but my objections only made matters worse, as she seized on them as an excuse for putting me through the most rigorous course of discipline and humiliation imaginable.

I was measured, and shortly after fitted, in spite of my struggles (which were soon subdued with the help of her maids) with very long and stiff corsets, which were pulled in at first to 24 inches, and tightened a little each day, till I measured only twenty-two inches at the end of the week; after that, except on special occasions, or for punishment, my waist was reduced ½ inch a month.

Tightly-fitting tunics and breeches of satin or velvet, black or coloured, were always my wear, with silk stockings, often open-worked for my extra humiliation; and either high-legged button boots, or low-cut or strapped shoes with French heels, which, starting at three inches, were rapidly increased in height, till finally, I could more or less successfully negotiate six inches on special occasions. These boots and shoes were always painfully tight and narrow, and usually of patent leather, though I sometimes wore satin at night, while my arms and hands were tightly buttoned up into strong kid gloves, often reaching well above my elbows, tan or black for morning, and white or light coloured for evening wear.

I was removed from my school, and, to my shame, a governess was engaged, who had a reputation as a severe disciplinarian and as a figure trainer and teacher of deportment; and who was even more exigent than my stepmother with regard to my deportment and personal appearance, while I had to obey her slightest orders instantly and without question.

Any objections were promptly met by punishments, many and varied in character. I classify them in three sections: 1st, punishment by humiliation, such as compulsory wearing of girls' underclothing, exhibiting frills and ruffles below my short sleeves and knickers; or in cases meriting severe treatment, the wearing of entire female dress – very short skirts with multitudes of laces and frills showing under them, and short-sleeved and even low-cut bodices, in which costume I was compelled to go about the house and have my meals, even decorated with brooches, bracelets and other jewellery on neck and ears. My hair also would be specially curled and crimped, my face powdered, etc. I hated this form of punishment intensely. The second punishment was by pain inflicted by dress, such as extra tight-lacing, tight narrow pointed boots, very high collars, etc. I have been strapped up by the hands, and my corset, an extra long and stiff one, tightened in till I could hardly breathe; and then my feet have been forced into the very tightest and most pointed extra high-heeled boots that could be got on; and then my hands have been tightly gloved, and strapped one on each side to a belt fixed firmly round my waist. In this condition, I would be compelled to stand where my stepmother or the governess could see me, sometimes for two or three hours, till I felt faint and sick with the pain and helplessness.

I think the torture of very tight and *short* extra high-heeled boots, especially when one is bound and helpless, is one of the worst punishments imaginable. My stepmother always seemed to enjoy proving to me my powerlessness, and constantly imprisoned my wrists and ankles with straps, or even locked handcuffs, keeping me in bonds for hours at a time. I have been placed in the stocks, both feet heel to heel in a straight line with one another, and with shoulders strapped back to a back-board, wearing a collar which held my head high and immovable in the air, my hands strapped to the board behind me. Sometimes she made me wear a jacket with a high stiff collar tightly fitting round my neck, with even three or four sharp points under the chin, a few hours of which would reduce the most unruly spirit to obedience; and as my hands were fastened, or steels sewn into the sleeves to prevent my bending my elbows, I was quite powerless to relieve myself in the least. *(continued next week)*

(Continued) 10th June 1911 (pp 18-19)

Sometimes, again, I had to wear an extra tight corset at night (I always wore night corsets with a locked belt to prevent removal), and tight boots and gloves, if she thought I needed punishment, the boots and shoes being secured by locked, tightly fitting bracelets and anklets; and if I attempted to tamper with them, I regretted it if discovered!

The third method of punishment was chastisement, either on the hands, in which case a thin and most stinging whalebone rod was applied over tight thin kid gloves, or a riding whip or cane; and on special occasions, the birch. These latter instruments were applied to the part Nature is said to have intended for the purpose, either over my knickers, or more often, I had to don a pair of very thin and tight silk breeches, fitting like a skin, before the whipping. I was always fastened down over a stool or cushion, and quite unable to resist or help myself.

The birch was applied over my bare skin, usually only for bad offences; and my stepmother made the whipping quite a ceremonial. I had to put on long white kid gloves, high heeled and high legged boots, lace cuffs and frills etc. while she herself was dressed in most fashionable evening dress, loaded with jewellery and wearing the smallest of corsets, very high heeled shoes, and long gloves. She whipped very slowly and severely, and the whippings were very hard to bear, the maids strapping me down over a high stool as tightly as possible, in order that I might get the full benefit of the rod.

One or two special punishments you may be interested to hear of. One evening, while in a low cut frock, I was rude to her; and she told the maids to strap me in my chair as I was, and sending out into the garden for some nettles, she whipped my back and shoulders until they were burning; and, after releasing me, strapped my gloved hands together behind my back, forcing me to bear the itching and irritation all the evening without any power of relief. Another day, after making me wear such high heels that I really could not walk in them, she got so angry at my failure, that she and the maids stripped my feet bare, and, laying me on my face on the floor, held up my feet and birched me on the soles in spite of my cries. They hurt horribly for hours, as they put on my boots and stockings again immediately afterwards.

I had nearly three years of this discipline, and could at last wear 18 inch corsets, and walk comfortably in five inch heels, wearing small fives in shoes and 6¼ in gloves. My experience made a permanent impression, and certainly had the effect of taming and subduing a decidedly unruly boy. Even now, over ten years since my experience of 'Petticoat Control' began, I still enjoy the feeling of a corset, tight gloves and high heeled boots, though I do not habitually wear them; and sometimes 'dress up' as in the days when my young and imperious stepmother compelled me to acknowledge her supremacy.

I should have said we had extensive grounds attached to our house, so I seldom went outside the gates, but if I did, though tightly corseted and gloved, and often in girl's underclothing, I wore outer garments like other boys, while my tight patent leather shoes had only very moderate heels, so as not to attract attention. In our own grounds, however, I had to show my figure fully to all – short sleeves, short breeches, glove-fitting tunics revealing my corsets, and boots and gloves."

THE FASCINATION OF SATIN   1st July 1911 (pp 16-17)

"COSMOPOLITE" has received the following letter from "GERTIE" (Leith) concerning his article, "The Fascination of the Fetish," which appeared in our issue of May 13th:–

I have been a regular reader of your charming paper for a considerable time. Your articles have always been of the greatest interest to me and my husband, and we have often longed to write to you about such subjects as Tiny Waists, High Heels, Garters, Frills *versus* Tights, and Boots *versus* Shoes. You seem, however, to be able to procure sufficient correspondence on these matters, and we have not thought it worth while to trouble you with our contributions.

We notice in this week's issue that you make a request for letters on Satin; and as I am devotedly attached–both literally and figuratively–to satin gowns, and my better half has always expressed great admiration for the "shimmering material," I have braced myself up to let you have my views on the question of its "sensational" fascination. If you publish my letter, I may let you have further views on similar topics.

"Satin," says my husband, "has always soothed my cares and revived my love for the beautiful. I remember well how I fell in love with you at the -----'s dance. You wore a dark satin dress then, and thin openwork violet stockings, with a petticoat of the same colour. My heart started fluttering dangerously during our first waltz; and when I had escorted you home, I said to myself, "I simply *must* marry that girl!" You were only eighteen then, dear Gertie; but ever since that eventful night, I have worshipped you when you wore satin, and merely admired you if you ever dressed in any other kind of costume."

I am only five feet two tall, and although it is usual for women of that height to avoid satin,

I find it an entrancingly delicious garb. My legs are longer, proportionately, than the upper part of my figure; and once I have clasped a pair of softly yielding garters just above my knees, over my skin-tight blue-violet stockings, and got my husband to lace up as tightly as possible my knee-high *bottines,* I feel that it is impossible for me to stand up on my four-and-a-half inch heels, or to endure my well-nigh painfully but yet delicately contrived pointed toes with their smart patent caps, unless I can feel the luscious pressure of the satin wavelets that billow gently about my ankles as I move.

I always feel awfully keen on enjoying life when dressed in tight-fitting eighteen-inch corsets and the clinging folds of a satin gown; and I notice invariably that the more "nice" I begin to feel, the more bewitching I seem to be considered. I suppose, therefore, that my smug little manner communicates an enthusiastic atmosphere; and, certainly, when I sit down and raise my gown slightly to cross my knees, I notice with a thrill of pride that a look of expectancy and joy comes into neighbouring eyes; and I seem to cheer people up considerably when I start talking.

Satin differs from all frock materials in that it appeals both to the eye and the ear. Coloured gowns, light summery blouses, delicately-fashioned dancing costumes, well-cut "tailor-mades"–all these make an appeal, sometimes an irresistible appeal, to the eye; they are very dainty, occasionally very tricky and elfish, and they *interest* the eye! But they possess no *music:* satin does. Satin not only interests the eye, it soothes it–*and it also has a charm of its own in its suggestive rustling movements, appealing inevitably to any ear that is not deaf to beauty.*

I think this is the main secret of the fascination of the soft ravishment that satin always has for the male heart. There is a thistledown, butterfly grace about it which can be found nowhere else; a quiet, almost dignified, suggestion of the Parisienne in its alluring power; an intermittent "swish" to retain the interest that is nearly always aroused at first sight; a radiant gloss about the surface which compels admiration; and enthralling, captivating glamour that haunts the ear for hours after one has heard it; a labyrinthine mystery about the ebb and flow of the folds; and an occasional magnetic flash of trim ankles and sweet high-heeled little boots or shoes as the dress is raised to prevent injury on a rainy day.

The zephyr-like breezes of the satin gown blow away worldly care from the masculine mind; its voluptuously sensuous charm and its languishing rapture inevitably and invariably provides the basis of love; and its verdure-like yielding pliancy appeals to the sense of touch quite as much as does the ecstatic, dream-like miasma exuded by its miniature orchestral equipment in the shape of a slow, clinging languor that can hardly fail to soothe the ear.

Such perhaps is the male conception of tall, satin-encased womanhood. Small women should not wear satin; their legs are not long enough to cause it to rustle; and unless satin rustles, it has no more charm than an ordinary dress. To the female mind, there is also the gentle sensation of soft squeezing that satin always provides; one unconsciously feels smart and neat and nice when thus attired. Perhaps I may add that a silk petticoat adds appreciably to the superiority of a satin gown over other varieties. The honey of bliss that one experiences can never be imagined; it must be realised by actually wearing a silk "pettie" underneath the satin. The two materials are not what alkali is to acid; they are what a slipping-on of a garter is to a divinely-fitting stocking, what a well-laced boot is to a soft little foot, what a pair of long, tightly-buttoned gloves is to a creamy hand and arm. They go so well together that one feels one has at last reached the consummate apotheosis of luxurious comfort and artistically moulded form-combination.

(This correspondent has answered the queries I set forth in my article in so complete and satisfactory a manner that it's doubtful if she has left anything else to be explained.–COSMOPOLITE)

[This is an interesting and amusing letter, but I am not entirely convinced that it was written by a woman. There are several odd things about it, not just the supposed husband's passion for satin. Satin does not really rustle more than any other fabric, or even at all: it is taffeta which does this *par excellence.* Again, fabrics come and go in and out of fashion, and are greeted with ecstasy each time they appear. The statement, "taffetas bids fair to become a veritable obsession this season" from *The Queen* of 6 April 1912 (p. 597) is the authentic voice of Fashion: it is an obsession, yes, but for this season. "Gertie" recognises the effect of petticoats, but there is more to it than that. The whole visual and *audible* effect is produced by the cut and construction of the gown, the dress material, the lining and the underskirts. While I am sure that a heavy satin cut in a wide flare would swish and swirl in a distinctive manner, especially if lined with taffeta, it would be uncharacteristic of a woman to value such an outfit for its sound alone.]

THE CUB AND THE KILT 8th July 1911 (pp 8-9)
[This article includes] I've had a letter from a Scotch lassie ("A Lover of Kilts") who at present has to put up with living at Dulwich, London, S.E. It seems evident that she has been following, with a great deal of interest, my articles on "The Cultivation of the Cub," she says:

"I believe that boys from six to sixteen can be trained and disciplined by us women for their own good. *You*, dear Mr Cosmopolite, think that tightly laced in stays etc. have a good effect in reducing to obedience, but *I* think that the best way of training the average human boy is to dress him in the Highland kilt. My brothers were kilted up to the age of sixteen, and I am convinced that their kilts were responsible for a great moral effect on their characters. Our mother was a good Highland Scotch woman with muscular arms; and if needful, she took the boys across her lap and chastised them well under their kilts with a thin leather strap. Nevertheless we all loved and respected our parents, and were a happy family.

A most interesting subject for discussion in your bright little paper would be this very one: 'The kilt as a garment of Moral Discipline for Boys'. You would have a lot of interesting letters from men and women, especially the latter, who would prove to you, that the beauty of the kilt is that it keeps the boys in the petticoat stage; and by depriving them of manly (?) trousers, keeps them more on a level with their sisters.

Many boys are very unaccomplished socially when they grow up: they cannot sing or dance or play any instrument. The wise mother who kilts her sons, easily overcomes this series of failings. She will find that the majority of boys like the Highland dress; and it needs little encouragement to get them to play the bagpipes, and dance the Sword-Dance, the Highland Fling, and the Highland Reel, as well as singing beautiful Scotch songs, which develops the artistic side of their natures and does away with stupid shyness. COSMOPOLITE

THE CUB AND THE KILT 2nd September 1911 (pp 8-9, 16)
(second ARTICLE)

The cultivation of the modern male cub seems to be a subject that not a few of my readers have studied consistently and carefully, if I am to judge by the following thoughtful letter received from a Liverpool correspondent, which bears out the facts and opinions contained in about a dozen others, which, unfortunately I have not the space today to give in full: "I see one of your readers advocates the wearing of kilts as a means of disciplining unruly boys. Kilts are worn at present by all classes of Scotchmen from the highest in the land down to the humblest gillie, and I have my doubts as to the moral effects of kilts pure and simple. If, however, a boy is made to feel that in wearing them he is on a level with his sister in short frocks, then it is another matter.

To produce this feeling, he must first of all be corsetted, not necessarily very tightly, but sufficiently so that he may experience the pressure, and that there may be some restriction in his movements. Further he must wear similar underclothing to his sister. Let him wear short trunk knickers with a little frill attached, and a white lace petticoat several inches shorter than

than his kilt; the petticoat should be of the 'Princess' shape, fitting closely to the figure. This costume would, I am sure, have a good moral effect. The boy would know that he was really garbed like a girl; and unless he were particularly boisterous in his movements, the casual passer-by in the street would be unaware of the fact, and the boy would not be exposed to ridicule.

When at home in the evening, he could wear longer knickers, and one or more petticoats of frilly character, than in the daytime; so that when he moved the laces and ribbons might be exposed to view, and remind him of the training he was undergoing. Girl's shoes, too, should be worn in the evening, but not with abnormally high heels. If this costume were more in vogue, the modern youngster would not be the young hooligan he so often is. Occasionally, he might be dressed entirely as a girl, which, besides tending to make him more obedient, would, I think, inculcate neatness and dispel the tendency to slovenliness that is so prevalent at the present day."

I have a letter before me from a man of thirty, who, as a boy, if I take his confession rightly, must have been the limit as regards unruliness and general unpleasant dirtiness and untidiness; and he asks me to believe honestly that the enforced wearing of a kilt and girl's lingerie entirely changed the trend of his character.

"At the beginning", he writes, "there were terrible scenes when the edict went forth as to the costume I was to adopt; and I didn't really bow to the inevitable until a cousin – a true type of your Muscular Girl – took me in hand one day from my mother and father, and favoured me with the soundest thrashing with a cane I had ever had! I was thin and slightly built, and she did me well, I can assure you!

After that, I regarded my kilted dress with resignation, if dully slumbering mutiny; but as time went on and I realised the delights of its freedom, I began to think I had been kicking against my own interests. My parents may have had the idea to shame me by making me wear girls' underclothing, by making me wear a pair of my youngest sister's corsets; but strange to say, the feeling that they had succeeded in their design, speedily wore off – and I wrote privately to my cousin – a rather wealthy woman – saying that if she wanted to give me a birthday present, she could buy me a kilted costume according to her own taste and fancy, which I promised to wear at a garden party she was about to have.

The woman, the conqueror, was delighted, perhaps as much by the knowledge that it had been *she* who had whipped me into submission as by my request; and the memory of the costume she gave me, will never be effaced from my memory, together with the exquisite corsets and lingerie that went with it. I don't know how much the lot cost her, but it must have been a pretty penny! As a Scotch costume, it was correct to an ace-shaped button on the black velvet coat, and the kilt itself was of silk and rustled and swished delightfully. The sensation of its contact around me was superfluously delicious – and the cure was complete! My only regret was that I could not wear that particular costume every day, but it was altogether too gorgeous for anything but sabbaths and gala times."

I regret that this correspondent has omitted several facts from his letter which would have been interesting to know – such as his waist measurement when the wearing of the kilt ceased at seventeen and he went into business, whether the charms of the corset have lasted until now, and whether the influence of that last gift costume still possesses anything for him beyond memory? Perhaps he will write and say. It may have developed a 'kink', especially as he says carelessly in one paragraph that I have not given here, that nothing pleases him more than to see his wife dressed in silk of a tartan pattern.

The influence of dress, seen or worn, is as much an influence as environment or surroundings, and has every bit as much effect upon character.

It seems pretty evident from the letters I have received from many parts of the country, from people who cannot possibly have met one another to compare notes, etc. that the kilt has a great restraining power, essentially for good in the case of a troublesome, wayward boy. The dress is feminine without being feminine, if I can apply such a phrase to it; and it's generally acknowledged by those who have been qualified to judge, that when a boy is put into anything like skirts by way of punishment, that boy is approaching one of the turning-points in his life; and unless he is past all human hope, a change in his moral behaviour *is* effected. But that change has to be brought about by systematic method; and the systematic method has been mentioned by both the correspondents I have quoted today; and those not mentioned have said precisely the same things. So there appears to be a standard code on the subject, which, being summarised, comes under three headings:– the kilt, the corset, and "flapper" lingerie.

I hope some of the foregoing will prove of interest to "A Distracted Parent" (Leamington), who has written me questioning the worth of attempting the Kilt-Cure for a young gentleman of perverse and untractable tendencies. I can only point out to her that it seems to have been practised with startling success by several who have been placed in her position, and that one lady added the wearing of the tightest black kid gloves to her offspring's "training" – occasionally binding his wrists behind his back and making him stand in a corner with his face to the wall, wearing a pair of her highest heeled button boots, for an hour at a time. I have also been told of a naughty little girl of fourteen who was kilted *minus* lingerie; and in this case a nice thin cane was fastened to her side ready for instant use, so wherever she was – well, the cane was there too! which was a marked economising of time and trouble – all round, so to speak!

A practical proof of the modern method of "cub-curbing" has been given me by a Liverpool correspondent, who has kindly forwarded a cutting from a Northern Sunday paper, headed "Boy in Petticoats".

"When a number of boys were charged at Liscard, recently, with stealing chocolate from automatic machines at Seacombe Ferry, by inserting cardboard discs, a detective said that one of them was of a roving disposition, and had slept out. On one occasion when he visited the home, he found the boy attired in petticoats to prevent him from leaving the house".

If the subject of the Cub and the Kilt has not been exhausted by this and my previous article, I should like to hear whatever else is to be said. COSMOPOLITE

THE ART OF THE FEMALE IMPERSONATOR 2nd September 1911 (p. 18)
Salisbury.

Dear Cosmopolite, I send you a cutting from an American paper, the Kalamazoo *Telegraph Press* which shows very plainly that "Amber" was not such an impossible creation after all, and that there are more cases of "transposition of sex" than people are aware of or would believe. It also shows that a man *can* live, work and mingle with his fellow-creatures in the garb of the opposite sex without betraying his secret, as witness this American stewardess who lived "her" life with complete success until Death revealed the truth. A SUBSCRIBER

The cutting referred to reads as follows:
FIND STEWARDESS IS REALLY A MAN.

Boston, Mass. June 23rd.–An autopsy performed on the charred remains of Harriet Kelly, stewardess, who was one of the two women burned to death in the fire that destroyed the excursion steamer "Governor Andrew" last Sunday morning, disclosed the fact that Harriet was a man. The fact became public today for the first time.

For thirty years Harriet had lived as a woman and was known on the "Governor Andrew" as a widow. No reason for his masquerade is known. For several years he was employed as a domestic in aristocratic Back Bay families, and always gave satisfaction.

ANSWERS TO CORRESPONDENTS 2nd September 1911 (p. 21)

GOY BIRL (Nottingham).–Pleased to hear from you. By all means let us have the photos to which you refer. Kindly put the fullest particulars on the back of each.

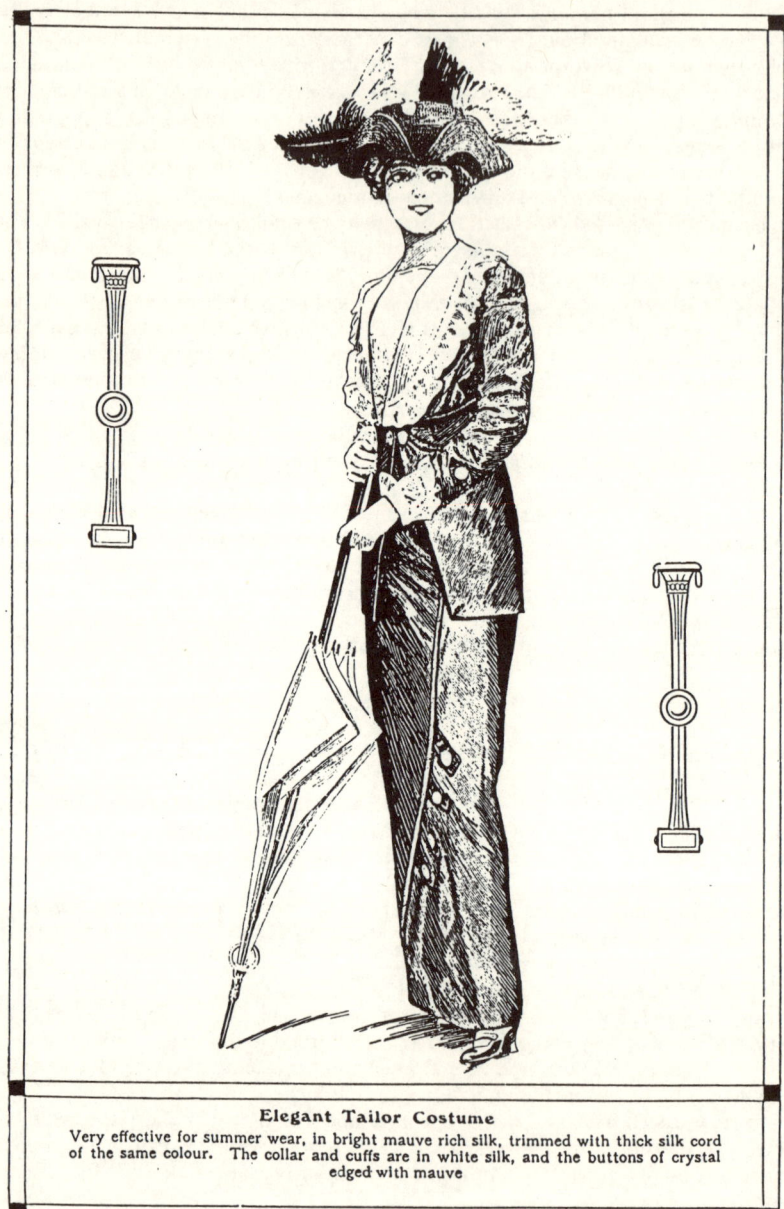

Elegant Tailor Costume

Very effective for summer wear, in bright mauve rich silk, trimmed with thick silk cord of the same colour. The collar and cuffs are in white silk, and the buttons of crystal edged with mauve

27. Elegant Tailor Costume. *The Lady's Realm*, July 1912, p.303.

A WOMAN'S SLAVE
9th September 1911 (pp 8-9)

And that's just what a man becomes when he, poor and probably obscure, marries for money!

It's a girl's prerogative to look out for herself and make the best pecuniary match she can; but when a fellow hikes out on the cash-bagging lay, he deserves all he gets, and more besides as soon as the public show and flummery is over, and he is fairly and squarely in his lady's hands. Therefore, you will understand that in this article I mean to deal only with my own errant sex, but I will be fair in one respect: I am taking the view of a man who has never married and who will never marry, either for love or gold. Perhaps I am looking at the matter with jaundiced eyes. If so, after reading this, you who have wed for the "ready" and obtained happiness, can write and tell me how wrong I am!

"The details of my abasement, of my marital bondage I have no time to tell you now. But if you are at all interested–*and my mistress permits*–I will do so later." So reads one of the closing paragraphs of a letter that I have received from a young man who signs himself "Alec in Petticoats," and gives the vague address of "Mayfair, W." I cannot hope to give his lengthy epistle *in extenso,* but summarised, it is this: he acted as secretary to a wealthy American lady, she proposed marriage, and now he is under her claws.

I know perfectly well that my leg has been most frightfully "pulled," but that doesn't matter a cent. I've been given a text that will enable me to stand up in my weekly pulpit once more and talk to you.

There's no doubt about the idea, which is running pretty free and easy in these days, that there's a certain class of woman who is out red-hot on the trail to subjugate a certain class of man; and to do that well and successfully, he's got to be bound up to her by what is generally termed "the holy bonds of matrimony." The fellow she catches is usually a waster and frankly servile to the subjugation of woman. He will invite or suffer any indignity as long as he, more or less of a hireling, has crawling access to her banking account, and is saved the trouble of working for a living.

The alleged case of "ALEC IN PETTICOATS" who had as a servant and has as a husband to dress in feminine attire whenever the dictatrix spoke in the past and speaks now, merely proves the depths to which some invertebrate specimens of the masculine gender will sink when their objective is a life of luxury and laziness, with the woman giving "wages." The whole of the yarn as it was written to me was "spoof" from beginning to end, but I am willing to concede that that "spoof" has an actuality *somewhere,* in fact and essence, but decidedly not in the case of "ALEC"–a name I have reason to dislike. He prejudiced me against himself by its mere fictitious employment; and we went to pains to find out whom he could be. Still, as I've said before, he provided me with a text for this chat.

[He goes on to say that marrying for money invites a penalty. There are plenty of wealthy women waiting to catch a tame bunny. I am SHE–you are IT." Boys, take heed. A rich woman will throw aside a rich suitor, if she can "boss" a poorer. Genuine experiences invited.]

COSMOPOLITE

COSMOPOLITIANA – THE CUB AND THE KILT
7th October 1911 (pp 18-19)

Dear Cosmopolite,

I have read with interest the letter you quoted from a Liverpool correspondent in your second article on the above subject and would like to give you my somewhat similar experience.

My mother was a confirmed invalid, and my sister and I were often sent to stay for long periods with an aunt. Although she was very fond of me, she held strong views about the upbringing of boys; and although not unwilling to use a cane sometimes, she generally preferred the form of punishment your correspondent describes.

For this purpose, she invented a rather original method. I was compelled to don the usual girls' underclothing except that my stockings were fastened to my very much beflounced knickers. My petticoat was always one of striped calico, and made so that nobody could possibly mistake what it was, and had a large flounce attached to its hem; and over the top of these garments were laced corsets in such a manner that I could not undo them myself. In this way, I was prevented from removing my underclothing, as the fastenings were under the corsets.

I had then to don short kilts about a quarter-of-an-inch longer than my petticoat and my knickers, which I could not pull higher as they were fastened to my stockings. High heeled shoes were then placed on my feet, and tied with knots of a particular kind, which I could not unfasten. My shoes prevented me from walking comfortably, my corsets prevented me from sitting comfortably, and, moreover, the slightest speck of dirt on my clothes was punished severely. Attired in this manner, I was often compelled to spend the greater part of the day, and I am not likely to forget the experiences I had to endure.

PETTICOATED MALE (Sunderland)

WHY DO WOMEN DRESS?　　　　　　　　　　　　　　　　　　4th November 1911 (p. 8-9)

Do women dress to please men or themselves?

I know this is a hoary old question that is turning up eternally, and that it has been beaten out of all shape long before today, chiefly by women; but for the moment I wish to state the case for the man alone, and, perhaps in a rather unconventional way. Please to remember, though, I do not speak for myself–merely on behalf of some male correspondents who have written me regarding the subject, and expressed their views, which I embody in my pregnant statements made this week.

Without any unnecessary preamble, let me get to work at once. "I don't care a bit for the opposite sex," writes "H.O.M." (Cricklewood, N.W.), "although I would do everything in my power to help or protect one of them should occasion arise. But I must own they have an attraction for me–and it lies entirely and essentially in their dress. I have certain ideals as regards hats, gloves, gowns and boots or shoes; and when I see the nearest approach to my certain ideals, I experience at once a combined sublimity of torture and pleasure. For the wearer herself, I have not the least hankering. My passion–if I may use such an abused and elastic word–is directed solely towards her attire."

Here is a rather vague and half-spoken confession, the true meaning of which could be thoroughly explained by any average girl of the world, which she knew all about as soon as she realised the significance of the dividing line between the man and the woman. To explain myself clearly, I will swing back to the extremest limit. I have known real, genuine man haters, young, pretty and accomplished girls, who, as the saying goes, invariably dressed "to kill," but the pleasure of being so arrayed was by no means wholly personal; they knew they circulated a torment and a torture to exist in the heart-cores of the masculine world, and that was sufficient satisfaction.

As far as I know, and I think that a few of you frankly speaking men will agree with me, a woman can either agitate or break a man's heart more easily by the sumptuousness of her apparel than by any coarse or common jilting–and she may be a stranger to him all the time! There, the mystery creeps in! Why should it be so? Why, for instance, should a man in a theatre feast his eyes upon a glorious creation of silk, satin or velvet in a box or in the stalls, lose all further interest in the play, detach the wearer of the magnificence from her magnificence, and think and dream only of her outward elegance? One answer may be that the feminine side of his nature, dormant or understood, has been reached. To my mind, such a man, if he were equipped by Nature for the part, would be a remarkably successful "Female Impersonator;" and if the truth were known and acknowledged, more than one living "Amber" would bear me out in my argument. But you can't coax them to speak, anyhow! Which is quite comprehensible.

Were there no men, there would be no feminine fashions of the style to which we are accustomed–to excite ridicule, admiration, or the sexual instinct. All these points go hand-in-hand with an inherent if innocently veneered cruelty–to tease and to distract. Otherwise, would any artist of the betrousered persuasion take the trouble to make alleged fun out of a passing whim of *la mode?*

The fact of the case is–the man is jealous, jealous of the turns and twists afforded to the ever-changing woman's wardrobe; and among those who are jealous, and who hug their secrets in the hidden chambers of their souls, are to be found those who confess anonymously to the delight that is afforded them by a temporary transposition of sex as far as outward appearances go. The idea as I give it here may belong to the mental equipment of a shop-boy–it may belong to the intelligence of My Lord; and there is no [*sic,* but surely should be omitted] more than one of the latter class who reflects in cloistral quietude the gratification of the "kink" peculiar to his train. The difference between them is this–My Lord can go to the top of his bent as regards elaborate falsification; the shop-boy has only a limited–a very limited–scope. But the sense of realisation is identical, and the Fraternity of Fudge is complete. Nevertheless, should the matter go so far, the shop-boy is locked up for "masquerading." My Lord, however, is exempt–for the excellent reason that he's cunning enough to keep within four walls. And don't ask me where those four walls exist.

Why do women dress? Simply to make men see to what extent they can go as regards the employment of their imaginations! I claim that–and I will claim it!–through thick and thin! The haunting remembrance of a fascinating costume will send a fellow home to a dowdily-dressed wife, and he will, by virtue of his creative faculties invest her with each and every one of the ineffable charms which are lingering in his memory–for a time! She may marvel and wonder at his outward affection; but, luckily for her, she doesn't know! Tell me truly–you whose workaday life takes you into the highways and bye-ways of busy traffic–for what length of time do you imagine you look at a girl's face–and for how much longer do you imagine you turn your head after she has passed and view her dress? You have to remember that the gown attracted you to begin with: the worth of the wearer's features was based entirely on idle curiosity. A streak of the artistic in your general make-up may have been responsible for a fleeting desire to know whether the natural touch agreed with the artificial; but the perfection or imperfection of the milliner, and the sensuous or otherwise work of the costumier, was primarily responsible for the optical line of magnetic inquisitiveness.

And now you may write, as you always do, and tell me exactly what you think, in your own way and your own words. COSMOPOLITE.

A WOMAN'S SLAVE, ETC. 4th November 1911 (p. 18)

Dear Cosmopolite, With reference to your article on "A WOMAN'S SLAVE," I am sorry that, owing to his offensive name, we shall not get the details of "ALEC'S" discipline by his wife. Many wise men have said that the only "true" tales extant are the old fairy tales. In the same way, the actual experiences of any human being are of little use in studying the nude human soul; but if under the protection of a *nom de guerre* anyone could be induced *to reveal the experiences he would like to undergo himself or to witness somebody else undergoing,* we get glimpses which are of the utmost interest. Of course, even under the most favourable circumstances, the revelation is generally only partial.

With reference to one of your recent letters from a correspondent–*vide* "H.A.P." in your issue of September 16th–if I was asked did any man really marry a widow much older than himself for the purpose of spanking her and her two grown-up daughters into good behaviour, I should say, "Yes, certainly!"–if not *here* and *now,* then *"Once upon a time"* in Vineland! Not that I would for a moment say that any experience was impossible. I have met with too many unbelievable cases myself not to allow that nearly anything is possible.

As to sexual inversion, otherwise female impersonation, I can recall half-a-dozen cases at this moment, and with a little trouble could no doubt double or treble the number; and I think for every case that is made public, there must be many that are never found out at all. Why the impersonators in real life do it, is a puzzle indeed, and it's a pity you can't get one of them to write and at least try to explain the matter as far as their own case is concerned.

HATINE TIE, London, W.

ANSWERS TO CORRESPONDENTS 4th November 1911 (p. 21)
CAP AND APRON (Blackheath).—The sense of your letter has been given by a number of correspondents in the past, and, we expect, will be repeated in the future. However, we may treat the subject, as you present it, later on, either in story or article form. We know of no books dealing with the life of a "Female Impersonator," and the only serial we have met with was our own "Amber the Actor," which recently appeared in these columns.

THE EFFEMINATE IN MAN (Second Article) 18th November 1911 (pp 8-9)
Here's a confession I received some time ago. Unfortunately, it has been overlooked, and I hope "PINAFORE" (London, N.W.) will forgive me the delay that has occurred in attending to him:

"I don't mind confessing that I am a 'Feminist,' and also that the 'fetish' holds its sway as far as I am concerned! I am not ashamed of either; and I owe much keen enjoyment to the fact that I am fortunately able to gratify my tastes to a greater extent than is probably possible to most of my fellow students of 'P.B.'

I am approaching middle age; and, to the outer world, I appear to be a rather unapproachable man, engaged in very dry literary work. I reside in a quiet London suburb–in one of those old houses with large gardens, which still survive the encroachments of the jerry-builder. My household consists of an elderly Scotch housekeeper and her two daughters, who do all the work of the place, thus ensuring me the perfect privacy that enables me to live my own life.

Those who know me in my private capacity, would be infinitely surprised to learn that I spend several days in every week dressed and living as a woman! During these periods, it is always understood that 'Mrs. Mac'–my housekeeper–is the absolute mistress of the house, and that I, as well as her daughters, have to submit to her rule in *every* respect. My own peculiar 'fetish' is that of not only delighting to see women and girls compelled to wear large, sensible white aprons and long, plain pinafores, but also to be dressed as a woman–and *forced to wear aprons and pinafores myself!* As I write, I am dressed entirely in feminine attire. My 'undies' are as fresh and dainty as you will find anywhere, and I am wearing a dark-blue linen frock with a "Quaker Girl" collar. Over this, I have been *compelled* to put on a long, plain, white diaper pinafore; and the feeling of delicious humiliation entailed in being *forced* to wear a pinafore is more exquisite than I can describe! I never get tired of it, although I have experienced it constantly for some years past.

Earlier this morning, I have been dressed as a housemaid–in a print frock, immense linen apron and a cap; and in this costume I have been working in the kitchen under 'Mrs. Mac's' orders. She is a stern disciplinarian, and I only wish that Derek had made 'Amber' dress and work under similar conditions (Wait and see what presently happens to Lord Teddie Cobhunter!–EDITOR.) A well-worn tawse always hangs besides the kitchen mantelpiece, which 'Mrs.Mac' does not hesitate to use, either on her daughters or me! The birch is reserved for more serious occasions.

I am also fond of dressing as a Lancashire mill girl–with a short skirt, no bodice, and a long, short-sleeved, close-fitting linen pinafore fastened in tightly round my waist with a leather belt, and gathered in closely round my neck by a tape passed through its hem at the top. This is what they call a 'brat' in Lancashire, and the costume is completed by a red handkerchief bound tightly round the head. Another delightful dress I often wear is that of the typical Yankee waitress, which consists of a plain white blouse–'shirt-waist' *they* call it–and an *immense,* stiffly starched, plain white linen apron. This apron is very fully gathered into a plain narrow band, the ends of which are pinned at each hip so as to overlap about six inches and cover one's skirts. My American aprons–they were specially made for me in Boston, U.S.A.– are fully forty inches wide at the band; and one hundred and twenty at the bottom hem. They are always stiffly starched, and, I can tell you, I 'feel good' when I have one of them pinned tightly round my waist.

In conclusion, I do not think the man with a 'fetish'–'mania,' if you like–is to be pitied. He is as different from the ordinary *debauché* as light is from darkness; and the fact of his 'fetishism' in itself argues a certain amount of brain-power."

Otherwise, "PINAFORE," the faculty of imagination. If some of you feel inclined to smile at the foregoing, let me tell you this: for some months past, letters have been dribbling into this office, addressed to me, from men, living abroad and in different parts of the country, who all confess to a passion for wearing *a feminine white apron,* over their own clothes or those of the opposite sex. I put their letters aside as none was sufficiently explicit and detailed to warrant opening up the subject. Instead, I preferred to wait a while for a more open-hearted, informative "confession"–and here it is!

Within recent years, there have been a number of pretty actresses, English and foreign, who have appeared on the stage in long, business-like looking aprons, for use in the theatrical *atelier* or domestic purposes involved by the plot of the piece; and I know a man the walls of whose "den" are covered with photographs of them showing this particular garment. Unconsciously, he laid bare to me his particular "kink," because who would buy pictures of charming ladies so respectably attired when one had the chance of securing more alluring revelations of undraped actuality of the same persons? Whether or not he has a cupboard full of the materiality of his "fetish," I don't know, but probably he has, although he certainly hasn't the same opportunity for displaying himself freely and openly *à la* "PINAFORE." I'm afraid his landlady would call in the police if he did!

Some time ago, the eternal servant question was supposed to be on the eve of solution by the introduction of the man-maid. I never met one, or had the chance of meeting one; but if I ever do, I shall put a few questions to him. Domestic work can appeal to no fellow unless there is somewhere a secret reason for his taking it up, which he will *not* give as his explanation for wishing to secure the job. Does the wearing of the white apron–that mysterious factor–supply any explanation? I heard from a correspondent some months ago–he said he had a private income–that he would give his services free to any household that would allow him to enter the place as a "maid" and wear the orthodox print gown, cap and apron! And he was so far in earnest that he asked me to insert an advertisement, at ten shillings per inch, under one of my articles, notifying his offer to the world at large!

I thought I had reached the end of the "kink" question, and had now only to ring the changes on what has gone before. But it seems I haven't! As I write, I remember a Streatham (London, S.W.) correspondent who once wrote asking us to have a competition in which the best photo of a servant in "uniform"– black dress, white cap and apron, etc. would be awarded a prize. Was he bitten like "PINAFORE?" If he sees this, he might write and say.

COSMOPOLITE

[The episode mentioned by the editor occurs in the last chapters to be published of the next serial, "The Society School," chapters 20 to 25, in the issues for 10 February to 2 March 1912. "Amber" was, however, compelled, as a punishment, to serve as a maid in chapters 14 to 21, entitled "My Life as a Maid" in the serial, "Amber the Actor," from 14 March to 15 April 1911. Presumably "Pinafore's" letter was written before that.]

A dainty summer frock for a child. It is of fine white embroidered lawn.
A Leghorn hat with ribbon strings should complete the costume

28. Child's Summer Frock.   *Every Woman's Encyclopædia*, Vol. VIII (1912), p.5166.

COSMOPOLITIANA – THE CUB AND THE KILT 18th November 1911 (p.20)

Dear Cosmopolite,

I have been more than interested in reading in your bright journal lately about "The Cub and the Kilt" problem and especially the last letter written by "Petticoated Male" in your issue of October 7th; but so far you have had no men write giving similar experiences.

I admit that I personally, although twenty-eight years of age, always and habitually wear girls' underclothing, including woollen vests, longcloth or nainsook chemises, knickers and suspenders to stockings and ordinary girls' boots, though not very high-heeled.

I think it is the most perfect of wear possible for comfort, and, I believe, produces a softening influence on man's otherwise austere nature. Of course with masculine trousers, petticoats are barred; but I regard the others above quoted as the true essentials.

I have only one curiosity – what do your lady readers think of myself and others who have got the craze?   ALL WHITE, Woolwich, S.E.

18th November 1911 (pp 20-21)

Dear Cosmopolite,

I have just come across a copy of "Photo Bits" and have found great interest in the series of letters on the "Cub and the Kilt" for I had somewhat similar experience meted out to me in my youth. For minor offences I was punished by being sent to bed; but if I had been extra cross or naughty, I was given my choice of being caned or dressed in my sister's clothes for the rest of the day. With manful disdain, I rejected the latter alternative; but one day, out of a spirit of bravado, I allowed myself to be arrayed in full feminine apparel. My mother dressed me completely in chemise, knickers with plenty of frills and ribbons above the knee, a corset which was laced in very tight indeed, and suspenders to my stockings. At this stage, she afterwards told me that I often howled, and begged for the cane instead; but no! she went on. Over my knickers went a short flannel petticoat, then a longer one, kilted and of a soft satin-like material; then a frock of bodice and skirt combined.

This was my punishment ever afterwards, and my mother actually procured a complete outfit of girls' clothes for winter and summer. This continued up to the age of twelve; and as I was usually punished for very slight offences, you will understand that sometimes for several days I was completely imprisoned in petticoats.

Somehow after a time, it became less and less of a punishment, and I began to derive a certain pleasure from my corsets and knickers; and as I was a rather good looking boy, I presented a not unpleasing picture. I was at the time of a retiring and contemplative nature; and my aesthetic sense was pleased by the soft clinging cambric, and by the satin and trimmings. When I grew older and went to school, I often looked back with pleasure to those days; and now I am well over twenty years of age, and tall and slight, I still feel the fascination of a thralldom in petticoats, and the various lingerie shops often catch and hold my attention when passing in the street – while, strange though it may appear, I have in my wardrobe in my bachelor rooms several elegant sets of dainty underclothing and corsets of satin and stockings of silk.

When my day's work is over, I often array myself in full costume and derive considerable pleasure from so doing. Now, I do not consider I am doing anything unmanly, for I see nothing peculiar in the natural attraction dainty clothing has over the uncouth undergarments we men are expected to wear.

My letter may be long, but it may interest some of your readers; and its purpose is to show that what was invented as a punishment, has provided me with some very real and dear pleasure.   TOGA, Camden Town, N.W.

THE MYSTERY OF SEX

(*Previous articles dealing with the strange but fascinating subject of the matter that is presented here to-day, appeared in our issues of August 20th and October 22nd, 1910; April 15th, April 29th, and November 18th, 1911. A few of these numbers are still in print.*)

Who was the first man who impersonated a woman in actual life, and what subtle sense of femininity actuated his transposition of sex?

If it were possible for these two questions to be answered together, minus the one of stimulus and excitation, I could once and for all solve the knotty problem that interests so many of my correspondents. But, alas! I can't do so! I want to be popularly scientific rather than rawly fleshly!

However, the skeins of meaning and suggestion which prompted the first man to masquerade as a woman, have been handed down in the form of isolated communicative threads to those who have since been impelled by peculiar natural forces to follow his example; and where form and stature, etc., have allowed it, the more or less remunerative "act" of the "Female Impersonator" on the stage has been the direct result, whatever has been said or written to the contrary. Of the "act" as practised by the *canaille* of the underworld, I have nothing to write about. It is no mystery of sex as regards them.

I deal exclusively with the man who confesses to a passion for attiring himself in entire feminine garb in private, and private only; who confesses to an esoteric pleasure derived from the sensation of his mock outward transposition, and who asks plaintively why he should be so "afflicted," but never asks that his "affliction" should be censured! . . . . The theory of reincarnation–the alleged fact that the "afflicted" has been a woman once or twice or thrice in a previous existence, and then that the Unfathomable Occult suddenly decided to place him for a second or a third or a fourth time upon the earth as a male, without having previously drained out of his mental composition every bit of the soul of the sex which was formerly his, gives one a pretty stiff dose to swallow! But what are you to accept in its place when proof is laid bare before you of mere boy-kids who have developed the "kink" immaturely almost as soon as they strayed out of the cradle and could walk? Here, surely in cases of this sort, there has been no chance for the reception of outward impressions? The tendency has arisen as soon as the sense of the difference between the clothing of the sexes has been realised in a kindergarten style–as it were and briefly, the boy-kid instinctively believes he is not properly dressed!

The funny part about this mystery of sex is–the man who confesses to a passion for attiring himself in entire feminine garb in private, and in private only, never gives himself away by his outward everyday appearance, and has rarely anything suggesting effeminacy about his exterior person or talk. He guards his secret so well that he is often offensively masculine, or so quiet and reserved and "indrawn" that you, without thought, label him as being either a boor or a fool afraid to open his mouth for fear of "putting his foot in it!" But, as I know, from confessions which have been made to me verbally, these men of one recognised sex, who possess the "fetish" that forms the subject of this article today, are far from being boors or fools, whatever the material and unimaginative may think; and for that class I am desperately sorry.

I have been told that the "kink" is a "debauchery of intellect." Looked at from one direction, it may be; but "a debauchery of intellect" is infinitely more preferable than a debauchery of a worse kind, which gives merely a transient pleasure and leaves behind scars that last to the grave.

I knew a man whose best and most brilliant work was only done when he was dressed wholly as a woman, in a woman's *complete* toilette. Of course, this part of his daily task was written in private–at home, but with his sympathetic wife's knowledge and co-operation. He claimed that his change of attire tuned his mental powers to the analysis and the realisation of the finest susceptibilities, which he was utterly unable to grasp and express when in the ordinary habiliments of his sex! That was all he could explain–nothing else; but as I had the opportunity of comparing the difference between his "out-door" and his "indoor" scribbling, and reading the abrupt, crude style of the first and the perfect word-building and neat terse diction of the second, I had to confess his "kink" had a sound, but incomprehensible, truth underlying it. I saw him once in his study, whilst he was engaged on the literary dissection of a ticklish social problem; and his transfiguration was amazing! I doubt if Julian Eltinge himself could have done much better! He admitted, however, that one hour's work under such conditions was as peculiarly exhausting as it was electric and thrilling and inspiring, and more tiring than three at the office. I understand why, and told him why. He was an intellectual "sensationalist," and the influence of the black satin he habitually wore *in camera* was a "fetish" that gave almost as much as it took. He never wore any other material whilst working as a "man-woman," and he could never properly explain his preference for it.

And nobody can explain the mystery of sex, except in a vague, nebulous way. With many, or rather, all so affected, it is a natural–some will say, unnatural–birthright, and may be suckled from maternity, which allows a claim to the effect that the more exquisitely feminine the mother, the stronger the feminine side of the masculine character, especially if he is the firstborn. I give this argument for what it may be worth, allowing that, in due course of time, impressions and environment may do the rest. Then we sometimes get the man who diverts, who lives his whole life as a woman, and whose secret is only betrayed by death.

I wonder how many "ladies" existing today are preparing this surprise for those they will leave behind them?

COSMOPOLITE

COSMOPOLITIANA: – THE CUB AND THE KILT 27th January 1912 (p.19)
Dear Cosmopolite,

I have read with interest the letters appearing in your columns on "The Cub and the Kilt". As a boy, I had to wear a kilt, and though while there was not much elaboration about that worn during the day, my evening one was very different. By day, I wore a plain tweed kilt with petticoat and knickers. I always had to wear corsets. My shoes were of the ordinary kind with buckles, and the heels were about two inches high. I was strictly gloved. If I wore a jersey, I had elbow length tan Cape gloves, pulled up over the sleeve; and if I wore a jacket and waistcoat, as in winter, tan gauntlets, the gauntlets being long.

In the house in the evening, I was subjected to much more "dressing". My kilt was of black satin, with lace trimmed petticoat and knickers underneath. Long black stockings, kept up by suspenders, covered my knees. White boots buttoned to the knee, with 4in. heels, came next. My corsets were longer and laced more tightly, and I wore a blouse with short sleeves and a red sash round my waist. Sixteen button length gloves, very tight of white kid, or a pale putty colour, covered my hands, and woe betide me if I soiled them!

I had many a deportment and dancing lesson dressed thus. My mother had a very small waist, and she devoted much pains to make mine small also. She was kind, but punished me sharply if I was troublesome. Although many years have passed since I was a boy, I have always kept on wearing corsets, and long four-buttoned gloves for ordinary day wear, and still longer ones for theatre and dances.

I hope some of your other readers will add to the experiences already given.

H.C.R., Brechin

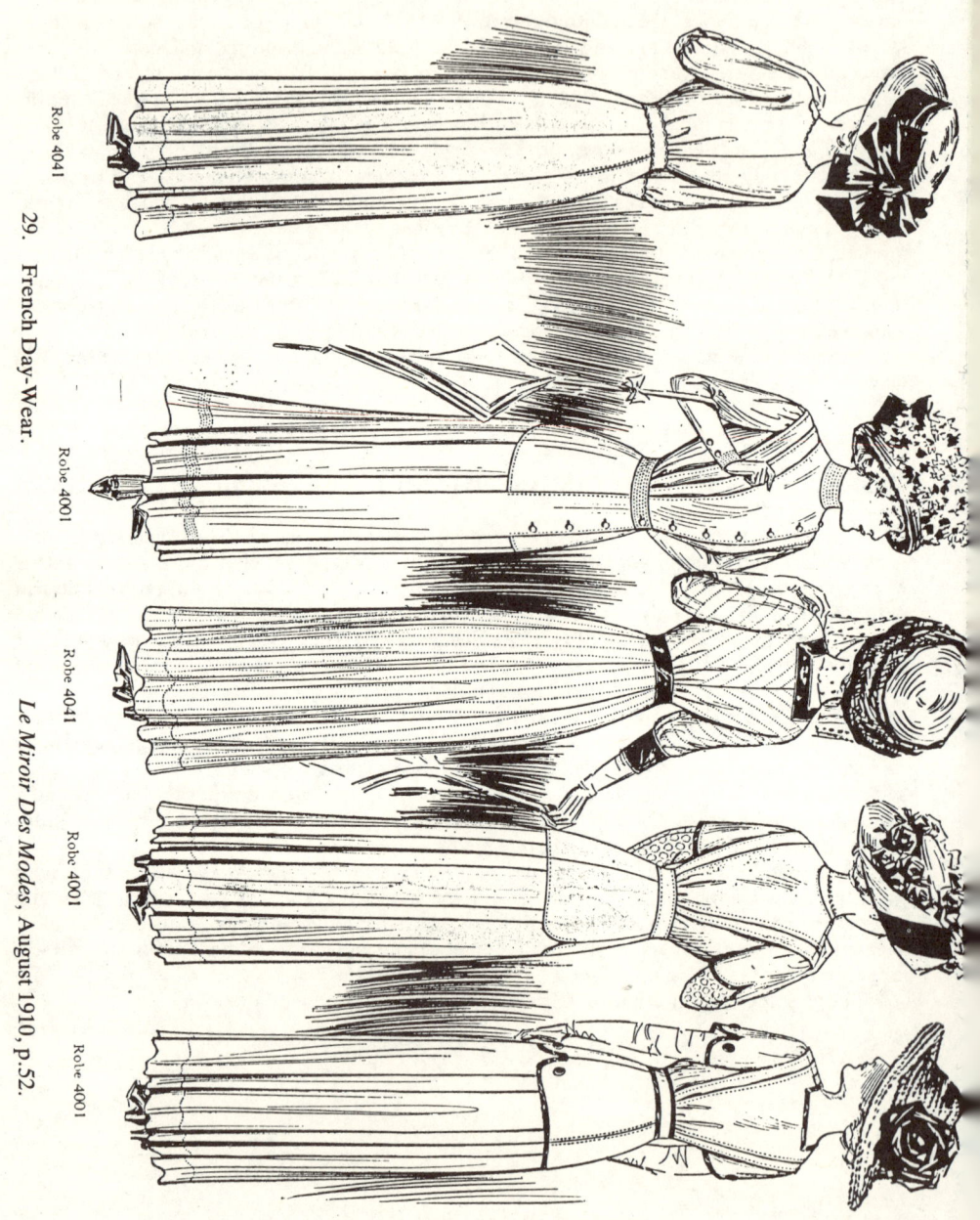

29. French Day-Wear. *Le Miroir Des Modes*, August 1910, p.52.